The OWNER'S MANUAL
for CHRISTIANS

The OWNER'S MANUAL *for* CHRISTIANS

THE ESSENTIAL GUIDE FOR A GOD-HONORING LIFE

CHARLES R. SWINDOLL

THOMAS NELSON
Since 1798

NASHVILLE   DALLAS   MEXICO CITY   RIO DE JANEIRO

The Owner's Manual for Christians

© 2009, 2011 by Charles R. Swindoll, Inc., a Texas corporation

Published in Nashville, Tennessee, by Thomas Nelson. Thomas Nelson is a registered trademark of Thomas Nelson, Inc.

Published in association with Yates & Yates, www.yates2.com.

Thomas Nelson, Inc., titles may be purchased in bulk for educational, business, fund-raising, or sales promotional use. For information, please e-mail SpecialMarkets@ThomasNelson.com.

Unless otherwise noted, scripture quotations are taken from the NEW AMERICAN STANDARD BIBLE®. © The Lockman Foundation 1960, 1962, 1963, 1968, 1971, 1972, 1973, 1975, 1977. Used by permission.

Scripture quotations marked NLT are from the *Holy Bible*, New Living Translation. © 1996. Used by permission of Tyndale House Publishers, Inc., Wheaton, Illinois 60189. All rights reserved.

Scripture quotations marked MSG are from *The Message* by Eugene H. Peterson. © 1993, 1994, 1995, 1996, 2000. Used by permission of NavPress Publishing Group. All rights reserved.

Scripture quotations marked NKJV are from THE NEW KING JAMES VERSION. © 1982 by Thomas Nelson, Inc. Used by permission. All rights reserved.

Scripture quotations marked KJV are from the King James Version of the Bible.

ISBN 978-1-4002-0301-7 (trade paper)

The Library of Congress has cataloged the hardcover edition as follows:

Swindoll, Charles R.
    The owner's manual for Christians : the essential guide for a God-honoring life / Charles R. Swindoll.
        p. cm.
    ISBN 978-0-8499-0191-1
    1. Christian life. I. Title.
BV4501.3.S955 2009
248.4—dc22   2009003615

Printed in the United States of America

15 16 17 18 19 RRD 10 9 8 7 6 5

Dedication

It has been my privilege to work alongside

some of God's choicest servants for many years.

The harmony we have enjoyed, the accomplishments we have achieved,

and the pleasures we have known while serving our Lord together

at Stonebriar Community Church and Insight for Living

have been among the highlights of my ministry.

Because of their mutual love for Christ as Lord

and their unswerving commitment to excellence in all they do,

I joyfully dedicate this volume to these five faithful friends:

Paul Brewer

Bill Gemaehlich

Charlton Hiott

Carol Spencer

Wayne Stiles

Table of Contents

QUICK START GUIDE

When all else fails, read the instructions." That little seven-word warning ought to appear on every electric train set, every plastic model, every backyard swing set in a two-ton package, every high-tech gizmo—anything that comes disassembled or requires electricity. Don't try to pretend this doesn't apply to you! I have no doubt that, just like me, you have looked at a seemingly harmless kit and tossed the manual aside, convinced that good old common sense would be good enough. Like most intelligent men and women, you thought you could put it together without the help of instructions.

I recall one particular time I looked at a simple swing set kit and thought, *Man, a guy with my ability shouldn't have any problem with that.* So an hour later, after making a complete mess of the project, I looked for the instructions. Obviously a sarcastic sage had prepared the instruction manual, because across the top of the first page in very small, inoffensive type, the opening line read, "Now that you have made a mess of things, please start over and follow these instructions." For a brief moment, I wondered if the author knew me personally and had written those words just for me! How could he have possibly known what I was going to do?

The fact is, he didn't know me. There was nothing supernatural going on. The sage simply understood human nature. It is part of our fallen, selfish, proud disposition to do things *our* way, and only when the consequences of failure become overwhelming do we seek help. Therefore, manufacturers have not only accepted this stubborn tendency, they have anticipated our shortsightedness by including a "Quick Start Guide" with the normal instruction manual. This is usually a condensed, need-to-know information pamphlet containing just enough information to keep the user from hurting himself or damaging the product.

Believe it or not, life comes with an owner's manual. The Creator has written His instructions in the pages of His Word, the sixty-six books of the Bible. Beginning in Genesis and ending with Revelation, He has described our origin, explained our purpose, confronted our need, prescribed our remedy, ordered our steps, and even revealed our future. Moreover, He has presented His instructions in the form of literature—the most engaging, compelling, and profound poetry and prose known to humanity. Nevertheless, we have all cast aside the owner's manual and rushed head-long into life with the assumption that our own common sense would be enough to get us through.

Many of you who read these words can nod with me in humble agree-ment because, like me, you have fouled up something far more significant than a child's swing set or an electronic gadget. You've fouled up a life . . . your own or perhaps someone else's . . . or both! So, let me encourage you with a basic truth that has given me hope throughout the years, especially after having made a mess of things: *It's never too late to start doing what is right.* It's never too late to pick up the owner's manual. In fact, after fouling up, it's the only right move.

Perhaps you are wiser than most. Maybe you have just removed the wrapping from the gift of life and you already appreciate the potential dan-gers of fouling up. Good for you! Let me challenge you with these words: *Read the instructions . . . or else!* If you are at all tempted to put your life together without reading the manual, the consequences of failure are grave. While you are certain to fail from time to time, and you will eventually make a mess of things, the damage will be far less than if you hadn't taken the time to read.

A FEW CLARIFICATIONS

I hope you will allow me a little creative latitude with the title of this volume. In reality, the only true "Owner's Manual for Christians" is the Bible. It is the only 100-percent-reliable source of truth from the Creator. If you prefer, think of this book as your "Quick Start Guide," a condensed, need-to-know information book about some of the most important teachings of Scripture.

Strictly speaking, this is a book of theology, but don't let that scare you or dissuade you from reading. Unfortunately, most theologians have given theology a bad rap by making their discipline more complicated than it needs to be. The purpose of theology is to consolidate the teaching of Scripture on any particular subject and then summarize that teaching in concise, understandable language so that the profound wisdom of the Bible is easier to understand and apply. When a theologian has made the principles of Scripture more difficult to grasp, he or she has failed. Hopefully, I have not failed in my task with this book. I have identified what I consider to be the most fundamental issues of life for believers and then focused the teaching of Scripture like a laser on each one . . . and I've stayed away from complicated words.

For the sake of clarity, let me also state that I have boldly assumed the reader has already placed his or her complete trust in Jesus Christ alone for salvation from sin and its eternal consequences; therefore, my treatment of such topics as grace, love, joy, God's will, and fellowship will only make sense for you who have "peace with God" (Romans 5:1). For example, I explain the implications of grace as a present reality, which is not applicable to those who have not yet received it through faith in the Son of God. Similarly, joy—true joy—cannot be found apart from Him, so the topic will be frustrating for anyone who is not already "in Christ."

So, let's pause and make sure you know where you stand. If you have not yet received the free gift of eternal life by grace alone, through faith alone, in Christ alone, I invite you to jump straight to the end, to that special section titled "How to Begin a Relationship with God." There you will discover how to receive God's life-changing gift of grace. Then, once you have begun your life as a believer, I encourage you to return to this spot and discover what God has waiting for you.

GETTING STARTED

In preparing this "owner's manual," I did not choose the topics haphazardly . . . and the order is no accident. First, I explore the foundation of our relationship with the Lord, which rests upon His gracious, loving care, His unblemished, holy character, and His absolute right to rule over His creation (including us). Naturally, all that we receive from Him has limitless potential to transform us from the inside out, which is the subject of the second section. While the Holy Spirit does the work of renovation, we are called to join Him by exercising spiritual disciplines. I will discuss a few of the most basic. Then, we must consider the purpose of our salvation and the results of God's transforming work, since the result of His bringing us into His family is good works (Titus 2:14). Not unlike assembling a kit by following the manufacturer's instructions, the Christian life is designed to be good for something (Ephesians 2:10).

As you review your life and assess the results of your time on earth so far, what do you see? Is your life worth emulating or a series of messes? Are others better off as the result of the time spent with you, or have your time and energy been focused on possessions that will be sold for pennies on the dollar after you are gone? What's down inside? A growing wisdom or repeated folly? Grace or grumbling? Be honest: Do you consider your life good for something?

Bottom-line questions like these are both depressing and challenging. Depressing because we all fall short; challenging because the Lord promises to accomplish far more than we can think or imagine. We cannot hope to be good for anything on our own; however, if we read and follow the instructions God provided, our lives can become monuments to His glory and models of His goodness. That is His promise (2 Corinthians 9:8; Ephesians 3:20).

Now, if I may be so bold, let me pass on some sage advice I received at a critical moment in my life: "Now that you have made a mess of things, please start over and follow these instructions."

—CHUCK SWINDOLL
Frisco, Texas

PART ONE

God's Character and the Foundation of Your Faith

I

GRACE

[The] moralizing and legalizing of the Gospel of God's grace is a dull heresy peddled to disappointed people who are angry because they have not received what they had no good reason to expect.

— RICHARD J. NEUHAUS

If there is any singular truth that distinguishes Christianity from all other religions, all other systems of belief, it is *grace*. In false religions, enough is never enough. They require followers to sacrifice more, achieve more, suffer more, learn more, or improve more. But the Christian enjoys peace with God by grace. We need not fear the animosity of evil spirits or the cruelty of demanding, angry deities. We never need to worry about whether our deeds were sufficiently good to earn a secure afterlife. We never need to fear death or divine judgment. We rest securely in the unearned, undeserved, freely given gift of eternal life with our Maker, who has promised to accept and embrace all who receive His grace through faith alone in Jesus Christ alone.

Grace is the bedrock truth upon which all of Christian belief and practice stand. While grace was not a new concept before Christ's arrival, the world could not fully understand grace until He came (1 Peter 1:10–13). That's because grace is heavenly by nature and therefore utterly foreign to the world. Only God, as a man, could reveal something so quintessentially divine.

While thinking back on his days with Jesus, John (one of the Twelve) remembered there was something about Him that was like no one else. During this time His disciples "beheld His glory" which was "full of grace and truth." Pause and let that sink in. The grace of heaven became tangible when Jesus, God's Son, became a human. It was His glory expressed as grace and truth that made Him different from all other religious teachers and all other philosophers. Jesus Christ, the God-man, revealed the truth about having peace with God. And this truth, this salvation by grace through faith, affects how believers live with one another. In a world of darkness and demands, rules and regulations, requirements and expectations demanded by hypocritical religious leaders, Jesus came and ministered in a new and different way—He alone, full of grace and full of truth, introduced a revolutionary, different way of life.

Remembering that uniqueness, John adds, "For of His fullness we have all received, and grace upon grace" (John 1:16).

Don't miss the tie-in with John 1:14. Initially, John wrote, "We beheld His glory," and then he added, in effect, "We received His fullness." John and the other disciples became marked men as a result. Grace heaped upon grace rubbed off, leaving them different. His style became theirs. His tolerance, theirs. His acceptance, love, warmth, and compassion were absorbed by those men, so much so that those things ultimately transformed their lives. By the end of the first century, the ministry of those same men had sent shock waves throughout the Roman world.

John puts the capstone on his introductory remarks by summing up the difference between contrastive styles of ministry: "For the Law was given through Moses; grace and truth were realized through Jesus Christ" (John 1:17).

With the Mosaic law came requirements, rules, and regulations, which fueled the Pharisees' heretical fire. With their own exacting demands came galling expectations. The Pharisees not only lengthened the list, they intensified everyone's guilt and shame. Obsessed with duty, external conduct, and a constant focusing only on right and wrong (especially in others' lives), they promoted a system so demanding there was no room left for joy. This led to harsh, judgmental, even prejudicial pronouncements as the religious system they promoted degenerated into external performance rather than internal authenticity. Obedience became a matter of grim compulsion instead of a joyous overflow prompted by love.

But when "grace and truth were realized through Jesus Christ," a long-awaited revolution of the heart began to set religious captives free. Fearful bondage motivated by guilt was replaced with a fresh motivation to follow Him in truth simply out of deep devotion and delight. Rather than focusing on dutiful adherence to the letter of the Law, He spoke of the heart. Instead of demanding that the sinner fulfill a long list of requirements, He emphasized faith, if only the size of a mustard seed.

The change spelled freedom, as the Lord Himself taught: "You shall know the truth, and the truth shall make you free" (John 8:32). Rigid, barren religion was, at last, replaced by a grace-oriented relationship—liberating grace. His followers loved it. His enemies hated it . . . and Him.

GRACE: LET'S UNDERSTAND THE TERM

What exactly is grace? You may be surprised to know that Jesus never used the word. He just taught it, and, equally important, He lived it. Furthermore, the Bible never gives us a one-statement definition, though grace appears throughout its pages . . . not only the word itself but numerous demonstrations of it. Understanding what grace means requires our going back to an old Hebrew term that meant "to bend, to stoop." By and by, it came to include the idea of "condescending favor."

If you have traveled to London, you have perhaps seen royalty. If so, you may have noticed sophistication, aloofness, distance. On occasion, royalty in England will make the news because someone in the ranks of nobility will stop, kneel down, and touch or bless a commoner. That is grace. There is nothing in the commoner that deserves being noticed or touched or blessed by the royal family. But because of grace in the heart of the royal person, there is the desire at that moment to pause, to stoop, to touch, even to bless.

The late pastor and Bible scholar Donald Grey Barnhouse perhaps said it best: "Love that goes upward is worship; love that goes outward is affection; love that stoops is grace."[1]

To show grace is to extend favor or kindness to one who doesn't deserve it and can never earn it. Receiving God's acceptance by grace always stands in sharp contrast to earning it on the basis of works. Every time the thought of grace appears, there is the idea of its being undeserved. In no way is the recipient getting what he or she deserves. Favor is being extended simply out of the goodness of the heart of the giver.

One more thing should be emphasized about grace: it is absolutely and totally free. You will never be asked to pay it back. You couldn't even if you tried. Most of us have trouble with that thought, because we work for everything we get. As the old saying goes, "There ain't no free lunch." But in this case, grace comes to us free and clear, no strings attached. We should not even try to repay it; to do so is insulting.

And now that Christ has come and died and thereby satisfied the Father's demands on sin, all we need to do is claim His grace by accepting the free gift of eternal life. Period. He smiles on us because of His Son's death and resurrection. It's grace, my friend, amazing grace.

SOME PRACTICAL EXPECTATIONS

Sir Edward C. Burne-Jones, the prominent nineteenth-century English artist, went to tea at the home of his daughter. As a special treat his young granddaughter was allowed to come to the table; she misbehaved, and her mother made her stand in the corner with her face to the wall. Sir Edward, a well-trained grandfather, did not interfere with his grandchild's training, but the next morning he arrived at his daughter's home with paints and palette. He went to the wall where the little girl had been forced to stand, and there he painted pictures—a kitten chasing its tail, lambs in a field, goldfish swimming. He decorated the wall on both sides of that corner with paintings for his granddaughter's delight. If she had to stand in the corner again, at least she would have something to look at. [2]

And so it is with our Lord. With the debt of sin paid by Christ on our behalf, we will never suffer punishment. When we do the things we should not, He may administer discipline, sometimes quite severely, but He never turns His back . . . He doesn't send His child to hell! Neither do we fall from grace and get slammed behind the iron bars of the law. He deals with His own in grace . . . beautiful, charming, unmerited favor. It is really amazing!

BEWARE THE KILLERS

Beware! Don't be taken by surprise. There are killers on the loose today. The problem is that you can't tell by looking. They don't wear little buttons that give away their identity, nor do they carry signs warning everybody to stay away. On the contrary, a lot of them carry Bibles and appear to be clean-living, nice-looking, law-abiding citizens. Most of them spend a lot of time in churches, some in places of religious leadership. Many are so respected in the community that their neighbors would never guess they are living next door to killers.

They kill freedom, spontaneity, and creativity; they kill joy as well as productivity. They kill with their words and their pens and their looks. They kill with their attitudes far more often than with their behavior. There is hardly a church or Christian organization or Christian school or missionary group or media ministry where such danger does not lurk. The amazing thing is that they get away with it, day in and day out, without being confronted or exposed. Strangely, the same ministries that would not tolerate heresy for ten minutes will step aside and allow these grace-killers all the space they need to maneuver and manipulate others in the most insidious manner imaginable. Their intolerance is tolerated. Their judgmental spirits remain unjudged. Their bullying tactics continue unchecked. And their narrow-mindedness is either explained away or quickly defended. The bondage that results would be criminal were it not so subtle and wrapped in such spiritual-sounding garb.

This day—this very moment—millions who should be free, productive individuals are living in shame, fear, and intimidation. The tragedy is they think it is the way they should be. They have never known the truth that could set them free. They are victimized, existing as if they are living on death row instead of enjoying the beauty and fresh air of the abundant life Christ modeled and made possible for all of His followers to claim. Unfortunately, most don't have a clue about what they are missing.

There is another danger lurking in the shadows. Rather than assault grace, some prefer to debate it to death. Similar to the days of the Protestant Reformation, grace has again become a theological football kicked from one end of the field to the other as theologians and preachers, scholars and students argue over terms. They behave like frustrated coaches trying to gain advantage over each other. Theirs is a classic no-win debate that trivializes God's great gift of love, leaving confused masses no other choice but to watch the fight from the stands confused, polarized, or, worst of all, bored. Grace was meant to be received and lived out to the fullest, not dissected and analyzed by those who would rather argue than eat. Enough of this! Grace must be awakened and released, not denied . . . enjoyed and freely given, not debated.

Grace received but unexpressed is dead grace. To spend one's time debating how grace is received or how much commitment is necessary for salvation, without getting into what it means to live by grace and enjoy the magnificent freedom it provides, quickly leads to a counterproductive argument. It becomes little more than another tedious trivial pursuit where the majority of God's people spend days looking back and asking, "How did we receive it?" instead of looking ahead and announcing, "Grace is ours . . . Let's live it!" Deny it or debate it, and we kill it. My plea is that we claim it and allow it to set us free. When we do, grace will become what it was meant to be—really amazing! When that happens, our whole countenance changes.

WAKE UP TO GRACE!

Most of you are familiar with the story of Rip Van Winkle, the man in the children's fairy tale who went to sleep for twenty years and awoke to a very different world from the one he had known before his two-decade slumber. All the while he was asleep, wonderful changes were taking place around him about which he was totally ignorant. Like Rip Van Winkle, many of us are slumbering under the oppressive opiate of those who would keep us from experiencing the marvelous grace-filled life. It is available to those of us who would be made fully alive to its liberating potential. Wake up! Sleep no longer! The grace awakening is upon us. And what can you expect upon rising from your uninformed stupor? Let me mention four practical expectations you can anticipate as you get a firm grasp on grace.

First, you can expect to gain a greater appreciation for God's gifts to you and others. What gifts? Several come to mind. The free gift of salvation (which we shall consider in depth in the next chapter). The gift of life. The gifts of laughter, of music, of beauty, of friendship, of forgiveness. Those who claim the freedom God offers gain an appreciation for the gifts that come with life.

Second, you can expect to spend less time and energy critical of and concerned about others' choices. Wouldn't that be a refreshing relief? When you get a grasp on grace—when you begin to operate in a context of freedom—you become increasingly less petty. You will allow others room to make their own decisions in life, even though you may choose otherwise.

Third, you can expect to become more tolerant and less judgmental. Externals will not mean as much to you as you recognize your need for grace and the abundance of God's supply. You'll begin to cultivate a desire for authentic faith rather than endure a religion based on superficial performance. You will find yourself so involved in your own pursuit of grace, you'll no longer lay guilt trips on those with whom you disagree.

Fourth, you can expect to take a giant step toward maturity. As your world expands, thanks to an awakening of your understanding of grace, your maturity will enlarge. Before your very eyes, new vistas will open. It will be so transforming, you will never be the same.

A LIFELONG PURSUIT

Lewis Sperry Chafer, the founder of the seminary I attended, died a few years before I began my theological studies in 1959, so I never had the honor of knowing him personally. Some of my mentors and professors, however, knew him well. Without exception they remembered him as a man of great grace. He was an articulate defender of the doctrine and an authentic model of its application throughout his adult life, especially during his latter years.

One of my mentors recalled the time when this dear man of God had concluded his final lecture on grace. It was a hot afternoon in Dallas, Texas, in the spring of 1952. The aging professor (who taught that particular semester from a wheelchair) mopped the perspiration from his brow. No one in the class moved as the session ended. It was as though the young theologues were basking in what they had heard, awestruck with their professor's insights and enthusiasm about God's matchless grace. The gray-haired gentleman rolled his chair to the door, and as he flipped the light switch off, the class spontaneously broke into thunderous applause. As the beloved theologian wiped away his tears, head bowed, he lifted one hand, gesturing them to stop. He had one closing remark as he looked across the room with a gentle smile. Amid the deafening silence, he spoke softly, "Gentlemen, for over half my life I have been studying this truth . . . and I am just beginning to discover what the grace of God is all about." Within a matter of three short months, the stately champion of grace was ushered into his Lord's presence at the age of eighty-one.

I seldom sing John Newton's eighteenth-century hymn "Amazing Grace" without remembering those final words of that giant of grace:

> Amazing grace! how sweet the sound
> That saved a wretch like me!
> I once was lost, but now am found,
> Was blind, but now I see.[3]

Nobody—not Lewis Sperry Chafer, not even John Newton—ever appreciated grace more than Paul, the first-century apostle. From a past of Pharisaic pride, cruel brutality, and religious unbelief, he was changed from a zealous persecutor of the church to a humble servant of Christ. And what was the reason? The grace of God. Hear his own testimony:

> For I am the least of the apostles, who am not fit to be called an apostle, because I persecuted the church of God. But by the grace of God I am what I am, and His grace toward me did not prove vain; but I labored even more than all of them, yet not I, but the grace of God with me. Whether then it was I or they, so we preach and so you believed. (1 Corinthians 15:9–11)

REAFFIRMING THE TRUTH OF GRACE

Whatever he became, according to his own statement, Paul owed it all to "the grace of God." When I ponder the words from that grand apostle, I come up with what we might call his credo. We can reduce it to three statements with only single-syllable words, the first consisting of only eight words; the second, ten words; and the third, twelve. Occasionally, it helps to take a profound, multifaceted theological truth and define it in simple, nontechnical terms.

First statement: *God does what He does by His grace.* Paul's first claim for being allowed to live, to say nothing of being used as a spokesman and leader, was "by the grace of God." Paul deserved the severest kind of judgment, but

God gave the man His grace instead. Humanly speaking, Paul should have been made to endure incredible suffering for all the pain and heartache he had caused others. But he didn't, because God exhibited His grace.

That leads us to the second statement: *I am what I am by the grace of God*. It is as if he was admitting, "If there is any goodness now found in me, I deserve none of the glory; grace gets the credit."

In our day of high-powered self-achievement and an overemphasis on the importance of personal accomplishments and building one's own ego-centered kingdom, this idea of giving grace the credit is a much-needed message. How many people who reach the pinnacle of their career say to the *Wall Street Journal* reporter or in an interview in *BusinessWeek*, "I am what I am by the grace of God"? How many athletes would say that kind of thing at a banquet in his or her honor? What a shocker it would be today if someone were to say, "Don't be impressed at all with me. My only claim to fame is the undeserved grace of God." Such candor is rare.

There's a third statement, which seems to be implied in Paul's closing remark: *I let you be what you are by the grace of God*. Grace is not something simply to be claimed; it is meant to be demonstrated. It is to be shared, used as a basis for friendships, and drawn upon for sustained relationships.

Jesus spoke of an abundant life that we enter into when we claim the freedom He provides by His grace. Wouldn't it be wonderful if people cooperated with His game plan? There is nothing to be compared to grace when it comes to freeing others from bondage.

There are those who seem to be waiting for the first opportunity to confront. Suspicious by nature and negative in style, they are determined to find any flaw, failure, or subtle weakness in your life and to point it out. There may be twenty things they could affirm; instead, they have one main goal: to make sure you never forget your weaknesses. Grace-killers are big on the "shoulds" and "oughts" in their advice. Instead of praising, they pounce!

OUR FINAL EXAM

Many (dare I say, most?) Christians live their lives as though they're going to be graded once a year by a God who stands there frowning with His hands stuck in the pockets of His robe. (I don't know why, but probably most people usually think of God with a robe on, never in sweats or cutoffs or a swimsuit . . . He's always wearing a beard and this white robe.) Glaring, He says, "Well, Johnson, that gets a C-." And, "Dorothy, you ought to be ashamed!" And, "Smith? Not bad. Could've been better, though." What heretical imaginations we have.

Why do we think like that? Who is responsible for such horror images of the Almighty? Where did we pick up the idea that God is mad or irritated? Knowing that all of God's wrath was poured out on His Son at His death on the cross, how can we think like that? As a matter of fact, the reason He brought Jesus back from the grave is that He was satisfied with His Son. Ponder this: if the Father is satisfied with His Son's full payment for sin, and we are in His Son, by grace through faith, then He is satisfied with you and me. How long must Christians live before we finally believe that? Perhaps our problem is that we will forever have bosses and friends and pastors and parents who will give us lists. There will always be those who will give us more and more and more to live up to. These are grace killers whether they know it or not. By using guilt trips, shame techniques, and sneaky manipulations, they virtually drive us to distraction! But never God. He's the One who assures us that if we are anything, it is by His marvelous, infinite, matchless grace. And once we truly get hold of it for our own lives—once we experience the grace awakening—it's amazing how we want to share it. We delight in letting others be what they are by the same grace of God.

In a fine little book titled *The Liberty of Obedience*, Elisabeth Elliot writes about a young man eager to forsake the world and to follow Christ closely. *What is it I must forsake?* he asks himself.

She records the following response and in doing so illustrates the foolishness of trying to please God by keeping man-made rules and legalistic regulations. What must he give up? Try not to smile:

Colored clothes, for one thing. Get rid of everything in your wardrobe that is not white. Stop sleeping on a soft pillow. Sell your musical instruments and don't eat any more white bread. You cannot, if you are sincere about obeying Christ, take warm baths or shave your beard. To shave is to lie against Him who created us, to attempt to improve on His work.[4]

"Does this answer sound absurd?" she asks. Then she surprises us with this statement:

> It is the answer given in the most celebrated Christian schools of the second century! Is it possible that the rules that have been adopted by many twentieth-century Christians will sound as absurd to earnest followers of Christ a few years hence?[5]

Before we cluck our tongues or laugh out loud at second-century grace-killers, we had better ask ourselves questions like: What message are we delivering to our brothers and sisters in the family of God? What list of dos and don'ts have we concocted and now require of others? What must they do to earn their way into the circle of our conditional love so that they can feel more accepted? And I must add this final question: Who gave us the right to give someone else the rules to live by?

If the great apostle had no list, if he was what he was by the grace of God, considering himself undeserving, I can assure you, we are all in the same camp, equally unqualified, undeserving, yet unconditionally loved by our Father. For there to be true maturity, people must be given room to grow, which includes room to fail, to think on their own, to disagree, to make mistakes. Grace must be risked, or we will be stunted Christians who don't think, who can't make decisions, who operate in fear and without joy because we know nothing but someone else's demands and expectations. When will we ever learn? God delights in choosing those most unworthy and making them the objects of His unconditional acceptance.

CONSIDERING AN EXAMPLE OF GRACE

In the ancient world, whenever a new king came into power, all those in the family of the previous king were exterminated once a new dynasty took control. Naturally, all members of the former monarch's family had every reason to live in fear once the new king took the throne.

In the case I'm thinking of, King Saul and his son Jonathan had died following a battle. When word of the dual tragedy reached David's attention, it grieved him; nevertheless, he was the Lord's choice as Saul's successor. Knowing that David was now Israel's new king, the members of Saul's family fled for their lives, erroneously thinking that David would treat them like all the other monarchs of Eastern dynasties. The scene portrayed in Scripture is one of pandemonium and panic:

> Now Jonathan, Saul's son, had a son crippled in his feet. He was five years old when the report of Saul and Jonathan came from Jezreel, and his nurse took him up and fled. And it happened that in her hurry to flee, he fell and became lame. And his name was Mephibosheth. (2 Samuel 4:4)

In the haste of escape, Saul's little grandson suffered a permanent injury. He lived the balance of his life lame in both his feet. We leave him as a five-year-old on the pages of the ancient record. Nothing more is said regarding Mephibosheth for fifteen to twenty years.

A Question Asked

Chapter 9 of 2 Samuel provides a link to the continuing story. Years have passed. Mephibosheth is now an adult, living out his days with a severe disability in both his feet. David has not only taken the throne, he has won the hearts of the people. The entire nation is singing his praises. As yet there is not a blemish on his integrity. He has expanded the boundaries of the united kingdom of the Jews in Palestine from approximately six thousand to sixty thousand square miles. The military force of Israel is stronger than ever in its history. Enemy nations now respect this powerful new country. David is healthy and happy. He has not known defeat on the battlefield, which means his immediate world is relatively peaceful. His economy and diplomacy are a refreshing change from Saul's. There is not only a chicken in every pot, there are grapes on every vine. It is a rare scene of incredible prosperity and God-given peace.

Overwhelmed by the Lord's goodness and grace, the middle-aged king muses over all his blessings. While doing so, he must have enjoyed a nostalgic moment, remembering his former friendship with Jonathan, which prompts him to ask:

Is there yet anyone left of the house of Saul, that I may show him kindness for Jonathan's sake? (2 Samuel 9:1)

I don't want you to miss the importance of one term David used for "kindness." It's the Hebrew word *chesed*, often rendered mercy, lovingkindness, or grace in the Old Testament. *Is there anyone still living in the family of Saul to whom I could demonstrate the same kind of grace that God has demonstrated to me?* That's the idea turning over in David's mind.

I love the question for what it does not ask. It does not ask, "Is there anyone who is deserving? Is there anyone who is qualified? Is there anyone who is sharp, whom I could use in government matters . . . or in good shape, whom I could add to my army?" No, he simply asks, "Is there anyone?" It is an unconditional desire, a question dripping with grace. "I'm wondering if there is anybody out there."

David does not stop searching until he discovers from a household servant named Ziba that Mephibosheth is living in Lo-debar. Interestingly, in Hebrew that town name means "a barren place." In English, the name of the place could be translated "no pastureland." It's as if the servant is saying that Jonathan's son is living in a place of stark barrenness—a place where there are no crops, a wilderness . . . a wasteland. There is not a moment's hesitation. David has heard enough to put a plan into action.

A Straggler Sought

Then King David sent and brought him from the house of Machir the son of Ammiel, from Lo-debar. And Mephibosheth, the son of Jonathan the son of Saul, came to David and fell on his face and prostrated himself. And David said, "Mephibosheth." And he said, "Here is your servant!" And David said to him, "Do not fear, for I will surely show kindness to you for the sake of your father Jonathan, and will restore to you all the land of your grandfather Saul; and you shall eat at my table regularly." (2 Samuel 9:5–7)

The disabled man was obviously frightened when he arrived at the king's palace in Jerusalem. The watchword of his life since he was a little boy had been anonymity. He never wanted to be found, certainly not by the king who succeeded his grandfather. To do so would mean sure death. And yet there was no way he could say no when David sent for him. Before he knew it, he was whisked away in a chariot provided for him; and before he could believe it, there he stood before the king.

All that explains why David's words must have stunned Mephibosheth. They fit David, however. When grace is in your heart, your hope is to release others from fear, not create it.

Let me interrupt this wonderful story to ask you a question about Jesus, the One who was "full of grace and truth." Do you know what was the most often-repeated command from His lips? Most people I ask are unable to answer that question correctly. Our Lord issued numerous commands, but He made this one more than any other. Do you happen to know what it was? It was this: "Fear not." Isn't that great? "Do not fear." Naturally, the most common reaction when someone stood before the perfect Son of God would have been fear. And yet Jesus, great in grace, repeatedly said, "Do not be afraid." He didn't meet people with a deep frown, looking down on them and swinging a club. He met them with open arms and reassuring words: "Don't be afraid." Those are the words David used before Mephibosheth. They drip with grace.

Mephibosheth's first reaction must have been the fear of a spear in his belly. Small wonder he says, "Here is your servant!" as he falls on his face before the king. "Don't be afraid," says David, but the crippled man cannot stop shaking. It is as if David wants to say, "I haven't sought for you to punish you for something you've done or not done. I have good in mind for you, not harm. I want to lift you up, not tear you down." The secret of David's entire message to the man could be stated in seven words: "I will surely show kindness to you."

A Privilege Provided

Don't miss something that's terribly important in the overall message of grace. David wanted to show kindness not because of Mephibosheth (he didn't even know the man before they met that day), but to show kindness "for the sake of your father Jonathan." Mephibosheth still can't believe what's happening. "Again he prostrated himself and said, 'What is your servant, that you should regard a dead dog like me?'" (2 Samuel 9:8). In calling himself "a dead dog," he uses the most descriptive words he can think of for a contemptuous, despicable, worthless creature. "I'm just a dead dog, living in Lo-debar. Why not just leave me alone in my misery?"

Remember when you said that to God? Has it been that long since you and He met? Or could you have already forgotten? Candidly, this is one of my all-time favorite stories in the Old Testament because its portrayal of grace is so powerful. Here is a man who is unknown, of no consequence to the king, and is disabled in both his feet. He can give nothing of benefit to the kingdom so far as physical strength is concerned. There is absolutely zero personal appeal, but David stoops in grace. Due to a relationship David had with his longtime friend Jonathan, the king is going to provide Mephibosheth the privileges and benefits he would have given his own son.

Swiftly and completely, the king kept his word:

> Then the king called Saul's servant Ziba, and said to him, "All that belonged to Saul and to all his house I have given to your master's grandson. And you and your sons and your servants shall cultivate the land for him, and you shall bring in the produce so that your master's grandson may have food; nevertheless Mephibosheth your master's grandson shall eat at my table regularly." (2 Samuel 9:9–10)

Four separate times in the biblical account we read that the cripple would eat at the king's table—verses 7, 10, 11, and finally verse 13: "So Mephibosheth lived in Jerusalem, for he ate at the king's table regularly. Now he was lame in both feet" (2 Samuel 9:13).

What a scene! What grace! From that time on he was welcome at the king's table of continual nourishment and uninterrupted provisions. Undeserving . . . yet unconditionally loved. Mephibosheth's head must have swirled for days as he forced himself to believe his new situation wasn't a dream.

Imagine a typical scene several years later. The dinner bell rings through the king's palace, and David comes to the head of the table and sits down. In a few moments Amnon—clever, crafty Amnon—sits to the left of David. Lovely and gracious Tamar, a charming and beautiful young woman, arrives and sits beside Amnon. And then across the way, Solomon walks slowly from his study—precocious, brilliant, preoccupied Solomon. The heir apparent slowly sits down. And then Absalom—handsome, winsome Absalom with beautiful flowing hair, black as a raven, down to his shoulders—sits down. That particular evening Joab, the courageous warrior and David's commander of the troops, has been invited to dinner. Muscular, bronzed Joab is seated near the king. Afterward, they wait. They hear the shuffling of feet, the clump, clump, clump of the crutches as Mephibosheth rather awkwardly finds his place at the table and slips into his seat . . . and the tablecloth covers his feet. I ask you: Did Mephibosheth understand grace?

Were he living today, I think he would quickly identify with the words from the hymn by John Newton:

> Through many dangers, toils, and snares
> I have already come;
> 'Tis grace hath brought me safe thus far,
> And grace will lead me home.[6]

2

LOVE

L ove—genuine love—is something that defies definition, yet like grace, it is fundamental to the Christian. For millennia, words have eluded the very best poets and philosophers in their quest to analyze love, quantify love, explain love, or define love. But where words leave the brain numb, the heart resonates in perfect pitch when we see love in action. Join me as we look in on some familiar scenes.

We're in a busy airport. An announcement over the intercom stirs a small commotion behind us as a man in uniform stands up. Tiny arms encircle each leg as an elderly couple looks on, weeping. He and his wife cling to each other in a long, desperate embrace. Tears and kisses and prayers and promises lead up to the inevitable "I love you . . . good-bye"—perhaps to be their last.

We're strolling down a dimly lit hospital hallway at 3:00 a.m. when the squeaks and coos of a nursing newborn draw our attention. There, in an island of soft light, is a new mother cradling the life that came from her body only hours before. Her husband sits behind her on the bed, his cheek pressed against hers as they stare in wonder at their baby. The expression on their faces reflects the miracle that has just occurred: love begat life.

The smell of fresh flowers and the jubilant chords of a pipe organ mingle together over our heads in a church sanctuary. A bride moves gracefully down the aisle, holding her father's arm. He wears the look of a man who's about to hand a million-dollar Stradivarius to a gorilla. At the altar, a young man stands on tiptoe, peering down the aisle for a glimpse of his bride. On his face we see innocence, fear, anticipation, delight, and enormous love.

LOVE ON DISPLAY

When we see love in action, our hearts cannot help but beat in perfect rhythm with those involved. Love is a universal language. When expressed authentically, no words are necessary. Furthermore, love is no less essential to human life than air, food, or water. Hard science proves the fact. And, as we'll see in the apostle Paul's towering treatise in 1 Corinthians 13, nothing is complete without love. Unfortunately, we love too little and we love too seldom. So, on occasion, we need a gentle reminder of what it means to love others with our whole hearts. That calls for wisdom and counsel from the Author of love.

Most of the essentials of love can be found in the first half of 1 Corinthians 13, Paul's grand discourse on love. As we examine this well-known passage, I fear that familiarity will obscure the genius it contains. Looking at something familiar from a fresh perspective requires mental discipline. So I ask, if this is not your first exposure to these verses, please pretend that it is. Determine to take Paul's words very personally. Let them slowly seep into your mind and then allow them to impact you.

THE PRIORITY OF LOVE

Paul begins his treatise with three statements, emphasizing the priority of love.

> If I speak with the tongues of men and of angels, but do not have love, I have become a noisy gong or a clanging cymbal. If I have the gift of prophecy, and know all mysteries and all knowledge; and if I have all faith, so as to remove mountains, but do not have love, I am nothing. And if I give all my possessions to feed the poor, and if I surrender my body to be burned, but do not have love, it profits me nothing. (1 Corinthians 13:1–3)

What amazing analogies! His first statement measures the importance of love against the gift of communication. If any of us knew the language of those mysterious, heavenly creatures that fill the throne room of God, or if we possessed the skill to capture the attention of audiences with our words and hold them spellbound with our eloquence yet at the same time lacked love, our words would be pointless, meaningless, and profitless. Without love, we have nothing of value to say. No amount of oratory giftedness or linguistic skill can substitute for love. Our mouth moves as sounds emerge, but everything falls flat if love is missing.

Ephesians 4:14–15 encourages us to speak the truth in love. Truth without love is cruel at worst, empty at best. If I confront someone with words and I don't do it because of love, I shouldn't be surprised to find them injured rather than healed. Loveless confrontation helps no one. If I attempt to comfort someone in pain without love as my motivation, my words will cause more sorrow than if I had just stayed away. Empty consolation fools no one. And if I try to instruct people without love as my guide, they will resist any application of the principles, however valid. They would only hear me for what I am: a heady, self-important, intellectual snob. Academic instruction changes no one.

Paul's second statement measures the value of love against spiritual giftedness and maturity. Take note of the spiritual gifts and skills he mentions:

Prophecy, the ability to speak the words and predict the works of God.
Omniscience, complete knowledge of all things, including the mind of God.
Faith, such oneness with God as to accomplish the physically impossible.

If we had that kind of spiritual maturity, we would be like Christ, wouldn't we? We may wield the powers of almighty God, yet if we didn't possess His uniquely defining quality of love, we are nothing. Think of it—nothing!

Then, perhaps thinking of Christ's gift to us, Paul's third statement measures love against sacrificial living and martyrdom. Selflessness that feeds the hungry, houses the homeless, cares for the sick, advances a great cause, even selflessness to the point of death accomplishes nothing if it lacks love.

THE SPECIAL NATURE OF AGAPE

The word Paul uses no fewer than nine times in this chapter is *agape*—rarely found outside the Bible—probably because the meaning is unique to the kind of love we experience with God. The Greek had *eros*, an intoxicating, impulsive love between men and women; and *philos*, the warm, noble affection of deep friendship. But *agape* was a seldom used and poorly understood term. The scholarly *Theological Dictionary of the New Testament* contrasts the meaning of *eros* and *agape* this way:

Eros	*Agape*
A general love of the world seeking satisfaction wherever it can.	A love which makes distinctions, choosing and keeping to its object.
Determined by a more or less indefinite impulsion towards its object [him or her].	A free and decisive act determined by its subject [us].
In its highest sense is used of the upward impulsion of man, of his love for the divine. Seeks in others the fulfillment of its own life's hunger.	Relates for the most part the love of God, to the love of the higher lifting up the lower, elevating the lover above others. Must often be translated "to show love"; it is a giving, active love on the other's behalf.[1]

Few put it better than Dr. Ron Allen in his footnote in *The Nelson Study Bible:*

> This word, *agape*, describes a love that is based on the deliberate choice of the one who loves rather than the worthiness of the one who is loved. This kind of love goes against natural human inclination. It is a giving, selfless, expect-nothing-in-return kind of love. . . .
>
> Our modern "throw-away" society encourages us to get rid of people in our lives who are difficult to get along with, whether they are friends, family, or acquaintances. Yet this attitude runs in complete contrast to the love described by Paul. True love puts up with people who would be easier to give up on.[2]

LOVE IN ACTION

There's nothing morally wrong with *eros* in the right context. In fact, every marriage needs a healthy dose of *eros*—a passionate, emotional, lusty appetite for each other. But that's not the kind of love that binds people together in a meaningful relationship. Where *eros* is a mystery that evokes good feelings, *agape* is a choice that reveals good character.

The Greek language also used the term *philos*, which stood for the kind of warm affection shared by family or close friends. The verb, *phileō* meant, literally, "to treat somebody as one of one's own people."[3] Less emotional than *eros*, and motivated more by character than emotion, *philos* was essentially synonymous with *agape* in the minds of most Greek speakers, including Christians. When Paul needed a term to describe the highest, purest form of love—divine love—he chose the rarely used *agape* and infused it with special meaning. For Paul, *agape* would best describe Christian love, which drew its inspiration and power from God Himself.

In 1 Corinthians 13:4–7, Paul gives us more than a dozen characteristics of *agape*, the life-blood of all Christian relationships.

Some of the characteristics are described positively ("love is . . ."), while most are expressed negatively ("love is not . . ."). Each description is worth noting on its own as you evaluate the strength and quality of your love for others. As we look at them, I challenge you to ask yourself two questions with each characteristic. First, "How am I doing in this area?" Second, "How would the behavior of others change if my love included this?"

Love Is Patient and Kind (v. 4)

In English, we use the term "short-tempered" to describe someone who is easily angered or has a volatile personality. You never know what will set this person off. The Greek for the opposite term is the compound of two words. The first is *thymia*. We get thermometer from this ancient term. It has in mind the idea of heat or, in this case, passion or anger. The second is *macro*, the opposite of micro. Love is "long-tempered." Love has a long fuse. One writer describes *macrothymia* as "the capacity to be wronged and not retaliate."[4] Love is patient. How are you doing with patience? How might the behavior of others change if your love were more patient?

Love is also kind. In our rapid-fire era, we've forgotten how to be kind. Jesus used a form of this word to describe wine that has aged and mellowed (Luke 5:38–39) and to describe a disciple's service to Him. He said:

> Come to Me, all who are weary and heavy-laden, and I will give you rest. Take My yoke upon you and learn from Me, for I am gentle and humble in heart, and you will find rest for your souls. For My yoke is easy and My burden is light. (Matthew 11:28–30)

Paul's word to describe love derives from the word Jesus used, translated "easy" in this passage. This quality of love is "serviceable," "useful," "adapted to its purpose," "good, of its kind."[5] A. T. Robertson called it "gentle in behavior." This is not a theological word, but it is a Jesus kind of love.

Think of a person who is mellow, not easily ruffled, someone who is both strong and gentle. Aren't people like that enjoyable to be around? You feel safe and relaxed in their presence. They have a love that is patient and kind.

Love Is Not Jealous or Arrogant (v. 4)

Think of these two terms in contrast to "patient and kind."

First, love is not jealous. Few things are less attractive than a suspicious, insecure, smothering protectiveness. A jealous lover's first concern is for self, which is the exact opposite of *agape*. Rather than being patient, the jealous lover zealously pursues what he or she wants, even to the extreme of controlling someone else.

Second, love does not brag, which is the chief occupation of the arrogant. An arrogant person has one exclusive concern: self. Paul selected a particular Greek word that sounds like what it is. The word is *phusio*, pronounced fffffooooooooo-zee-o. It means "to blow, to puff up, to inflate." The verb comes from a noun meaning "bellows." Years ago, every fireplace had an accordion-like contraption next to it. If the fire decreased to embers, someone would grab the bellows, pull the handles apart so it would fill with air, then quickly squeeze. The result was a long blast of air that would fan the dying coals into a flame again.

We've all been around someone like that. The handles pull apart as he or she puffs up, then the handles squeeze and out comes a long blast of meeeeeeeeeee. You may have noticed that it never inspires admiration. If anything, the arrogant blowhard only draws more criticism. Like the mother whale warning her young, "Don't go up there and blow so hard. That's when you get harpooned!"

On the other hand, how pleasant and surprising it is to be around individuals who are well known, gifted, and sought after, but who never make demands or expect special treatment. Cynthia and I have a longtime friend who left his former career to work as a business manager for a small Bible college. As Joe got underway in that job, he and the leadership of that school decided that a good athletic program would help put the institution on the map. Football required far more money than they could invest, so they chose basketball. The Lord seemed to affirm that decision by sending—virtually out of the blue—a Christian man who also happened to be a very gifted coach. Recruiting top-notch players without the clout of a big-name school or money for scholarships would be their next challenge.

One day, the phone rang and a voice on the other end said, "I understand you're the business manager. We've never met. My name is John."

After a polite exchange, the man continued, "I've followed basketball for a long time, and I hear you'd like to get a team going. I think that's wonderful. I love your school, and I've watched it grow from almost nothing. As a matter of fact, I know your new coach, and I also know a very gifted kid he'd like to meet. He could easily become an All-American, in my opinion, but for some reason recruiters have overlooked him. I could arrange a meeting if you would like that."

Of course, Joe agreed. They ended up recruiting the young man along with two of his friends. That combination gave them a winning squad almost immediately. Some time later Joe began to wonder who John was. His call had made everything possible. So he did some digging only to discover that John, who called him, was John Wooden, the six-time NCAA Coach of the Year for the UCLA Bruins who took his teams to ten national championship victories in twelve seasons! His introduction? "Hi, I'm John. I've followed basketball for a long time."

Keep in mind, *agape* is a humble love. If we love our mates with this kind of love, we will be more concerned with serving and helping him or her rather than inflating ourselves. Love isn't arrogant.

Love Is Charming (v. 5)

Paul says, "[Love] does not act unbecomingly; it does not seek its own." The word "unbecoming" describes someone who is rude or crude, someone without class or decorum. In the positive sense, love is tactful, courteous—I would use the word "charming." Merriam-Webster defines charming as "extremely pleasing or delightful."[6]

Charming love brings out the best in other people. Howie Stevenson, our minister of worship for many years in the church I served in Fullerton, California, taught me that people are charmed into righteousness. I've never heard anyone say, "You know what? He slammed me over the head with a baseball bat, and I realized I need to be more like Christ" or, "She treated me like dirt, and now I want to see things her way and follow Jesus." Of course not! The kind of love that bonds people is a winsome, charming love that thinks more of others than of self.

This is important because we often want the person we love to behave in a certain way, which then influences how we behave toward him or her. This is the very self-serving attitude that Paul warns against with the words "love does not seek its own." Love for our mates will seek to bring out the best in them by giving without conditions or expectations.

Love Has a Thick Skin (v. 5)

Paul uses two negative descriptions—"is not provoked" and "doesn't take into account a wrong suffered." In other words, genuine love isn't fragile. *Agape* applies lots of grace to every relationship; it leaves lots of room for other people to make mistakes. And in marriage for example, when you live in close proximity to someone for the majority of a lifetime, there will be lots of them to overlook.

I've seen both men and women who are constantly irritated by other people, especially close family. The smallest error—a wrong look, a misplaced word, a simple oversight—causes miniature explosions throughout the day. These little outbursts of irritability must certainly be the result of keeping a long list of wrongs close at hand. Paul uses an accounting term to caution us against keeping a mental ledger of bad deeds. When we do that, we're the losers. Warren Wiersbe writes:

One of the most miserable men I ever met was a professed Christian who actually kept in a notebook a list of the wrongs he felt others had committed against him. Forgiveness means that we wipe the record clean and never hold things against people.[7]

The truth is, we can keep a list without writing anything down or even realizing it. If you find that friends and loved ones irritate you for reasons that you must admit are minor, the chances are good they have something on the wrong side of your ledger sheet. Either address your anger appropriately and promptly, or simply let it go.

Love Loves Truth (v. 6)

Paul then combines a negative with a positive statement to describe the role of truth in a love relationship. Let me caution you: the implications of this powerful statement run deep.

> [Love] does not rejoice in unrighteousness, but rejoices with the truth.
> (1 Corinthians 13:6)

For Paul, *agape* is the intersection of truth, salvation, and obedience to God.

Stop. Read that again slowly and, preferably, aloud.

Your love for your mate, your friends, and your family should encourage their love relationship with the Lord. Righteousness is a shared goal because individually it is your highest calling as a believer. You are encouraging them to pursue truth because the Author of truth called you to Himself. He's also the One who gave you each person as a helper in life's journey. That's why love and truth have been inseparable companions since before time. They always go together. Where you find love, you find truth. And when you seek the highest good of another, truth is absolutely essential.

Sometimes you must tell the truth, even though that truth is not pleasant. The truth may be something difficult to hear about yourself, which will require all the courage you can gather. Your trust will be put to the test. Your friends, family, or spouse may fail to respond with grace. But to enjoy an authentic relationship, your love must be based upon truth. Sometimes, the truth will be something about those around you that they may find difficult to hear. If you are eager to reveal it, I suggest you wait. If you are reluctant, you are probably in the best position to apply the needed tact and gentleness to help your mate discover a difficult truth. When telling the truth in love, the sole motivation is the good of the other person, which means your speech will be laced with patience and kindness.

Where there is love, there is transparent and unguarded honesty, even when the honesty is not easy to express.

The Limits of Love (v. 7)

For Paul, *agape* has limits like the universe has edges. He measures the dimensions of love in four directions: patience, trust, confidence, and endurance. Observe how he weaves the four threads together, forming a tapestry of love.

> [Love] bears all things, believes all things, hopes all things, endures all things.
> (1 Corinthians 13:7)

Your love shelters the relationship from anything that should fall upon it. Your love chooses to trust and believe the best of people in the midst of challenging circumstances. Your love expresses confidence in their faithfulness and goodness despite how hopeless things may seem. And your love chooses to remain steadfast, opting for a long-term view through short-term difficulties. The insightful British commentator Alfred Plummer summarized this verse well when he wrote, "When love has no evidence, it believes the best. When the evidence is adverse, it hopes for the best. And when hopes are repeatedly disappointed, it still courageously waits."[8]

APPLYING THE GLUE

Love, like glue, has the potential to create a bond, but only when released from its container. If you want something to stick, you have to apply it. Authentic love is demonstrative. What we have discovered so far is convicting enough; so let me keep this simple with three short phrases. These are merely a place to start.

Tell Them Often

I'm not sure why, but most of us have a tendency to keep compliments, affirmations, and other expressions of love and appreciation bottled up for years. Later, when our loved one lies cold in a casket, we pour out all the things we should have said but didn't in a grand eulogy for all to hear . . . except the most important person of all can't hear a word of it. Why do we wait? Why not tell our loved ones now how much we love them and why we most appreciate them? Why not do all that now, while our words still have the power to bring them joy? We don't have to be witty or eloquent, just vulnerable and sincere.

Furthermore, some people assume their family and friends know they are loved, so years pass between the times they utter the words, "I love you." Why? In all my years of pastoral ministry, I have never met a single person who regretted saying "I love you" too often. On the other hand, I have rarely conducted a funeral in which at least one person didn't say, "I don't think she knew just how much I loved her," or "I wish he could have known how much he meant to me."

Don't wait. Say it today, say it to someone who needs to hear it, and say it often.

Risk It Often

I know this can be a tough one for some. You may have a long history of people taking advantage of your good nature and stepping on your heart. Perhaps the idea of being vulnerable enough to love without reservation feels too risky for you. Unfortunately, you have no alternative. Love and risk cannot be separated. C. S. Lewis wrote some of his most memorable words on the subject of love in his work *The Four Loves*.

To love at all is to be vulnerable. Love anything, and your heart will certainly be wrung and possibly broken. If you want to make sure of keeping it intact, you must give your heart to no one, not even to an animal. Wrap it carefully round with hobbies and little luxuries; avoid all entanglements; lock it safe in the casket or the coffin of your selfishness. But in that casket—safe, dark, motionless, airless—it will change. It will not be broken; it will become unbreakable, impenetrable, irredeemable. The alternative to tragedy, or at least to the risk of tragedy, is damnation. The only place outside Heaven where you can be perfectly safe from all the dangers and perturbations of love is Hell.[9]

Risk loving without reservation or qualification or condition. You have survived being hurt in the past, and the Lord will not allow you to suffer more than you can manage. Pain is likely if you choose to love, but a living death is certain if you don't. So, you see? You really don't have any other alternative. Risk it. Risk it often.

Do It Now

It's easy to substitute life for work and pat ourselves on the back—that is, until something threatens our lives. After Senator Paul Tsongas was diagnosed with cancer, a friend wrote to him, affirming his decision not to run for reelection. We would do well to remember his sobering words: "No man ever said on his deathbed, 'I wish I had spent more time in the office.'"[10]

Don't wait until tomorrow. Satan would love to lull you into a procrastinating complacency that always believes there will be time enough tomorrow, or next week, or once the big project is done, or after things settle down just a little, or . . . or . . . or . . . Trust me, having lived for more than seventy years, there will never come a more convenient time to love the people in your life the way 1 Corinthians 13 describes. The time is now.

So, love them now. Don't wait for the atmospheric conditions to be right, don't expect that with less stress it will come naturally, don't hope that it will take care of itself once this or that is resolved. As my friends at the Minirth Clinic like to say, "Love is a choice." In small ways, a dozen times a day, you show what you've chosen. Your next opportunity is coming soon. Be on the lookout for it.

3

JOY

Someone once asked Mother Teresa what the job description was for anyone who might wish to work alongside her in the grimy streets and narrow alleys of Calcutta. Without hesitation she mentioned only two things: the desire to work hard and a joyful attitude. It has been my observation that both of those qualities are rare. But the second is much rarer than the first. Diligence may be difficult to find, but compared to an attitude of genuine joy, hard work is commonplace.

Unfortunately, our fast-paced, affluent culture seems to have lost its spirit of fun and laughter. Recently, a Brazilian student studying at a nearby university told me that what amazes him the most about Americans is their lack of laughter. I found myself unable to refute his criticism.

Just look around. Bad news, long faces, and heavy hearts are every-where—even in houses of worship (especially in houses of worship!). Visit most congregations today and search for signs of happiness and sounds of laughter and you often come away disappointed. Joy, "the gigantic secret of the Christian,"[1] is conspicuous by its absence. I find that inexcusable. The one place on earth where life's burdens should be lighter, where faces should reflect genuine enthusiasm, and where attitudes should be uplifting and positive is the place this is least likely to be true.

Some critics would be quick to point out that our times do not lend themselves to such an easygoing philosophy. They would ask, "Under these circumstances how could I be anything but grim?" To which I reply, "What are you doing under the circumstances?" Correct me if I'm wrong, but isn't the Christian life to be lived above the circumstances?

A good sense of humor enlivens our discernment and guards us from taking everything that comes down the pike too seriously. By remaining lighthearted, by refusing to allow our intensity to gain the mastery of our minds, we remain much more objective. People who live above their circumstances usually possess a well-developed sense of humor, because in the final analysis that's what gets them through.

I met such a person at a conference in Chicago several years ago. We shared a few laughs following a session at which I had spoken. Later she wrote to thank me for adding a little joy to an otherwise ultraserious conference. (Why are most Christian conferences ultraserious?) Her note was a delightfully creative expression of one who had learned to balance the dark side of life with the bright glow of laughter. Among other things she wrote:

> Humor has done a lot to help me in my spiritual life. How could I have reared twelve children, starting at age 32, and not have had a sense of humor?
>
> After your talk last night I was enjoying some relaxed moments with friends I met here. I told them I got married at age 31. I didn't worry about getting married; I left my future in God's hands. But I must tell you, every night I hung a pair of men's pants on my bed and knelt down to pray this prayer:
>
> Father in heaven, hear my prayer,
> And grant it if you can;
> I've hung a pair of trousers here,
> Please fill them with a man.

The following Sunday I read that humorous letter to our congregation, and they enjoyed it immensely. I happened to notice the different reactions of a father and his teenaged son. The dad laughed out loud, but the son seemed preoccupied. On that particular Sunday the mother of this family had stayed home with their sick daughter. Obviously neither father nor son mentioned the story, because a couple of weeks later I received a note from the mother:

> Dear Chuck:
> I am wondering if I should be worried about something. It has to do with our son. For the last two weeks I have noticed that before our son turns the

light out and goes to sleep at night, he hangs a woman's bikini over the foot of his bed. . . . Should I be concerned about this?

I assured her there was nothing to worry about. And I am pleased to announce that the young man met and married his sweetheart soon after that, so maybe the swimsuit idea works.

Perhaps you find yourself among those in the "if-only" group. You say you would laugh if only you had more money . . . if only you had more talent or were more beautiful . . . if only you could find a more fulfilling job. I challenge those excuses. Just as more money never made anyone generous and more talent never made anyone grateful, more of anything never made anyone joyful.

> The happiest people are rarely the richest, or the most beautiful, or even the most talented. Happy people do not depend on excitement and fun supplied by externals. They enjoy the fundamental, often very simple, things of life. They waste no time thinking other pastures are greener; they do not yearn for yesterday or tomorrow. They savor the moment, glad to be alive, enjoying their work, their families, the good things around them. They are adaptable; they can bend with the wind, adjust to the changes in their times, enjoy the contests of life, and feel themselves in harmony with the world. Their eyes are turned outward; they are aware, compassionate. They have the capacity to love.[2]

Without exception, people who consistently laugh do so in spite of, seldom because of, anything. They pursue fun rather than wait for it to knock on their door in the middle of the day. Such infectiously joyful believers have no trouble convincing people around them that Christianity is real and that Christ can transform a life. Joy is the flag that flies above the castle of their hearts, announcing that the King is in residence.

Meet a Man Who Smiled in Spite of . . .

There once lived a man who became a Christian as an adult and left the security and popularity of his former career as an official religious leader to follow Christ. The persecution that became his companion throughout the remaining years of his life was just the beginning of his woes. Misunderstood, misrepresented, and maligned though he was, he pressed on joyfully. On top of all that, he suffered an affliction so severe he called it a "thorn in my flesh"—some have suggested it was a physical ailment, perhaps an intense form of migraine that revisited him on a regular basis.

I am referring to Saul of Tarsus, later called Paul. Though not one to dwell on his own difficulties or ailments, the apostle did take the time to record a partial list of them in his second letter to his friends in Corinth. Compared to his first-century contemporaries, he was

> . . . in far more imprisonments, beaten times without number, often in danger of death. Five times I received from the Jews thirty-nine lashes. Three times I was beaten with rods, once I was stoned, three times I was shipwrecked, a night and a day I have spent in the deep. I have been on frequent journeys, in dangers from rivers, dangers from robbers, dangers from my countrymen, dangers from the Gentiles, dangers in the city, dangers in the wilderness, dangers on the sea, dangers among false brethren; I have been in labor and hardship, through many sleepless nights, in hunger and thirst, often without food, in cold and exposure. Apart from such external things, there is the daily pressure upon me of concern for all the churches. (2 Corinthians 11:23–28)

Although that was enough hardship for several people, Paul's journey got even more rugged as time passed. Finally, he was arrested and placed under the constant guard of Roman soldiers to whom he was chained for two years. While he was allowed to remain "in his own rented quarters" (Acts 28:30), the restrictions must have been irksome to a man who had grown accustomed to traveling and to the freedom of setting his own agenda. Yet not once do we read of his losing patience and throwing a fit. On the contrary, he saw his circumstances as an opportunity to make Christ known as he made the best of his situation.

Read a Letter with a Surprising Theme

Interestingly, Paul wrote several letters during those years of house arrest, one of which was addressed to a group of Christians living in Philippi. It is an amazing letter, made even more remarkable by its recurring theme—joy. Think of it! Written by a man who had known excruciating hardship and pain, living in a restricted setting chained to a Roman soldier, the letter to the Philippians resounds with joy! Attitudes of joy and contentment are woven through the tapestry of these 104 verses like threads of silver. Rather than wallowing in self-pity or calling on his friends to help him escape or at least find relief from these restrictions, Paul sent a surprisingly lighthearted message. And on top of all that, time and again he urges the Philippians (and his readers) to be people of joy.

Let me show you how that same theme resurfaces in each of the four chapters.

- When Paul prayed for the Philippians, he smiled!

I thank my God in all my remembrance of you, always offering prayer with joy in my every prayer for you all. (Philippians 1:3–4)

- When he compared staying on earth to leaving and going to be with Jesus, he was joyful.

For to me, to live is Christ, and to die is gain. But if I am to live on in the flesh, this will mean fruitful labor for me; and I do not know which to choose. But I am hard-pressed from both directions, having the desire to depart and be with Christ, for that is very much better; yet to remain on in the flesh is more necessary for your sake. And convinced of this, I know that I shall remain and continue with you all for your progress and joy in the faith. (Philippians 1:21–25)

- When he encouraged them to work together in harmony, his own joy intensified as he envisioned that happening.

If therefore there is any encouragement in Christ, if there is any consolation of love, if there is any fellowship of the Spirit, if any affection and compassion, make my joy complete by being of the same mind, maintaining the same love, united in spirit, intent on one purpose. (Philippians 2:1–2)

- When he mentioned sending a friend to them, he urged them to receive the man joyfully.

But I thought it necessary to send to you Epaphroditus, my brother and fellow worker and fellow soldier, who is also your messenger and minister to my need; because he was longing for you all and was distressed because you had heard that he was sick. For indeed he was sick to the point of death, but God had mercy on him, and not on him only but also on me, lest I should have sorrow upon sorrow. Therefore I have sent him all the more eagerly in order that when you see him again you may rejoice and I may be less concerned about you. Therefore receive him in the Lord with all joy, and hold men like him in high regard. (Philippians 2:25–29)

- When he communicated the "core" of what he wanted them to hear from him, he was full of joy.

Finally, my brethren, rejoice in the Lord. To write the same things again is no trouble to me, and it is a safeguard for you. (Philippians 3:1)

- When he was drawing his letter to a close, he returned to the same message of joy.

Rejoice in the Lord always; again I will say, rejoice! (Philippians 4:4)

- Finally, when Paul called to mind their concern for his welfare, the joy about which he writes is (in my opinion) one of the most upbeat passages found in Scripture.

But I rejoiced in the Lord greatly, that now at last you have revived your concern for me; indeed, you were concerned before, but you lacked opportunity. Not that I speak from want; for I have learned to be content in whatever circumstances I am. I know how to get along with humble means, and I also know how to live in prosperity; in any and every circumstance I have learned the secret of being filled and going hungry, both of having abundance and suffering need. I can do all things through Him who strengthens me. Nevertheless, you have done well to share with me in my affliction. And you yourselves also know, Philippians, that at the first preaching of the gospel, after I departed from Macedonia, no church shared with me in the matter of giving and receiving but you alone; for even in Thessalonica you sent a gift more than once for my needs. Not that I seek the gift itself, but I seek for the profit which increases to your account. But I have received everything in full, and have an abundance; I am amply supplied, having received from Epaphroditus what you have sent, a fragrant aroma, an acceptable sacrifice, well-pleasing to God. And my God shall supply all your needs according to His riches in glory in Christ Jesus. (Philippians 4:10–19)

Needed: a Joy Transfusion

I strongly suspect that after the Philippians received this delightful little letter from Paul, their joy increased to an all-time high. They had received a joy transfusion from someone they dearly loved, which must have been all the more appreciated as they remembered Paul's circumstance. If he, in that irritating, confining situation, could be so positive, so full of encouragement, so affirming, certainly those living in freedom could be joyful.

Life's joy stealers are many, and you will need to get rid of them if you hope to attain the kind of happiness described by Paul's pen. If you don't, all attempts to receive (or give) a joy transfusion will be blocked. One of the ringleaders you'll need to do battle with sooner rather than later is that sneaky thief who slides into your thoughts and reminds you of something from the past that demoralizes you (even though it is over and done with and fully forgiven) or conjures up fears regarding something in the future (even though that frightening something may never happen). Joyful people stay riveted to the present—the here and now, not the then and never.

If God Is God . . . Then Laughter Fits Life

As I attempt to probe the mind of Paul, trying to find some common denominator, some secret clue to his joy, I have to conclude that it was his confidence in God. To Paul, God was in full control of everything. Everything! If hardship came, God permitted it. If pain dogged his steps, it was only because God allowed it. If he was under arrest, God still remained the sovereign director of his life. If there seemed to be no way out, God knew he was pressed. If things broke open and all pressure was relieved, God was responsible.

My point? God is no distant deity but a constant reality, a very present help whenever needs occur. So? So live like it. And laugh like it! Paul did. While he lived, he drained every drop of joy out of every day that passed. How do I know? This little letter to the Philippians says so.

In the first chapter of Philippians we learn there is laughter in living—whether or not we get what we want, in spite of difficult circumstances, and even when there are conflicts.

In the second chapter we learn there is laughter in serving. It starts with the right attitude (humility), it is maintained through right theology (God is God), and it is encouraged by right models and mentors (friends like Timothy and Epaphroditus).

In the third chapter, we learn there is laughter in sharing as Paul shares three happy things: his testimony, his goal of living, and his reason for encouragement.

Finally, in the fourth chapter we learn there is laughter in resting. These have to be some of the finest lines ever written on the principle of personal contentment.

What a treasure house of joy! Frankly, I'm excited—and I know you will be too. Before we are very far along, you will begin to realize that joy is a choice. You will discover that each person must choose joy if he or she hopes to laugh again.

Jesus gave us His truth so that His joy might be in us. And when that happens, our joy is full (John 15:11). The tragedy is that so few choose to live joyfully.

Will you? If you will, I can make you a promise: laughter and enthusiasm will follow.

I came across a story in one of Tim Hansel's books that points this out in an unforgettable way. It's the true account of an eighty-two-year-old man who had served as a pastor for more than fifty of those years. In his later years he struggled with skin cancer. It was so bad that he had already had fifteen skin operations. Tim writes:

Besides suffering from the pain, he was so embarrassed about how the cancer had scarred his appearance, he wouldn't go out. Then one day he was given *You Gotta Keep Dancin'*, in which I tell of my long struggle with the chronic, intense pain from a near-fatal climbing accident. In that book, I told of the day when I realized that the pain would be with me forever. At that moment, I made a pivotal decision. I knew that it was up to me to choose how I responded to it. So I chose joy. . . .

After reading awhile, the elderly pastor said he put the book down, thinking, "He's crazy. I can't choose joy."

So he gave up on the idea. Then later he read in John 15:11 that joy is a gift. Jesus says, "I want to give you my joy so that your joy may be complete."

A gift!, he thought. He didn't know what to do, so he got down on his knees. Then he didn't know what to say, so he said, "Well, then, Lord, give it to me."

And suddenly, as he described it, this incredible hunk of joy came from heaven and landed on him.

"I was overwhelmed," he wrote. "It was like the joy talked about in Peter, a 'joy unspeakable and full of glory.' I didn't know what to say, so I said, 'Turn it on, Lord, turn it on!'" And before he knew it, he was dancing around the house. He felt so joyful that he actually felt born again—again. And this astonishing change happened at the age of 82.

He just had to get out. So much joy couldn't stay cooped up. So he went out to the local fast food restaurant and got a burger. A lady saw how happy he was, and asked, "How are you doing?"

He said, "Oh, I'm wonderful!"

"Is it your birthday?" she asked.

"No, honey, it's better than that!"

"Your anniversary?"

"Better than that!"

"Well, what is it?" she asked excitedly.

"It's the joy of Jesus. Do you know what I'm talking about?"

The lady shrugged and answered, "No, I have to work on Sundays."[3]

Every time I read Tim's story, I shake my head. What a ridiculous response on the part of that woman! But not unusual. Basically there are two kinds of people: people who choose joy and people who don't. People who choose joy pay no attention to what day of the week it is . . . or how old they are . . . or what level of pain they are in. They have deliberately decided to laugh again because they have chosen joy. People who do not choose joy miss the relief laughter can bring. And because they do not, they cannot. And because they can't, they won't.

Which one are you?

4

FELLOWSHIP
AND FRIENDSHIP

I f I have learned anything during my journey on planet Earth, it is that
people need one another. The presence of other people is essential—
caring people, helpful people, interesting people, friendly people, thought-
ful people. These folks take the grind out of life. About the time we are
tempted to think we can handle things all alone—*boom*! We run into some
obstacle and need assistance. We discover all over again that we are not
nearly as self-sufficient as we thought.

In spite of our high-tech world and efficient procedures, people remain
the essential ingredient of life. When we forget that, a strange thing happens: we start treating people like inconveniences instead of assets.

This is precisely what humorist Robert Henry, a professional speaker,
encountered one evening when he went to a large discount department
store in search of a pair of binoculars.

As he walked up to the appropriate counter he noticed that he was the only
customer in the store. Behind the counter were two salespersons. One was so
preoccupied talking to "Mama" on the telephone that she refused to acknowledge that Robert was there. At the other end of the counter, a second salesperson was unloading inventory from a box onto the shelves. Growing impatient,
Robert walked down to her end of the counter and just stood there. Finally,
she looked up at Robert and said, "You got a number?"

"I got a what?" asked Robert, trying to control his astonishment at such an absurdity.

"You got a number? You gotta have a number."

Robert replied, "Lady, I'm the only customer in the store! I don't need a number. Can't you see how ridiculous this is?" But she failed to see the absurdity and insisted that Robert take a number before agreeing to wait on him. By now, it was obvious to Robert that she was more interested in following procedures than helping the customer. So, he went to the take-a-number machine, pulled number 37 and walked back to the salesperson. With that, she promptly went to her number counter, which revealed that the last customer waited on had been holding number 34. So she screamed out, "35! . . . 35! . . . 36! . . . 36! . . . 37!"

"I'm number 37," said Robert.

"May I help you?" she asked, without cracking a smile.

"No," replied Robert, and he turned around and walked out.[1]

Now, there's a lady who's lost sight of the objective. I might question whether something like that ever happened if I had not experienced similar incidents in my own life. How easily some get caught up in procedures and lose sight of the major reason those procedures were established in the first place. Without people there would be no need for a store. Without people, who cares how efficient a particular airline may be? Without people a school serves no purpose, a row of houses no longer represents a neighborhood, a stadium is a cold concrete structure, and even a church building is an empty shell. I say again: *We need each other.*

Since none of us is a whole, independent, self-sufficient, super-capable, all-powerful hotshot, let's quit acting like we are. Life's lonely enough without our playing that silly role.

The game's over. Let's link up.

People are important to each other. Above all, people are important to God. Which does not diminish His authority and self-sufficiency at all. The creation of humanity on the sixth day was the crowning accomplishment of the Lord's creation handiwork. Furthermore, He put into humankind His very image, which He did not do for plant life or animals, birds, or fish. It was for the salvation of humanity, not brute beasts, that Christ came and died, and it will be for us that He will someday return. The major reason I am involved in a writing ministry and a broadcasting ministry and a church ministry is that people need to be reached and nurtured in the faith. This could be said of anyone serving the Lord Christ.

Couldn't God do it all? Of course, He is God—all-powerful and all-knowing and all-sufficient. That makes it all the more significant that He prefers to use us in His work. Even though He could operate completely alone on this earth, He seldom does. Almost without exception, He uses people in the process. His favorite plan is a combined effort: God plus people equals accomplishment.

I often recall the story of the preacher who saved up enough money to buy a few inexpensive acres of land. A little run-down, weather-beaten farmhouse sat on the acreage, a sad picture of years of neglect. The land had not been kept up either, so there were old tree stumps, rusted pieces of machinery, and all sorts of debris strewn here and there, not to mention a fence greatly in need of repair. The whole scene was a mess.

During his spare time and his vacations, the preacher rolled up his sleeves and got to work. He hauled off the junk, repaired the fence, pulled away the stumps, and replanted new trees. Then he refurbished the old house into a quaint cottage with a new roof, new windows, new stone walkway, new paint job, and finally a few colorful flower boxes. It took several years to accomplish all this, but at last, when the final job had been completed and he was washing up after applying a fresh coat of paint to the mailbox, his neighbor (who had watched all this from a distance) walked over and said, "Well, preacher—looks like you and the Lord have done a pretty fine job on your place here."

Wiping the sweat from his face, the minister replied, "Yeah, I suppose so . . . but you should have seen it when the Lord had it all to Himself."

God has not only created each one of us as distinct individuals, He also uses us in significant ways. Just stop and think: Chances are you are where you are today because of the words or the writings or the personal influence of certain people. I love to ask people how they became who they are. When I do, they invariably speak of the influence or the encouragement of key people in their past.

I would be the first to affirm that fact. When I look back across the landscape of my life, I am able to connect specific individuals to each crossroad and every milestone. Some of them are people the world will never know, for they are relatively unknown to the general public. But to me personally? Absolutely vital. And a few of them have remained my friends to this very day. Each one has helped me clear a hurdle or handle a struggle, accomplish an objective or endure a trial—and ultimately laugh again. I cannot even imagine where I would be today were it not for that handful of friends who have given me a heart full of joy. Let's face it, friends make life a lot more fun.

SPECIAL FRIENDS IN PAUL'S LIFE

It is easy to forget that the late, great apostle Paul needed friends too. Being ill on occasion, he needed Dr. Luke. Being limited in strength and unable to handle the rigors of extensive travel alone, he needed Barnabas and Silas. Being restricted in freedom, he needed other hands to carry his letters to their prescribed destinations. And on several occasions he needed someone to actually write out his letters. But isn't it interesting that though we know quite a bit about Paul, we know very little about his circle of friends? Yet in reality, they were part of the reason he was able to move through life as well as he did.

Returning to the letter he wrote to the Philippians, we come upon the mention of two names—a man Paul calls "my son" in another of his writings and a man he calls here "my brother." Since these two men played such significant roles in Paul's life that they deserved honorable mention, let's spend the balance of this chapter getting better acquainted with both. They were friends who made Paul's life richer and more enjoyable.

A "Son" Named Timothy

Being held under Roman guard in his house arrest, Paul found himself unable to travel back to Philippi, so he decided to send his young friend Timothy. More than any other individual, Timothy is mentioned by Paul in his writings. We saw his name earlier, in fact, in the opening line of this very letter: "Paul and Timothy, bond-servants of Christ Jesus."

Who was Timothy?

He was a native of either Lystra or Derbe, cities in southern Asia Minor—today called Turkey.

He was the child of a mixed marriage: Jewish mother (Eunice) and Greek father (never named).

Since he remained uncircumcised until he was a young adult, Timothy's childhood upbringing was obviously more strongly influenced by the Greek than the Jewish parentage.

However, his spiritual interest came from the maternal side of his family. Both Eunice and her mother Lois reared him to be tender toward the things of the Lord. We learn this from two comments Paul makes later in life in his second letter to his young friend.

> For I am mindful of the sincere faith within you, which first dwelt in your grandmother Lois, and your mother Eunice, and I am sure that it is in you as well. (2 Timothy 1:5)

> You, however, continue in the things you have learned and become convinced of, knowing from whom you have learned them; and that from childhood you have known the sacred writings which are able to give you the wisdom that leads to salvation through faith which is in Christ Jesus. (2 Timothy 3:14–15)

Paul, no doubt, led Timothy into a personal relationship with the Lord Jesus Christ. This explains why the older referred to the younger as "my beloved and faithful child in the Lord" (1 Corinthians 4:17).

Once Timothy joined Paul (and Luke) as a traveling companion, the two remained close for the rest of Paul's life. We read of the beginning of their friendship in the early part of Acts 16.

> And he [Paul] came also to Derbe and to Lystra. And behold, a certain disciple was there, named Timothy, the son of a Jewish woman who was a believer, but his father was a Greek, and he was well spoken of by the brethren who were in Lystra and Iconium. Paul wanted this man to go with him; and he took him and circumcised him because of the Jews who were in those parts, for they all knew that his father was a Greek. (Acts 16:1–3)

So much for a quick survey of Timothy's background. What is of interest to us is how Paul wrote of him to the people of Philippi.

> But I hope in the Lord Jesus to send Timothy to you shortly, so that I also may be encouraged when I learn of your condition. For I have no one else of kindred spirit who will genuinely be concerned for your welfare. For they all seek after their own interests, not those of Christ Jesus. But you know of his proven worth that he served with me in the furtherance of the gospel like a child serving his father. Therefore I hope to send him immediately, as soon as I see how things go with me; and I trust in the Lord that I myself also shall be coming shortly. (Philippians 2:19–24)

As I ponder those words, three things jump out at me. All three have to do with how Paul viewed his friend. First, Timothy had a unique "kindred spirit" with Paul. The single Greek term Paul used for "kindred spirit" is a combination of two words, actually: "same souled." This is the only time in all of the New Testament the term is used. We might say Paul and Timothy possessed an "equal spirit," or that they were "like-minded." Mathematically speaking, their triangles were congruent. Just think of the implications of the comment Paul makes: "I have no one else of kindred spirit."

First, they thought alike. Their perspectives were in line with each other. Timothy would interpret situations much like Paul, had the latter been there. In today's slang, they hit it off. When the older sent the younger on a fact-finding mission, he could rely on the report as being similar to one he himself would have brought back. Being of kindred spirit in no way suggests they had the same temperament or even that they always agreed. What it does mean, however, is that being alongside each other, neither had to work hard at the relationship; things flowed smoothly between them. I would imagine that it was not unlike the closeness David enjoyed with Jonathan, about which we read "the soul of Jonathan was knit to the soul of David, and Jonathan loved him as himself." And a little later, "he loved him as he loved his own life" (1 Samuel 18:1; 20:17).

Coming across a person with a kindred spirit is a rare find. We may have numerous casual acquaintances and several good friends in life, but finding someone who is like-souled is a most unusual (and delightful) discovery.

And when it happens, both parties sense it. Neither has to convince the other that there is a oneness of spirit. It is like being with someone who lives in your own head—and vice versa—someone who reads your motives and understands your needs without either having to be stated. No need for explanations, excuses, or defenses. Paul enjoyed all these relational delights with Timothy, along with a spiritual dimension as well.

Second, Timothy had a genuine concern for others. That statement opens a window for us into the young man's makeup. When Timothy was with others, his heart was touched over their needs. Compassionate individuals are hard to find these days, but they were hard to find back in those days too. Remember what Paul wrote?

> For they all seek after their own interests, not those of Christ Jesus. (Philippians 2:21)

Not Timothy. Timothy modeled what Paul wrote earlier concerning an unselfish attitude.

> Do nothing from selfishness or empty conceit, but with humility of mind let each of you regard one another as more important than himself; do not merely look out for your own personal interests, but also for the interests of others. (Philippians 2:3–4)

That was Timothy. No wonder Paul felt so close to him. Friends like that remind us of the importance of helping others without saying a word. One man writes with understanding:

> A few years ago I stood on the banks of a river in South America and watched a young man in western clothes climb out of a primitive canoe. The veteran missionary with whom I was traveling beamed at the young man and whispered to me, "The first time I saw him he was a naked Indian kid standing right on this bank, and he pulled in my canoe for me. God gave me a real concern for him, and eventually he came to Christ, committed himself to the Lord's work and is just returning home after graduating from seminary in Costa Rica." I could understand the beam on the missionary's face, and I

think Paul beamed when he talked of his men. And he had good cause to be thrilled with them.[2]

Third, Timothy had a servant's heart. Paul also mentioned Timothy's "proven worth," meaning "caliber"; he was that caliber of man. And what was that? He served like a child serving his father.

Question: How can one grown man serve on behalf of another grown man "like a child serving his father"?

Answer in one word: Servanthood.

In the world of leadership we are overrun with hard-charging, tough-minded, power-loving people who equate position with power. But people can wield power in any position, just as long as they maintain control over something others want.

That reminds me of a homey little story that illustrates positional power. A new factory owner went to a nearby restaurant for a quick lunch. The menu featured a blue plate special and made it clear—absolutely no substitutions or additions. The meal was tasty, but the man needed more butter. When he asked for a second pat of butter, the waitress refused. He was so irritated he called for the manager . . . who also refused him and walked away (much to the waitress's delight). "Do you people know who I am?" he asked indignantly. "I am the owner of that factory across the street!" The waitress smiled sarcastically and whined, "Do you know who I am, sweetie? I'm the one who decides whether you get a second pat of butter."

Unlike that waitress, Timothy conformed to the Jesus model. He didn't strut his stuff. Like Paul, he served. By sending Timothy to the people of Philippi, Paul felt he was sending himself. No fear of offense. No anxiety over how the young man might handle some knotty problem he might encounter. Not even a passing thought that he might throw his weight around, saying, "As Paul's right-hand man. . . ." The aging apostle could rest easy. Timothy was the man for the job. Paul must have smiled when he finally waved good-bye. Friends like Timothy relieve life's pressure and enable us to smile.

A "Brother" Named Epaphroditus

Because the two men were closer, Paul wrote of who Timothy was. But when he mentions this second gentleman, Epaphroditus, he puts his finger on what he did. Another contrast: Timothy would be going to Philippi sometime in the future, but Epaphroditus would be sent immediately, probably carrying this letter Paul was writing.

Epaphroditus had been sent to Rome to minister to Paul, but shortly after arriving, the man became terribly ill. Ultimately he recovered, but not before a long struggle where he lingered at death's door. News of his illness might have traveled back to Philippi, and the man was concerned that his friends back home would be worried about him. Furthermore, when he returned earlier than expected, some might think he returned as a quitter, so Paul was careful to write strong words in his defense.

> But I thought it necessary to send to you Epaphroditus, my brother and fellow worker and fellow soldier, who is also your messenger and minister to my need; because he was longing for you all and was distressed because you had heard that he was sick. For indeed he was sick to the point of death, but God had mercy on him, and not on him only but also on me, lest I should have sorrow upon sorrow. Therefore I have sent him all the more eagerly in order that when you see him again you may rejoice and I may be less concerned about you. Therefore receive him in the Lord with all joy, and hold men like him in high regard; because he came close to death for the work of Christ, risking his life to complete what was deficient in your service to me. (Philippians 2:25–30)

And toward the end of the same letter:

> But I have received everything in full, and have an abundance; I am amply supplied, having received from Epaphroditus what you have sent, a fragrant aroma, an acceptable sacrifice, well-pleasing to God. (Philippians 4:18)

When Epaphroditus first arrived, he brought a gift of money from the Philippians. This tells us the people back home trusted him completely. When he gave the gift to Paul, he brought enormous encouragement to the apostle . . . but shortly thereafter, Epaphroditus fell ill. So the apostle writes with deep affection, referring to him as, "brother . . . fellow worker . . . fellow soldier . . . messenger . . . minister to my need." I'd call those admirable qualities in a friend. Bishop Lightfoot says that Epaphroditus was one in "common sympathy, common work, and common danger and toil and suffering" with the great apostle. When you've got someone near you with credentials like that, life doesn't seem nearly as heavy.

Why did Paul send Epaphroditus back? To put the people at ease and to cause them to rejoice (there's that word again) upon hearing from Paul by letter.

What was to be their response back home? Extend a joyful welcome and hold Epaphroditus in high regard.

Why did he deserve their respect? Because he had risked his life in coming to minister to Paul. He had exposed himself to danger. We would say he had flirted with death to be near his friend.

In those days when people visited prisoners who were held captive under Roman authority, they were often prejudged as criminal types as well. Therefore, a visitor exposed himself to danger just by being near those who were considered dangerous. The Greek term Paul uses here for "risking"—*paraboleuomai*—is one that meant "to hazard with one's life . . . to gamble." Epaphroditus did just that.

In the early church there were societies of men and women who called themselves the *parabolani*, that is, *the riskers or gamblers*. They ministered to the sick and imprisoned, and they saw to it that, if at all possible, martyrs and sometimes even enemies would receive an honorable burial. Thus in the city of Carthage during the great pestilence of A.D. 252, Cyprian, the bishop, showed remarkable courage. In self-sacrificing fidelity to his flock, and love even for his enemies, he took upon himself the care of the sick, and bade his congregation nurse them and bury the dead. What a contrast with the practice of the heathen who were throwing the corpses out of the plague-stricken city and were running away in terror![3]

A special joy binds two friends who are not reluctant to risk danger on each other's behalf. If a true friend finds you're in need, he or she will find a way to help. Nor will a friend ever ask, "How great is the risk?" The question is always, "When do you need me?" Not even the threat of death holds back a friend.

This reminds me of the six-year-old girl who became deathly ill with a dreadful disease. To survive, she needed a blood transfusion from someone who had previously conquered the same illness. The situation was complicated by her rare blood type. Her nine-year-old brother qualified as a donor, but everyone was hesitant to ask him since he was just a lad. Finally they agreed to have the doctor pose the question.

The attending physician tactfully asked the boy if he was willing to be brave and donate blood for his sister. Though he didn't understand much about such things, the boy agreed without hesitation: "Sure, I'll give my blood for my sister."

He lay down beside his sister and smiled at her as they pricked his arm with the needle. Then he closed his eyes and lay silently on the bed as the pint of blood was taken.

Soon thereafter the physician came in to thank the little fellow. The boy, with quivering lips and tears running down his cheeks, asked, "Doctor, when do I die?" At that moment the doctor realized that the naive little boy thought that by giving his blood, he was giving up his life. Quickly he reassured the lad that he was not going to die, but amazed at his courage, the doctor asked, "Why were you willing to risk your life for her?"

"Because she is my sister . . . and I love her," was the boy's simple but significant reply.

So it was between Epaphroditus and his brother in Rome . . . and so it is to this day. Danger and risk don't threaten true friendship; they strengthen it. Such friends are modern-day members of *the parabolani*, that reckless band of friends—riskers and gamblers, all—who love their brothers and sisters to the uttermost. Each one deserves our respect. When we need them, they are there. I have a few in that category. Hopefully, you do too.

THREE PEOPLE WHO DESERVE A RESPONSE

As I think about how all this ties in with our lives today, I am reminded of three categories of special people and how we are to respond to them.

First, there are still a few Timothys left on earth, thank goodness. When God sends a Timothy into our lives, He expects us to relate to him. It is often the beginning of an intimate friendship, rarely experienced in our day of superficial companionship. With a Timothy, you won't have to force a friendship; it will flow. Nor will you find yourself dreading the relationship; it will be rewarding. When a Timothy comes along, don't hesitate . . . relate.

Second, there may be a modern-day Epaphroditus who comes to your assistance or your rescue. When God sends an Epaphroditus to minister to us, He expects us to respect him. This is the type of person who reaches out when he has nothing to gain and perhaps much to lose . . . who gambles on your behalf for no other reason than love. His or her action is an act of grace. Don't question it or try to repay it or make attempts to bargain for it. Just accept it. Grace extended in love is to be accepted with gratitude. The best response to an Epaphroditus? Respect.

And there is a third person. His name is Jesus Christ. Since God sent Christ to take away our sins and bring us to heaven, He expects us to receive Him. If you think a Timothy can mean a lot to you or an Epaphroditus could prove invaluable, let me assure you that neither can compare as a substitute for Jesus. With nail-scarred hands He reaches out to you and waits for you to reach back in faith. I tell you without a moment's hesitation, there is no one you will ever meet, no friend you will ever make, who can do for you what Jesus can do. No one else can change your inner heart. No one else can turn your entire life around. No one else can remove not only your sins but the guilt and shame that are part of that whole ugly package. And now that the two of you have been introduced, only one response is appropriate. Only one. Receive.

I began this chapter by stating that people need other people. You need me. I need you. Both of us need a few kindred spirits, people who understand us and encourage us. Both of us need friends who are willing to risk to help us and, yes, at times, to rescue us. Friends like that make life more fun. But all of us—you, me, Timothy-people, Epaphroditus-people, all of us—need a Savior.

In the beginning, the Creator of humanity stated that it was not good for the first human to be alone. He created us for relationship—first with Himself and then with other people. After sin separated us from our Maker and from each other, He didn't leave us alone in our sin and sorrow. God became a man in the person of Jesus Christ. Emmanuel. "God with us." Keep in mind, He came to be "with us." And we need never be alone again.

If you're still going it alone, stop kidding yourself. As it was with the first human, it's not good for *you* to be alone. You need others, starting with the Son of God. Then, through Him, you have fellowship with an enormous family. You need them, and they need you. So, no more delay. Get plugged in. Today!

5

GOD'S WILL

The way of God is complex, He is hard for us to predict. He moves the
pieces and they come somehow into a kind of order.

— EURIPIDES,
   Helen

There is something fundamentally flawed about a purely academic
interest in God. God is not an appropriate object for cool, critical,
detached, scientific observation and evaluation. No, the true knowledge of
God will always lead us to worship. . . . Our place is on our faces before
Him in adoration.

— JOHN R. W. STOTT,
   Romans: God's Great News for the World

Thinking theologically is a tough thing to do. It works against our
human and horizontal perspective on life. Thinking vertically is a
discipline few have mastered. We much prefer to live in the here-and-now
realm, seeing life as others see it, dealing with realities we can touch, analyze,
prove, and explain. We are much more comfortable with the tactile, the familiar, the logic shaped by our culture and lived out in our times.

But God offers a better way to live—one that requires faith as it lifts us
above the drag and grind of our immediate little world, opens new dimensions of thought, and introduces a perspective without human limitations.
In order to enter this better way, we must train ourselves to think theologically. Once we've made the switch, our focus turns away from ourselves,

removing us from a self-centered realm of existence and opening the door of our minds to a God-centered frame of reference, where all things begin and end with Him.

A prophet named Jeremiah was called by God to minister on His behalf. Jeremiah was afraid to accept the assignment because, from his perspective, he was too young, too inexperienced—simply too inadequate. The Lord silenced such horizontal thinking by telling Jeremiah that He knew him even before he was conceived and had set him apart even before he was born. God also promised to protect him and to deliver him and to use him mightily. That started Jeremiah thinking theologically. God had decreed certain things. Jeremiah needed to obey without fear or hesitation. Hard times would surely come—all of which God would permit to happen. But Jeremiah could take great comfort in knowing that God would have His way in spite of the hardships ahead. God had called him and would protect him. And even the opposition Jeremiah would encounter (which God permitted to occur) would not stop or alter God's plan (which He had decreed would occur).

For the rest of this chapter I urge you to think theologically. It will help. By doing so, you will grasp the importance of both the decreed will of God and the permitted will of God.

GOD'S DECRETIVE WILL

The first facet of God's will is what we shall call His decretive will: His sovereign, determined, immutable will. Our friend Job spoke of this when he said:

> Man, who is born of woman,
> Is short-lived and full of turmoil. . . .
> Since his days are determined,
> The number of his months is with Thee,
> And his limits Thou hast set so that he cannot pass. (Job 14:1, 5)

Job's words tell us that the decreed will of God is running its course precisely as arranged by our great God. This aspect of the will of God is not something that we can anticipate ahead of time; we can only know it after it has happened.

It may seem to many that the One who made us is too far removed to concern himself with such tiny details of life here on planet Earth. But that is not the case. His mysterious plan is running its course right on schedule, exactly as He decreed it. This world is not out of control, spinning wildly through space. Nor are earth's inhabitants at the mercy of blind fate or meaningless chaos. I don't know why a tornado destroys one neighborhood and not another. I just know that even in this calamity God's plan is not frustrated or altered. He is not sitting on the edge of heaven, wondering what will happen next. That's not the God of the Scriptures. So while we cannot fathom the "Why?" of this age-old question, we do know that Scripture states that God is not surprised by calamity. Somehow or other, it's all part of His mysterious will.

Now that is a tough concept to justify. So my advice is quite simple: quit trying. While Job's declaration is not something you would want to include in a note of comfort to somebody who has just gone through a great tragedy, it is a verse you need to comfort yourself with when you are going through your own calamity. Remember, nothing is a surprise to God. His plan may seem unfair, humanly illogical, even lacking compassion, but that's because we dwell in the here and now. We lack the vertical view. In fact, we sometimes quarrel with God, as the prophet Isaiah testifies:

> "Woe to the one who quarrels with his Maker—
> An earthenware vessel among the vessels of earth!
> Will the clay say to the potter, 'What are you doing?'
> Or the thing you are making say, 'He has no hands'? . . .
> It is I who made the earth, and created man upon it.
> I stretched out the heavens with My hands,
> And I ordained all their host.
> I have aroused him in righteousness,
> And I will make all his ways smooth;
> He will build My city, and will let My exiles go free,
> Without any payment or reward," says the LORD of hosts. (Isaiah 45:9, 12–13)

At one time in my life statements like that made me cringe and become resentful. Not until I released my grip on my horizontal perspective did I find any comfort in God's sovereignty. Little by little, it began to settle in my mind, bringing relief instead of fear. God is in charge, not us!

This determined, decreed dimension of God's will has four qualities: (1) It is absolute. (2) It is immutable, which means "unchangeable." (3) It is unconditional. (4) It is always in complete harmony with His nature. In other words, the decreed will of God will be holy, it will be just, it will be good, it will be righteous; therefore, it will be best. And everything—even the evil intended by others and the afflictions of a world given over to evil—will work toward God's predetermined ends.

The subject of God's will is woven throughout the tapestry of God's truth as revealed in Scripture. We have seen it in Isaiah. Now let's observe it in Romans:

> We know that God causes all things to work together for good to those who love God, to those who are called according to His purpose. For whom He foreknew, He also predestined to become conformed to the image of His Son, that He might be the first-born among many brethren; and whom He predestined, these He also called; and whom He called, these He justified; and whom He justified, these He also glorified. (Romans 8:28–29)

Mark in the margin of your Bible beside these verses: "Decreed will of God." His decreed will is at work in your life. He's chipping away in your life, causing you to take on the character of His Son, Jesus Christ.

Even the death of our Savior was part of the determined will of God:

> Men of Israel, listen to these words: Jesus the Nazarene, a man attested to you by God with miracles and wonders and signs which God performed through Him in your midst, just as you yourselves know—this Man, delivered up *by the predetermined plan and foreknowledge of God*, you nailed to a cross by the hands of godless men and put Him to death. (Acts 2:22–23, emphasis added)

Though unbelieving men nailed Jesus to His cross, it occurred, "by the predetermined plan and foreknowledge of God." It was exactly at the time and in the place and by the means God had determined. And what looked to the eleven confused disciples as mysterious, as well as unfair and unjust (humanly speaking, it was all of the above and more), God looked at it and said, "That is what I've planned. That's the mission that My Son came to accomplish."

That's why Jesus' final words from the cross before He died were, "It is finished." God's redemption plan had been completed—Jesus' payment for our sin. And then He slumped in death.

And God raised Him up again, putting an end to the agony of death, since it was impossible for Him to be held in its power. (Acts 2:24)

That's exactly what will happen beyond our death. He will raise us up by His grace, putting an end forever to the agony of death, since we will not be held by its power. God has decreed it so. That is a wonderful thought to claim at a graveside, isn't it?

This means, however, that there are some things God cannot and will not do because they do not conform to His nature. For example, God cannot and will not lie (Numbers 23:19; Hebrews 6:18). God cannot and does not tempt anyone to sin (James 1:13–15). Those actions would be against His nature and, therefore, against His will.

"Let no one say when he is tempted, 'I am tempted by God,'" writes James, and he uses an interesting syntax when he writes this. In the original language James used a more subtle expression, meaning, "Let no one say when he is tempted, 'I've been tempted indirectly by God.'"

That's a familiar angle, isn't it? Remember the first couple, Adam and Eve? "The woman You gave me, she caused me to sin." (Indirectly, "Lord, You're the one who made me sin.") And we've been doing that ever since. "Lord, if You hadn't given me this nature, I wouldn't have checked into the Internet, and I wouldn't have gone to that chat room, and I wouldn't have gotten involved with that woman, which led to the affair. I mean, if You hadn't given me the time to do this . . ." Not only is that nonsense, it's terrible theology. God cannot, does not, and will not tempt us. He never solicits us to do evil.

Also, God will never contradict His own nature to make a point. "If we are faithless, He remains faithful; for He cannot deny Himself," Paul writes in 2 Timothy 2:13. God is eternally consistent.

Of course we haven't even scratched the surface of this subject of the decretive will of God, but this at least gives us a place to start.

Just remember: no one ultimately is able to frustrate God's plan . . . no one. No one who lets us down surprises God. No one who walks away from his or her responsibilities causes God to wonder why.

In the final analysis, God will have His way. What He has determined will transpire.

But what about evil? What is God's role regarding earthly matters that do not reflect His holy character?

GOD'S PERMISSIVE WILL

The other realm of the will of God is His permissive will, which represents what God allows. For example, God allowed Job to go through suffering. God didn't cause the suffering. He permitted it. Satan came to God and accused Job of being one of those individuals whom the Lord had carefully protected. "Who wouldn't trust a God who protects His servant from harm? But you touch Job, you touch his life, you touch his family, you touch his health, and he'll curse You."

"All right," said the Lord. "I will allow you to do all that."

I don't know why God did that. How could He call that fair or merciful? From my perspective, it wasn't. It's part of His mysterious will. But I'm not God. I'm merely the clay; He's the Potter. Admittedly, when we read the whole story, we see what wonderful things Job learned about God through this ordeal.

> Then Job answered the LORD, and said,
> "I know that Thou canst do all things,
> And that no purpose of Thine can be thwarted. . . .
> Therefore I have declared that which I did not understand,
> Things too wonderful for me, which I did not know." (Job 42:1–3)

As a result, for succeeding generations, Job's name has been synonymous with patience.

Another example and element of the permissive will of God is found in 2 Peter 3:9:

> The Lord is not slow about His promise, as some count slowness, but is patient toward you, not wishing for any to perish but for all to come to repentance.

There's the very top of God's "wish list." He wishes that all would come to Him and repent—that none would perish. But all will not repent; some never will. The apostle Paul said, in effect, "I've done all of these things that I might by all means save some" (1 Corinthians 9:19–22). He knew that all would not be saved.

God does not wish for anyone to perish but for all to come to repentance. He does not cause sin, but He does permit it. He is not pleased when His creation yields to temptation, but He uses even that to accomplish His purposes.

Pause right now and read Acts 4:27–31.

> "For truly in this city there were gathered together against the holy servant Jesus, whom Thou didst anoint, both Herod and Pontius Pilate, along with the Gentiles and the peoples of Israel, to do whatever Thy hand and Thy purpose predestined to occur.
>
> "And now, Lord, take note of their threats, and grant that Thy bond-servants may speak Thy word with all confidence, while Thou dost extend Thy hand to heal, and signs and wonders take place through the name of Thy holy servant Jesus."
>
> And when they had prayed, the place where they had gathered together was shaken, and they were all filled with the Holy Spirit, and began to speak the word of God with boldness.

In His permissive will, God used godless Gentiles like Pontius Pilate and Herod to carry out His purposes and plans. No matter what our station or status in life, we're all servants—one way or the other—of the sovereign Lord of the universe. He can do whatever He wills with any of us.

DO WE KNOW ANYTHING FOR SURE?

God's Word clearly declares that certain things are not the will of God and never will be the will of God in the Christian life. It also clearly teaches that certain things are the will of God for the believer. We don't have to pray to "find leading" on this. We only have to dig through the Scriptures to mine it for ourselves. Once unearthed, these truths sparkle like the richest ore or brightest gemstone.

This is solid, immutable, unchangeable, biblical, God-given truth. The unsaved will never understand it, nor should we try to make them live up to it. This is strictly the will of God for the child of God. For example, sexual immorality is never the will of God.

> For this is the will of God, your sanctification; that is, that you abstain from sexual immorality. (1 Thessalonians 4:3)

I'm reminded of the Ten Commandments here—a full and complete list of divine prohibitions (read Exodus 20:3–17). Another clearly stated set of actions God hates is conveyed in Proverbs 6:16–19.

Now that we've looked at a few of the negatives, let's consider some of the things that Scripture explicitly tells us are the will of God for our lives.

> Rejoice always; pray without ceasing; in everything give thanks; for this is God's will for you in Christ Jesus. (1 Thessalonians 5:16–18)

"Should I give thanks? Is that the will of God for my life?" You don't have to pray about that. He says it here loud and clear: Rejoice. Pray without ceasing. Give thanks in everything. Give thanks when you are being tested, stretched, and forced to wait. Yes, give thanks. Give thanks for the patience you are learning. Give thanks for the way God is working in your life through this trial. Give thanks.

Peter, one of Jesus' closest friends, reminds us of two more responses that are always the will of God. The first has to do with submission. The second relates to an obedient walk in a wayward world.

Submit yourselves for the Lord's sake to every human institution, whether to a king as the one in authority, or to governors as sent by him for the punishment of evildoers and the praise of those who do right.

For such is the will of God that by doing right you may silence the ignorance of foolish men. (1 Peter 2:13–15)

While we may not know what the will of God is for the future, He has given us a whole list of requirements that are in His will for every believer:

Obey your parents (Ephesians 6:1).

Marry a Christian (1 Corinthians 6:15).

Work at an occupation (1 Thessalonians 4:11–12).

Support your family (1 Timothy 5:8).

Give to the Lord's work and to the poor (2 Corinthians 8–9; Galatians 2:10).

Rear your children by God's standards (Ephesians 6:4).

Meditate on the Scriptures (Psalm 1:2).

Pray (1 Thessalonians 5:17).

Have a joyful attitude (1 Thessalonians 5:16).

Assemble for worship (Hebrews 10:25).

Proclaim Christ (Acts 1:8).

Set proper values (Colossians 3:2).

Have a spirit of gratitude (Philippians 4:6).

Display love (1 Corinthians 13).

Accept people without prejudice (James 2:1–10).

And the list goes on and on.

This is the will of God for your life as a child of God, no matter who you are or where you live. Nothing mysterious here!

The better you get to know the Word of God, the less confusing is the will of God. Those who struggle the least with the will of God are those who know the Word of God best. We see the importance of the Scriptures clearly when we consider another of those often-asked questions: How did God reveal His will in biblical times? And does He do the same today?

LOOKING FOR GUIDANCE

"God's guidance in the Old Testament reached down into the details of daily life while His guidance in the New Testament is expressed in more general commands and principles," says Garry Friesen in his book *Decision Making and the Will of God*.[1]

In biblical times, God revealed His will in a number of ways, but most of them fall into three categories that are clearly verified in Scripture.

First, God used miraculous events to reveal His will.

Before there was Genesis through Revelation, before there was a completed, written revelation of the mind of God, He occasionally used miracles to reveal His will. Examples? The burning bush (Exodus 3:1–10). How did Moses know it was God telling him to return to Egypt and deliver the Israelites? The burning bush. The fact that a bush burned in the wilderness wasn't a miracle. That happens to this day. Lightning strikes, and poof, foliage catches fire and burns. But this brush fire wouldn't go out. Miraculously, it burned and burned. And that's what caused Moses to stop and listen and hear God's will.

Or what about the Red Sea? How did Moses know he should cross the Red Sea? The sea miraculously opened up, making a dry pathway for Moses and the Israelites (Exodus 14:21–29). Pretty sure indication that it was God's will for him to walk across, right?

In the time of the Judges, Gideon wanted to know God's will. He left a lamb fleece out overnight, and God indicated His will by leaving dew on the fleece one time, and another time, no dew (Judges 6).

In the days of the early church, how did Peter know that it was God's will for him to leave prison? God opened the doors and brought him out miraculously (Acts 12:1–17).

Today, God doesn't reveal His will through miraculous events. People may think they see a miracle—like a parking place at the mall during Christmas season or the face of Jesus in an enchilada—but that's not the way God works today. As my friend Gary Richmond says, "If miracles happened that often, they'd be called regulars." Nevertheless, we don't need miracles to discern God's will. We have something far greater. We have His Word in our hands and His Spirit in our hearts!

Not that God no longer does miracles. He does. But miracles, by their very definition, are extremely rare. In my lifetime, I probably could name three I've been aware of, and they were so obviously miracles of God that no other explanation would work. But God's standard method of revealing His will is not through miracles. So, please, don't get caught in that trap. Guard against anticipating or searching for miracles to find God's will. You don't need them.

God used miracles in ancient times because that was the way He spoke to His people prior to His Word being written. Today He speaks to us through His Word.

Second, God spoke through visions and dreams.

Abraham saw visions, and Joseph dreamed dreams (Genesis 15:1; 40:8; 41:25). God spoke to Abraham through visions, just as He spoke to Joseph through dreams. He even used an Egyptian pharaoh's dreams and Joseph's interpretation of those dreams to preserve Egypt from the ravages of a terrible drought and famine. God worked His will for both the Israelites and the Egyptians through visions and dreams.

In New Testament times, Peter saw a sheet coming down from heaven with all kinds of food on it—including what would have been the equivalent of a ham sandwich to a Jew. He saw food that God had forbidden the Jews to eat. Now, however, God said, "Eat." Peter said, "I can't eat." And God said, "Eat." Through this vision of the sheet and the miraculous provision of this food, Peter discovered that it was God's will for him to take the gospel message to the Gentiles (Acts 10:10–23).

Third, God revealed His will through direct revelation.

God spoke His will to His prophets, who in turn delivered the message to the people. "Amos, do this." "Isaiah, say that." "Jeremiah, go over there." The prophets spoke as oracles of God. "For no prophecy was ever made by an act of human will, but men, moved by the Holy Spirit spoke from God" (2 Peter 1:21).

The Greek word here is *phere*, and it literally means to be "moved along apart from one's own power." It's a nautical term used for a ship without a rudder or a sail, carried along at the mercy of the waves and the wind and the current. Here the word is used for the prophets, moved not by their own power, but by the power of God as He spoke through them and revealed His will.

The last occurrence in the Bible of the formula "the word of God came to" refers to John the Baptist (Luke 3:2). He was a true prophet.

Now that the written Word of God is available to us all, the word of God in prophetic utterance is no longer needed. The word of God does not come to people today. It has come once and for all; people must now come to it.

How many times have you heard someone say, "The Lord told me to do so and so"? I confess to you, in my unguarded moments I want to ask, "Was His voice a baritone or a bass? You're telling me you heard His voice?" Of course, when people say they have actually heard God's voice, I get even more spooked!

Have you exhausted His Word so completely that you now must have a literal voice to guide you? Never! We have an inexhaustible source of truth in God's Word. Go there. It will never contradict God's plan or work against God's nature. You can rely on it. It has come down to us through the centuries. As we derive precepts and principles from the Scriptures, based on a careful, intelligent interpretation of His truth, we're able to apply it in numerous ways to our circumstances today. God's Word and God's will are inseparably connected. His Word is God's final revelation, until He sends His Son and takes us home to be with Him. Yes . . . final.

> God, after He spoke long ago to the fathers in the prophets in many portions and in many ways, in these last days has spoken to us in His Son, whom He appointed heir of all things, through whom also He made the world. (Hebrews 1:1–2)

God's Word provides all the light we will ever need on our journey through this life. It's "a lamp to [our] feet, and a light to [our] path" (Psalm 119:105). It brings light to our darkened minds. It helps us think theologically. Strange and mysterious though His leading may seem, when we derive our understanding from a serious investigation of the written Word of God, we will not be led astray. And we will continue to stand on the solid rock of God's Word of Truth.

All other ground is sinking sand.

PREREQUISITES FOR FOLLOWING
THE WILL OF GOD

First and foremost, you must be a Christian. "For all who are being led by the Spirit of God, these are sons of God" (Romans 8:14).

When you accept Christ as the Savior and Lord of your life, the Holy Spirit comes to dwell within you. Among other things, He is there to reveal the will of God to you. Only the believer has the Spirit's presence within, and we must have this inside help if we are going to follow the will of God.

Second, you must be wise. "Therefore be careful how you walk, not as unwise men, but as wise, making the most of your time, because the days are evil" (Ephesians 5:15–16).

At the beginning of the chapter, I gave you a couple of examples of the foolishness that can occur when people attempt to decipher God's will in the wrong way. God tells us not to be foolish, but wise, making the most of our time, taking every opportunity that comes our way and using it wisely.

Before his twentieth birthday, Jonathan Edwards, the brilliant and godly philosopher-theologian who became God's instrument in the Great Awakening revival of the eighteenth century, resolved "never to lose one moment of time, but to improve it in the most profitable way I possibly can." That is exactly what he did, using well the intellectual gifts God had given him. He entered Yale at thirteen and at seventeen graduated at the head of his class. At twenty-six he was the minister of one of the largest congregations in Massachusetts.

Scripture says that doing the will of the Lord requires wisdom, for, as Paul writes in the next verse, those who are wise, those who are not foolish, "understand what the will of the Lord is" (Ephesians 5:17).

Following the will of God requires wisdom, clear thinking, and, yes, even good old garden-variety common sense. Such a mixture helps us understand the Father's will.

Third, you must really want to do the will of God. "If any man is willing to do His will, he shall know of the teaching, whether it is of God, or whether I speak from Myself" (John 7:17).

Your "want to" is a green light: you really will do what He wants you to do. You really want to do the will of God more than anything else. More than completing your education, more than getting married, more than getting your house paid for; more than anything else you want to do the will of God.

Looking back on my own life, I know that there have been times when I said I wanted to do His will but I really didn't. That's a tough thing to confess, but looking back with 20/20 hindsight, I realize that at times I resisted His will. I've learned that serious consequences follow selfish resistance.

The apostle Paul offers words of counsel to those who were enslaved. They have great meaning for us in this context. "Slaves, be obedient to those who are your masters according to the flesh, with fear and trembling, in the sincerity of your heart, as to Christ," wrote Paul, "not by way of eyeservice, as men-pleasers, but as slaves of Christ, doing the will of God *from the heart*" (Ephesians 6:5–6, emphasis added).

Doing the will of God from the heart—that's as deep as it gets. More than pleasing people, more than staying comfortable and safe, you want to please God. You want to follow His will with all of your being.

Fourth, you must be willing to pray and to wait. "Ask, and it shall be given to you; seek, and you shall find; knock, and it shall be opened to you. For everyone who asks receives, and he who seeks finds, and to him who knocks it shall be opened" (Matthew 7:7–8). "And this is the confidence which we have before Him, that, if we ask anything according to His will, He hears us. And if we know that He hears us in whatever we ask, we know that we have the requests which we have asked from Him" (1 John 5:14–15).

Fifth, following the will of God means you must be willing to give up your creature comforts. "'And now, behold, bound in spirit, I am on my way to Jerusalem, not knowing what will happen to me there, except that the Holy Spirit solemnly testifies to me in every city, saying that bonds and afflictions await me. But I do not consider my life of any account as dear to myself, in order that I may finish my course, and the ministry which I received from the Lord Jesus, to testify solemnly of the gospel of the grace of God'" (Acts 20:22–24).

Here, Paul speaks of the direction in which the Spirit is leading him as being "bound in the spirit." He is caught up in following the will of God, committed to it, bound by it. "I'm leaving you folks here in Ephesus," he says, "and I'm going where it's not going to be as comfortable. In fact, there will be struggles, pressures, discomforts, and afflictions—dangerous risks, even imprisonment. But none of that matters. Even my life doesn't matter."

Now we know some of the essentials that are required before we can even think of following the Lord's will. If we are going to follow, we have to be able to sense the presence and pleasure of our Leader. So, then, how does God lead us into His will today? Without removing all the mystery that often accompanies His will, I have found several absolutes that assist me in following the Lord.

How Does God Lead Today?

I could probably list at least ten ways that God leads His children today, but I will limit myself to the four that I think are the most significant methods of God's leading.

First and most basic, God leads us through His written Word. As the psalmist said, "Thy word is a lamp to my feet, and a light to my path" (Psalm 119:105).

Whenever you see the scriptural phrase "This is the will of God," you know for sure that's His will. You also know that to disobey is to break His Word. Other clear indications of His leading are the precepts and principles in the Scripture.

There are precepts in Scripture, but mainly God has given us principles to follow. These principles require wisdom and discernment. "Teach me good discernment and knowledge," wrote the psalmist, "for I believe in Thy commandments" (Psalm 119:66).

We need to be very clear about the way God leads His people today. God leads us through His written Word. However, keep in mind that this does not mean that we must have a particular Bible verse for every single decision or move we make.

Second, God leads us through the inner prompting of the Holy Spirit. Read the following statement carefully: "So then, my beloved, just as you have always obeyed, not as in my presence only, but now much more in my absence, work out your salvation with fear and trembling; for it is God who is at work in you, both to will and to work for His good pleasure" (Philippians 2:12–13).

Now that you've been born again, Paul says, work out your salvation. In other words, be discerning, think it through, use your head, pay attention, get serious about your Christian walk. For it is God (the Holy Spirit) who is working His will in you. That's why the apostle can say in the next verse, "Do all things without grumbling or disputing" (Philippians 2:14). As the Spirit of God within you engages in various ways of leading you, working out God's will in you, you come to accept it, regardless of the challenges the future brings.

I think of a young Christian couple who for the past fifteen years have been living through unbelievably difficult circumstances. When they were in their late twenties, parents of four children, the young mother was diagnosed with multiple sclerosis. Now in their thirties, with her condition worsening severely, they are still living witnesses of God's grace "without grumbling and disputing." That is clearly the result of the Holy Spirit's work within.

The book of Jude offers a wonderful example of the powerful prompting of the Holy Spirit: "Beloved, while I was making every effort to write you about our common salvation, I felt the necessity to write to you appealing that you contend earnestly for the faith which was once for all delivered to the saints" (v. 3). Jude started to write a letter to his fellow Christians about salvation, about the finished work of Christ on the cross. That was his original plan . . . until the Holy Spirit prompted him to do otherwise. "I felt the necessity to do so," Jude admits. I've underlined that phrase in my Bible: "I felt the necessity." That was nothing less than the inner prompting from the Spirit of God.

Nothing wrong with planning. Nothing wrong with thinking it through, listing all the pros and cons, and talking it over. But as you are moving along, stay sensitive to the quiet, yet all-important prompting of God through His Holy Spirit. By doing so, you may well sense inner promptings that will spur a thought, such as, "I can't believe I'm still interested in that. I wonder what the Lord is doing? I wonder where He's going with this?"

That inner prompting is crucial, because much of the time we just can't figure it out. "Man's steps are ordained by the LORD, how then can man understand his way?" (Proverbs 20:24). (I love that!) When all is said and done, you'll say, "Honestly, I didn't figure this thing out. It must have been God." Talk about mysterious! The longer I live the Christian life, the less I know about why He leads as He does. But I do know that He leads.

The third way God leads us is through the counsel of wise, qualified, trustworthy people. This does not mean some guru in Tibet or serious-looking stranger at the bus stop. This is an individual who has proven himself or herself wise and trustworthy and, therefore, qualified to counsel on a given matter. Usually such individuals are older and more mature than we. Furthermore, they have nothing to gain or lose. This also means that they are often not in our immediate family. (Immediate family members usually don't want us to do something that will take us away from them or cause us or them discomfort or worry.)

One well-known exception to this is Moses, who listened to the wise counsel of his father-in-law, Jethro (Exodus 18:17–27). "Moses, you're trying to take on too much," said Jethro. "You can't do everything. You need help." Moses listened, and he found that the will of God was that he delegate most of his numerous responsibilities.

At critical moments in my own life, I have sought the counsel of seasoned individuals—and they've seldom been wrong. That's been my experience. But you must choose your counselors very carefully. And just as the best counselors are often not your family, often they are not your best friends either. Wise and trustworthy counselors are persons who want for you only what God wants. Such persons will stay objective, listen carefully, and answer slowly. Often they won't give you an answer at the time you ask for it. They want to sleep on it; they want to think about it.

Finally, God leads us into His will by giving us an inner assurance of peace. "And let the peace of Christ rule in your hearts," Paul writes to the Colossians, "to which indeed you were called in one body; and be thankful" (Colossians 3:15). God's inner assurance of peace will act as an umpire in your heart.

Although peace is an emotion, I have found it wonderfully reassuring as I've wrestled with the Lord's will. This God-given peace comes in spite of the obstacles or the odds, regardless of the risk or danger. It's almost like God's way of saying, "I'm in this decision . . . trust Me through it."

The will of God for our lives is not some high-sounding theory; it is reality. We have discussed some of the prerequisites and requirements for following the will of God, and we have looked at some of the ways God leads us into His will. Now comes the bottom line: we have to live out His will in the real world.

Two Searching Questions

Let me ask you two pointed questions as we wrap up our thoughts in this chapter. First: *What makes risk so difficult for you?* Be painfully honest as you answer that question. Blow away the fog in your thinking. Clear out the nettles and overgrown vines of tradition or bad habits or just plain sloth. Change, for most folks, is enormously challenging. Walking with the Lord is a risky path, and everything within us, when we live and lean on our own understanding, screams, "Just keep it like it is. Just leave it alone. If it ain't broke, don't fix it." But sometimes things need to be rearranged even though they aren't broken. Sometimes we need a major change of direction—not because we are necessarily going in an evil direction, it's just not the direction God wants for us. God does not want us to substitute the good for the very best.

Now, here's my second question: *Are you willing to make a major change in your life—assuming that it's the Lord's will?* I'm now convinced that the real issue is not so much, "What does the Lord want me to do?" as it is, "Am I willing to do it once He makes it clear?"

Before moving on, stop and answer those two questions. Not until they are answered are you ready to move ahead, fleshing out the will of God.

PART TWO

What's True About God Becomes True About You

6

Intimacy:
Deepening Our Lives

We live in a society that tries to diminish us to the level of the antheap
so that we scurry mindlessly, getting and consuming. It is essential to
take counteraction. . . . Every one of us needs to be stretched to live at
our best, awakened out of dull moral habits, shaken out of petty and
trivial busy-work.[1]

— Eugene Peterson

Let's go on a brief spiritual pilgrimage together.

Journey back in your mind to your first days as a brand-new believer
in Jesus Christ, no matter how recent. Return to that time when your love
was budding and emerging into full bloom. Remember when you would
speak of Christ and it would ignite your heart with an exciting burst of zeal
and delight? Remember when prayer was new and untried, and you felt its
power as you communed with the Almighty? Remember when the Bible was
that delicious book of truth filled with delectable insights you had never
known before? Remember when sharing Him with someone else repre-
sented the highlight of your week? Remember when your devotion was
consistent, fulfilling, enriching . . . deep?

What happened to all of that? When you ponder those questions—not
just in passing, but taking time to concentrate as you ponder them—you
may find yourself feeling like one of the Ephesian Christians that we're about

to discuss, whom Jesus urged, "Remember from where you have fallen, and repent and do the deeds you did at first" (Revelation 2:5).

The book of Revelation recounts a church, known only as "the church at Ephesus," that worked diligently and was known for its zeal and encouragement. This is what the Lord Himself had to say about this church as He sized it up:

> I know your deeds and your toil and perseverance, and that you cannot tolerate evil men, and you put to the test those who call themselves apostles, and they are not, and you found them to be false. (Revelation 2:2)

They would have nothing to do with apostolic pretenders. This discerning group of believers formed a church famous for its doctrine. It was biblically sound and probably had strong leaders, with many courageous people willing to take a stand in opposition to wrong. They gave no time to folks who were phony. They were zealous and firm and relentless in their pursuit of truth. So far, so good. Who can argue with orthodoxy? However, all was not well in the Ephesian church, and they will show us that not all change can be counted as growth.

Verse 4 begins with what linguists call a particle of contrast: *but*. For three verses we read of nothing but commendable things, attributes of a local assembly of believers that would have drawn you and hundreds of other first-century worshipers like you to the church at Ephesus. "But I have this against you," the Lord says with a sigh. "You have left your first love."

A. T. Robertson, in his *Word Pictures in the New Testament*, writes, "This early love, proof of the new life in Christ . . . had cooled off in spite of their doctrinal purity. They had remained orthodox, but had become unloving."[2]

John R. W. Stott, in a small but wonderful work entitled *What Christ Thinks of the Church*, adds these thoughts about the Ephesian believers:

> They had fallen from the early heights of devotion to Christ which they had climbed. They had descended to the plains of mediocrity. In a word, they were backsliders. . . . Certainly the hearts of the Ephesian Christians had chilled.[3]

I can't speak for you, but it puts a shiver up my back when I see the word *chilled*. What an indictment! What a horrible way to describe the heart of a Christian! I think of death when I hear that word used to describe a heart.

A little later Stott continues, "Their first flush of ecstasy had passed. Their early devotion to Christ had cooled. They had been in love with Him, but they had fallen out of love."[4]

How much had changed since Paul had penned his last comment to that church in his letter to the Ephesians: "Grace be with all those who love our Lord Jesus Christ *with a love incorruptible*" (Ephesians 6:24, emphasis added).

In that benediction, I feel a longing in the great apostle's heart that the Ephesian Christians experience no waning of love. By the time John wrote the book of Revelation thirty years later, Paul's dreams were dashed. Jesus said, in effect, "You left that love. You once had a love that was incorruptible, but you abandoned it. You once enjoyed a devotion that was consistent, meaningful, satisfying. In fact, the warmth of your love transformed your thinking and your attitudes; it revolutionized the way you related to Me, to your heavenly Father, and to your brothers and sisters. But you have cooled off."

John Stott aptly portrays the scene:

> The tide of devotion had turned and was ebbing fast. They toiled with vigour, but not with love. They endured with fortitude but without love. They tested their teachers with orthodoxy but had no love in their hearts.[5]

Remember, we said earlier that growth is change, but not all change is growth. Cynthia and I would never choose to return to those early days, not even to when our love was in springtime, delightfully new and fresh. Those were wonderful days and wonderful feelings, but our love has grown. The love we enjoy now is deeper, characterized by a comfortable ease and a profound sense of security that nearly fifty years of life shared together has earned.

Not so for the Ephesians! And perhaps not so for you in your relationship with God. Look again at what Jesus commanded. Your spiritual life may be in need of some major changes. A new perspective is essential in order to rekindle that first-love kind of relationship where God is real again, where you and He are on much closer speaking terms. The kind of intimacy that doesn't require a stirring message from the pulpit and doesn't depend upon a great worship event or concert but simply exists as a natural part of your walk.

INTIMACY WITH GOD REQUIRES ACTION

Distance from God is a frightening thing. God will never adjust His agenda to fit ours. He will not speed His pace to catch up with ours; we need to slow our pace in order to recover our walk with Him. God will not scream and shout over the noisy clamor; He expects us to seek quietness, where His still, small voice can be heard again. God will not work within the framework of our complicated schedules; we must adapt to His style. We need to conform to His way if our lives are to be characterized by the all-encompassing word *godliness.*

Godliness is still our desire as believers, isn't it?

But the great question is, how? How do busy people, living fast-paced and complicated lives, facing relentless pressures, consistently walk with God? Whatever would be included in the answers, we can be assured that they will not come naturally, automatically, quickly, or easily. I do not think a person on this earth has ever been automatically godly or quickly godly or easily and naturally godly. "This world is no friend of grace to help us on to God."[6] Everything around us is designed to make us dissatisfied with our present condition.

Henri Nouwen said that while he was driving through Los Angeles on one occasion, he felt like he was driving through a giant dictionary—words everywhere, sounds everywhere, signs everywhere, saying, "Use me, take me, buy me, drink me, smell me, touch me, kiss me, sleep with me."[7] He found himself longing to get away from all those words, all those giant signs and sounds. Why? Not because there was something innately wrong with those things—some, but not all. He grieved that it was all so empty, so devoid of God.

So how do we pull it off? How, in a world bent on distracting us from growing deeper in our first love, always enticing us to pursue the pointless, do we find closeness with God? How do you and I become godlier?

This question has led me back to a word that I used much more in my early days in ministry than I have in recent years. The word is *discipline*. The secret lies in our returning to the spiritual disciplines.

DISCIPLINE YOURSELF
FOR INTIMACY WITH GOD

Pause long enough to read the following scripture slowly. It is Paul's advice to Timothy, his son in the faith:

> But the Spirit explicitly says that in later times some will fall away from the faith, paying attention to deceitful spirits and doctrines of demons, by means of the hypocrisy of liars seared in their own conscience as with a branding iron, men who forbid marriage and advocate abstaining from foods which God has created to be gratefully shared in by those who believe and know the truth. For everything created by God is good, and nothing is to be rejected if it is received with gratitude; for it is sanctified by means of the word of God and prayer.
>
> In pointing out these things to the brethren, you will be a good servant of Christ Jesus, constantly nourished on the words of the faith and of the sound doctrine which you have been following. But have nothing to do with worldly fables fit only for old women. *On the other hand, discipline yourself for the purpose of godliness*; for bodily discipline is only of little profit, but godliness is profitable for all things, since it holds promise for the present life and also for the life to come. (1 Timothy 4:1–8, emphasis added)

Paul was sitting alone in a dungeon when he wrote this letter to Timothy. His younger friend was serving as the pastor of a church—interestingly, the church in Ephesus. This instruction came sometime after the letter Paul wrote to the Ephesians and before the letter Jesus wrote to that same church in Revelation 2. Consider Eugene Peterson's paraphrase of that passage in *The Message*:

> The Spirit makes it clear that as time goes on, some are going to give up on the faith and chase after demonic illusions put forth by professional liars. These liars have lied so well and for so long that they've lost their capacity for truth. They will tell you not to get married. They'll tell you not to eat this or that food—perfectly good food God created to be eaten heartily and with thanksgiving by Christians! Everything God created is good, and to be

received with thanks. Nothing is to be sneered at and thrown out. God's Word and our prayers make every item in creation holy.

You've been raised on the Message of the faith and have followed sound teaching. Now pass on this counsel to the Christians there, and you'll be a good servant of Jesus. Stay clear of silly stories that get dressed up as religion. Exercise daily in God—no spiritual flabbiness, please! Workouts in the gymnasium are useful, but a disciplined life in God is far more so, making you fit both today and forever. (1 Timothy 4:1–8 MSG)

I think verse 7 represents the climax of Paul's instruction to Timothy. Don't miss this advice: "Discipline yourself for the purpose of godliness." In other words, "Timothy, get serious about your walk with God! It's time to step up, young man . . . godliness won't just happen."

Guess what, churchgoing men and women: religion won't cut it! We live in a spiritual hothouse where we talk religious talk and send religious letters and write religious pamphlets and do religious Bible study guides and answer religious phones (religiously) and deal with religious concerns. It is so easy to get religious instead of godly. And all the while, a chilling religion slowly cools our hearts. Ironic, isn't it? The general public may have this marvelous idea about how godly we are, when if the truth were known, many of us would have to say, "I am stagnant, and I have been that way longer than I want to admit."

What's missing? Stop and think. It's that "first love," the great fountain that both generates the spiritual disciplines and feeds on them. Yet I find it absolutely amazing that in the process of doing spiritual things (not religious things, but truly *spiritual* things), we can fail to "discipline" ourselves "for the purpose of godliness." I can, and I have.

Therefore in recent months I have sensed a genuine need—in my own life first (before I ever speak or write to someone else, I have to address it in my own life)—for the cultivation of intimacy with the Almighty. Those words are carefully chosen. They are put forth in deliberate contrast. The almighty, awesome God loves it when we are intimate with Him. So, our goal is intimacy, and according to Scripture, intimacy with God requires spiritual disciplines. In this book I will address eight disciplines that are essential in our pursuit of godliness.

INTIMACY WITH GOD CULTIVATES WISDOM

While rummaging through an old bookstore some time ago, I came across Dallas Willard's excellent work *The Spirit of the Disciplines*. Bedside reading, it is not. This convicting piece of literature is not something you plop down on the sofa and read alongside *People* magazine. Willard's words require you to think with him. For example:

> The modern age is an age of revolution—revolution motivated by insight into the appalling vastness of human suffering and need. Pleas for holiness and attacks on sin and Satan were used for centuries as the guide and the cure for the human situation. Today such pleas have been replaced with a new agenda. On the communal level, political and social critiques yield recipes for revolutions meant to liberate humankind from its many bondages. And on the individual level various self-fulfillment techniques promise personal revolutions bringing "freedom in an unfree world" and passage into the good life. Such are modern answers to humanity's woes.
>
> Against this background a few voices have continued to emphasize that the cause of the distressed human condition, individual and social—and its only possible cure—is a spiritual one. But what these voices are saying is not clear. They point out that social and political revolutions have shown no tendency to transform the heart of darkness that lies deep in the breast of every human being. That is evidently true. And amid a flood of techniques for self-fulfillment, there is an epidemic of depression, suicide, personal emptiness, and escapism through drugs and alcohol, cultic obsession, consumerism, and sex and violence—all combined with an inability to sustain deep and enduring personal relationships.
>
> So obviously the problem is a spiritual one. And so must be the cure.
>
> But if the cure is spiritual, how does modern Christianity fit into the answer? Very poorly, it seems, for Christians are among those caught up in the sorrowful epidemic just referred to. And that fact is so prominent that modern thinking has come to view the Christian faith as powerless, even somehow archaic, at the very least irrelevant. . . .
>
> There is a deep longing among Christians and non-Christians alike for the personal purity and power to live as our hearts tell us we should. What we

need is a deeper insight into our practical relationship with God in redemption. We need an understanding that can guide us into constant interaction with the Kingdom of God as a real part of our daily lives.[8]

"The Kingdom of God as a real part of our daily lives." I want that. I want that for you more than any other thing. I want that for every soul reading this book. But the hardest thing in the world, it seems, is for God to have our full attention so that intimacy with Him glows from within and can be seen by others as a passion that is authentic. He wants no mere show of religion but a passionate spirituality, where God still does miraculous things through His people—often in spite of us—where God reveals His will in ways that are full of mystery and surprise and wonder. A humble spirituality that leaves us, the clay, willingly soft and malleable in the hands of the Potter, our sovereign God. I repeat, I want that for me, and I want that for you.

Again and again and again the words *deep* and *deeper* appear in Willard's book. I want depth; I don't want heights. I want substance; I don't want speed. I want to be able to think theologically and biblically, not be entertained with theological theories and biblical stories. I believe you want that, too, or you wouldn't be reading these pages.

WITH WISDOM COMES CHRISTLIKENESS

We need wisdom, not just knowledge. God is willing to give wisdom, but not on our terms. As we go deeper, He begins to entrust us with more and more of His mind. In the process we become more and more like Christ.

When tragedy strikes, we don't need more intelligence. We don't need a greater number of skills. We need depth, the kind of depth Job had. When the bottom dropped out of his life, Job had the wisdom to say:

"But He knows the way I take;
When He has tried me, I shall come forth as gold.
My foot has held fast to His path;
I have kept His way and not turned aside.
I have not departed from the command of His lips;

I have treasured the words of His mouth
more than my necessary food. (Job 23:10–12)

We need the depth of Paul, who prayed three times for the horrible stake in his flesh to leave (the word often translated "thorn" means a pointed instrument, like a sword), and three times the Lord said no. In response, Paul said, "Most gladly I will rather boast in my infirmities, that the power of Christ may rest upon me" (2 Corinthians 12:9 NKJV). That's depth. That's an example of wisdom at work. Rather than throw a pity party for himself, Paul boldly declared, "I choose to embrace my affliction so that I can have the privilege of experiencing even more of Christ's power over me."

What depth of character. What intimacy with the Almighty these men had. I want that too. I want what they had, so that my walk is such that I walk in step whether I feel good or not. Whether I get a yes or no to my prayers, I walk consistently, even when I don't get my own way.

WISDOM IS CULTIVATED ON GOD'S TERMS, NOT OURS

God often does His best work in us when He catches us by surprise and introduces a change that is completely against our own desire.

A couple of years after Cynthia and I were married, I had an obligation to fulfill in the military, so I joined the Marine Corps. I endured boot camp and advanced infantry training, which I completed at Camp Pendleton. I then received orders to serve my tour of duty in San Francisco. Cynthia and I were elated. Other guys were going to hot deserts, like Barstow, California, and lonely places like Okinawa, out in the middle of nowhere. Some were assigned to guard duty aboard a ship and would have to be at sea for six months at a time.

Not me. My assigned duty was at 100 Harrison Street in San Francisco, an enviable, plum assignment. We bought a new car and took off on our first road trip through the Sierras to that beautiful and romantic city on the California peninsula. It was fabulous! While we were settling into our little studio apartment in Daly City, we got connected with a fine church located south of us, Peninsula Bible Church.

Then . . . an unexpected letter came in the mail. At first I didn't even bother to open it; it was one of those form letters the military sends out by the truckloads. I sat staring out into the San Francisco bay. I could see Alcatraz straight ahead. Eventually I pulled the letter out of my pocket, sliced it open, and immediately noticed the printed signature at the bottom: Dwight D. Eisenhower, the president. It was a speed letter containing the official order for me to change from San Francisco to Okinawa. And, of course, I did what anybody would have done. I checked the envelope to make sure it was sent to the right person. No mistake. It was mine. Immediately my whole frame of reference changed.

Cynthia and I wept ourselves to sleep that night. Early on in our marriage, that tour of duty would take me sixty-five hundred miles away from her for no fewer than sixteen months. It felt like our world had spun off its axis and come to an end.

Little did I realize how that one small sheet of paper would change my entire life. It opened doors I would never have otherwise passed through. It forced me out of my familiar, somewhat pampered existence and into a world of stretching opportunities that laid the groundwork for a ministry I would never have known or pursued. But at that moment—the moment it began—I could not imagine anything good coming from such a shocking disappointment.

Before I left, my brother shoved a book in my hand titled *Through Gates of Splendor*, the story of five missionaries who were martyred in Ecuador and their widows, who went on to evangelize the same Auca Indians who had murdered their husbands. On that troop ship, during the seventeen days between California and Okinawa, I discovered a whole new frame of reference. For the first time since I received the speed letter, my mind stopped resisting. For the first time I stopped focusing on myself. For the first time I began to think, *Maybe there's a divine plan at work here.*

I met a man named Bob Newkirk on the island of Okinawa. And one of the first things Bob gave me was a newly released translation of the New Testament—really, a paraphrase—called the Amplified New Testament. When I opened to read that paraphrase of the Scriptures for the first time, I found that Bob had marked only one verse: Philippians 3:10. I read that volume through at least three times before I left the island, but this verse kept coming back to me:

> [For my determined purpose is] that I may know Him—that I may progressively become more deeply and intimately acquainted with Him, perceiving and recognizing and understanding [the wonders of His Person] more strongly and more clearly, and that I may in that same way come to know the power outflowing from His resurrection [which it exerts over believers]; and that I may so share His sufferings as to be continually transformed [in spirit into His likeness even] to His death. (Philippians 3:10 AMP)

That's it! That's why I wound up on Okinawa! Humanly speaking, I never would have met Bob Newkirk in the safe haven of Houston or during our idyllic honeymoon in San Francisco. But halfway around the world, away from all the crutches, separated from all of those things that made me comfortable, I was given a chance to see God at work cross-culturally like never before. And the government paid my way! For the first time I would spend time in a missionary home. For the first time I would be surrounded by another culture and baffled by another language. For the first time in my life I would be the foreigner. And I found myself again and again and again having to look to heaven and learn a whole new way of walking. And best of all, my first love really began to bloom.

"My determined purpose" [perhaps Paul means 'my focus'] is *that I may know Him.*

INTIMACY WITH GOD MUST BE INTENTIONAL

Intimacy is marked by a very close association, contact, or familiarity. Relationally, intimacy is a warm and satisfying friendship developing through long association on a very personal and private level.

As I was preparing to preach on marriage at the Dallas Theological Seminary chapel, I came to the twenty-fifth verse in Genesis 2: "And the man and his wife were both naked and were not ashamed." The thought hit me: *That's the best description of intimacy.* It includes being emotionally naked and unashamed. You can be physically naked and unashamed with your partner in marriage. You can be so personally unguarded, you're able to share your deepest fear, your most guarded secret, or your most frightening thought, and you have no shame. That's intimacy.

> *But the ultimate is not an intimacy with one's partner in life; it is intimacy with the living God.*

Paul says, in effect, "My determined purpose is to be inwardly naked yet unashamed before Him, understanding the wonders of His person and the mystery of His will." Such divine intimacy is rare.

How distant are you from God right now? Has your closeness with Him chilled? Could that be why your worship has become so perfunctory? Do you sing the songs while thinking about something else? Are you so critical of your brothers and sisters in God's family that you sound just like an unbeliever, even though you know your place after death will be with God in heaven?

Paul would respond this way: "My determined purpose is for that never to be true of me. I will pursue a relationship with Him that becomes so close, He and I will walk consistently together through whatever pressures that occur." That's intimacy. That's our goal.

And the way we secure that intimacy? *Discipline.*

Discipline is training that corrects and perfects our mental faculties or molds our moral character. Discipline is control gained by enforced obedience. It is the deliberate cultivation of inner order.

So how are intimacy and discipline connected? If intimacy is the goal, discipline is the means to that end. Remember, intimacy is never natural, automatic, quick, or easy. Show me someone who is intimate with God, and I'll show you someone who can be compared to a beautiful garden without weeds. Because all gardens grow weeds, you can bet that someone has taken time to cultivate the good plants while rooting out the bad ones. People who are close to God cultivate a personal intimacy with Him like a good gardener cultivates beautiful flowers.

So intimacy is both a discipline and a goal—much like humility and prayer and sacrifice, and any of the other disciplines. Our great tendency in this age is to increase our speed, to run faster, even in the Christian life. In the process our walk with God stays shallow, and our tank runs low on fumes. Intimacy offers a full tank of fuel that can only be found by pulling up closer to God, which requires taking necessary time and going to the effort to make that happen. Remember, Paul said that his "determined purpose" (the discipline) was that he might "know God more intimately and personally" (the goal). Intimacy and discipline work together—and in the process, in a very real way, the means (discipline) leads to the very satisfying end (intimacy).

PRAYER: CALLING OUT

Prayer is listening as well as speaking, receiving as well as asking; and its deepest mood is friendship held in reverence. So the daily prayer should end as it begins—in adoration.[1]

— GEORGE A. BUTTRICK

UNDERSTANDING PRAYER

Understanding any spiritual discipline begins with a good definition. Put succinctly, prayer is communicating with God. A conversation that can be spoken or silent, and even expressed in song. Many of the psalms are prayers set to music. A primary purpose of prayer is connecting with God in order to transfer His will into your life. It's collaborating with God to accomplish His goals.

Prayer is a vital expression of trust in the Lord that emerges from our devotion and commitment. E. M. Bounds put it this way: "When the angel of devotion has gone, the angel of prayer has lost its wings, and it becomes a deformed and loveless thing."[2]

Prayer often involves other disciplines, such as meditation, worship, silence, solitude, and surrender—always surrender.

Effective prayer will have a believer deliberately seeking the mind of God on a particular matter that's on his or her heart. Whether it's confessing a sin or praising His name or pursuing His will or interceding for a friend or petitioning for our own needs, prayer must be God-centered, never self-centered.

> *To reduce prayer to a cheap marketing scheme insults God's character. He is holy and righteous, and He will always act in your best interests whether you behave correctly or not.*

Sincere prayer comes from a heart that longs for God to reveal what He desires. So prayer must also allow adequate time for listening, waiting intently before the Father.

God never hides His will. If we seek direction, He delights in providing it.

WHAT PRAYER IS NOT

Since prayer is one of the most powerful of all spiritual disciplines, we shouldn't be surprised that it is among the most misunderstood as well. Christian prayer has some important distinctions from the discipline in other religions, yet it's a temptation for Christians—even those who have known the Lord for years—to make prayer complicated. It is easy to have a distorted perspective.

While He was on earth, Jesus clearly addressed what should be avoided when His followers pray:

> When you pray, you are not to be like the hypocrites; for they love to stand and pray in the synagogues and on the street corners so that they may be seen by men. Truly I say to you, they have their reward in full. But you, when you pray, go into your inner room, close your door and pray to your Father who is in secret, and your Father who sees what is done in secret will reward you. And when you are praying, do not use meaningless repetition as the Gentiles do, for they suppose that they will be heard for their many words. So do not be like them; for your Father knows what you need before you ask Him. (Matthew 6:5–8)

Prayer is not bargaining or pleading. As Douglas V. Steere, a Quaker scholar, wrote, "It's not a question of changing God's mind or of exercising some magical influence or spell."[3] Pagan religions worshiped gods that could be charmed with incantations and influenced by offerings. But attempts to coerce God didn't stop with ancient rituals; they are ever-present among us! "Name it and claim it" until your face turns blue, sow all the "seeds of faith" until your checkbook gasps, but God will not be manipulated. Jesus opened the way for us to have direct access to the throne of heaven—an awesome privilege that would have boggled the minds of the Old Testament saints.

Prayer is not a get-rich-quick scheme. Despite what many of the media hucksters may tell you, prayer does not release the powers of good fortune from heaven, filling your pocketbook with an abundance of cash. Difficult as it is to understand, His will may be for His people to live as poor as dirt, just as His own Son and the apostles who followed Him did.

Prayer is not presenting God with a wish list as though He were a genie. Neither is prayer a laborious, painful marathon of monotonous misery entered into for hours each day to prove one's piety to God. It is not the repetition of the same religious words. Remember? Jesus condemned "meaning-less repetition." On the contrary, rather than trying to motivate or impress God to gain what we want, prayer is an authentic seeking of His plan as we willingly adjust our will to match His.

WHAT PRAYER IS

Our hope in doing so is to glean His perspective, or as Paul called it, "the mind of Christ" (1 Corinthians 2:16). Thankfully we can have this conversation anywhere and at any time.

Before I moved to Frisco, Texas, it took me about twenty-five minutes early on Sunday mornings to drive from our home in Dallas to Stonebriar Community Church. It took much longer during the week. Usually I left the radio off in order to use that time for prayer. The habits I picked up during those years have remained, so my time behind the steering wheel is a regular opportunity to pray. I'll walk through the morning message in my mind and ponder snags that emerge in the sermon. I'll ask for guidance on how to transition between complex points or how to illustrate a difficult truth. I'll also talk with Him about special needs, like how to blend the worship service that morning into a meaningful service of praise, or ask His guidance

> *Prayer is one's personal conversation with the Almighty that includes both expressing our concerns and listening to His response.*

regarding some matter of church business, easily switching back and forth between large and small issues.

I pray for my wife. I pray for all four of our children. I pray for our ten grandchildren, mentioning each one before the Lord. I pray for Dallas Theological Seminary, our government leaders, and sometimes for world affairs—tragedies, conflicts, or efforts for peace. I am often amazed by how many concerns I'm able to cover while driving between appointments or to run errands.

Often I speak to God out loud. Sometimes I sing to Him. Occasionally the entire prayer will be in my mind. Each time I commit myself to prayer, I notice that God becomes my focus rather than some personal struggle. I am relieved of worry. I am able to release anything concerning me so that I could become altogether lost in the majesty of His presence and the joy of ministry. When I arrive, I'm excited to do as God pleases. I find myself refreshed, relieved, and ready. My mind is focused. My heart is prepared. My emotions are clear, and whatever was troubling me when I began that drive no longer concerns me. Prayer has made that possible.

Now, I wish that I could say that I use every commute every day for time in prayer. But, like many people, I often forget. My mind will be spinning from one problem to the next and rather than pray, I churn. At times I'll be so anxious that it doesn't occur to me that I should quit worrying and commence praying. (More about worry in a moment.)

THE PRIORITY OF PRAYER

Prayer is not a natural response; it's a Spirit response. If we fail to cultivate this discipline, prayer winds up being our last resort rather than our first response. Sometime after Timothy became the pastor in Ephesus, Paul wrote him a letter of instruction. In the second chapter of 1 Timothy, Paul communicated to his son in the faith many of the fundamentals of ministry.

Not surprisingly he started with the discipline of prayer, beginning with the words, "First of all . . ."

> First of all, then, I urge that entreaties and prayers, petitions and thanks-givings, be made on behalf of all men, for kings and all who are in author-ity, so that we may lead a tranquil and quiet life in all godliness and dignity. (1 Timothy 2:1–2)

Note the priority Timothy was admonished to give to prayer. In effect, Paul wrote, "First of all, I urge you. I plead with you, Timothy, *first* pray. *First*, before you slide out of bed. *First*, before you take a shower to start your day. *First*, before you make your way to work. *First*, before any appointment. *First of all*, pray, pray, pray."

Long before Paul wrote Timothy, we are able to see how important prayer is to building a ministry by returning to the amazing growth of the first church in Jerusalem. In the very beginning, according to Acts 2:42, the first Christians devoted themselves to four essentials: "They were continually devoting themselves to the apostles' teaching and to fellowship, to the *break-ing of bread* and to *prayer*" (emphasis added).

We could call these the four corners of a church foundation. No church is complete without all four. Leave out any one of them and you may have a school, a prayer group, a Bible study, or a social gathering—and each of those is a good thing—but you won't have a church. The church in Jerusalem was established and sustained on prayer.

Shortly after the new church in Jerusalem began, Peter and John were busy in their day, yet the text tells us that they were "going up to the temple at the ninth hour" (Acts 3:1). Three o'clock in the afternoon was the hour of prayer for Jews. The apostles took time in the middle of their afternoon to attend a gathering for the purpose of prayer.

But this didn't stop the pressure that was mounting against those early Christians. Matter of fact, those early believers began to experience such intense persecution, some were thrown into jail. Prayer went up for them. When they were released, their companions again "lifted their voices to God with one accord" (Acts 4:24) as they prayed for the success of the gospel and the faithfulness of the church. Their first response to persecution was not panic; it was prayer. They interrupted the course of events to seek God's mind, to plead for His protection, to ask for His strength and sustaining grace.

Ben Patterson, chaplain at Westmont College, wrote, "That's what prayer does, says the Lord. It's radical, it goes down deep beneath the surface to uproot evil and upset the status quo."[4] When your day is rolling along at its own pace and in its own direction, interrupt it with prayer. As your day builds toward a crisis, deliberately stop to pray. When your morning begins to go south, pull away for a few moments of solitude to seek God's mind and ask for His instruction. When your attitude starts to sour, pause for an attitude adjustment, prompted by prayer. Don't wait—pray immediately.

The church that started (Acts 2) and grew through persecution (Acts 4–5) kept multiplying. Acts 6 describes a church that had grown so large in size and in responsibility—the members numbered in the multiple thousands—that the apostles could not meet all the needs. For example, some widows weren't getting the food they needed in order to survive, so the twelve recognized the need for a radical change. They urged the congregation to select qualified people to handle this and other practical matters. Once done, they delegated several duties to those men in order to keep their priorities straight as the spiritual leaders of the congregation. "But we will devote ourselves to prayer, and to the ministry of the word" (6:4). Wise decision. The needs were addressed and dealt with, allowing the apostles to stay with their priorities.

I am especially fortunate to serve in a church whose elders are mature spiritual leaders. Their dedication to prayer reveals their maturity. Our meetings are punctuated by times of prayer. We begin by praying and then dive into general matters of the church only to realize it's time once again . . . time for more prayer. We may see matters on the agenda that are beyond our ability to handle, so we lay them before the Lord in prayer. We stop everything to spend at least fifteen to twenty minutes each meeting in prayer as each one of us comes before the Lord with specific concerns.

This would probably seem like a huge waste of valuable time to a corporation. Some might say, "You can't keep doing that; you've got a church to run." No. Actually, we don't. It's not *our* church; it's God's—and it's not our responsibility to run it! Fortunately, He is responsible for the church's success, however that should be defined. Our priority is to devote ourselves to prayer and to the ministry of the Word. In the end, we find that our time praying is an investment that pays for itself many times over. When each elder or pastor has his will aligned with the Lord's, we waste no time arguing for our own. It's amazing what effect prayer has on our relationships with one another. Barriers are broken down. Hearts are softened. Wills become submissive. And fresh ideas flow freely.

Stonebriar Community Church is sustained by prayer. Behind the scenes are prayer groups meeting to intercede on behalf of the church, sometimes scheduled in advance and other times completely spontaneous. During a typical day, an e-mail or a phone call will come in representing a need, and almost without exception, the one who presents the need to me will say, "We have to stop right now and pray over this." And we'll pray right then. Some needs are so grave or so urgent that several of us will gather during the day for prayer. And I wouldn't have it any other way. Our commitment as spiritual leaders in the church is, first of all, to be people dedicated to prayer and to the ministry of the Word.

Acts 7 recounts a tragic day in the life of the first church. Enemies of the gospel dragged Stephen, a deacon, before a mock court and condemned him to die by stoning. As the stones crushed him, he prayed, "Lord, do not hold this sin against them!" (v. 60). Standing nearby, a man held the robes of Stephen's brutal executioners. His name was Saul, later called Paul.

Saul had seen firsthand the results of prayer in building a movement he couldn't destroy. Stephen's prayer quite probably haunted him. Enraged, perhaps by conviction, Saul multiplied his efforts to destroy every Christian he could find. But the Lord disabled him on the road to Damascus and made him a champion of the very movement he tried to wipe out—the movement built and sustained by prayer.

No wonder he told Timothy, "First of all, pray!"

THE CURE FOR WORRY

May I get very personal here? The pressures of our times have many of us caught in the web of the most acceptable, yet energy-draining sin in the Christian family: worry. Chances are good you awoke this morning, stepped out of bed, and before doing anything, strapped on your well-worn backpack of anxiety. You started the day, not with a prayer on your mind but loaded down by worry. What a dreadful habit!

Jesus challenged His followers with the question, "And who of you by being worried can add a single hour to his life?" (Matthew 6:27). Worry solves nothing. It creates unrest, uneasiness, and left unchecked, it can churn our waves of anxiety into a perfect storm of emotions. Add a little imagination and creativity, and our worst fears come to life in Technicolor brilliance.

The stress from worry drains our energy and preoccupies our minds, stripping us of our peace. Few in God's family are exempt. We fret over big things and little things. Some of us have a laundry list of concerns that feed our addiction to worry. It's a very unattractive addiction, yet we somehow manage to make a joke out of it. I've heard people say with a smile, "If I don't have something to worry about, I get worried about not having something to worry about." Anxiety has become a favorite pastime that we love to hate. And worse, we're passing it on to our children. As they see the worry on our faces and they hear it from our lips, we're mentoring them in the art of anxiety.

PRAY WITHOUT CEASING

As always, Scripture has the answer. Paul, again, is the writer. Hoping to relieve the anxiety of his friends in Philippi, he wrote from his imprisonment:

> Rejoice in the Lord always; again I will say, rejoice! Let your gentle spirit be known to all men. The Lord is near. Be anxious for nothing, but in everything by prayer and supplication with thanksgiving let your requests be made known to God. And the peace of God, which surpasses all comprehension, will guard your hearts and your minds in Christ Jesus. (Philippians 4:4–7)

His prescription for anxiety can be boiled down to this: Worry about nothing. Pray about everything.

Before moving on, read those six words again slowly, several times. Notice that the remedy to worry involves a choice. He's not asking you to exist in a state of denial. "Don't worry; be happy" fails to appreciate the seriousness of the concerns you have. You worry because the problems you face are difficult to solve. Furthermore, they have grave consequences if you don't find a resolution. God doesn't expect you to suddenly stop caring. Instead, He offers an alternative to the pointless and exhausting habit of worry: "Be anxious for nothing, but in everything by prayer and supplication with thanksgiving let your requests be made known to God" (Philippians 4:6).

Before this day is done, you will have another occasion to choose between worry and prayer. Determine now what you will do. Decide now that when the crisis arises you will transform the worry into prayer. If at the end of praying, your emotions are still in turmoil, pray more. By cultivating the discipline of prayer, you will discover the ability to remain calm and quiet. As you wait before the Lord, you'll find relief from fear's grip on your spirit.

You might be tempted to think that your prayer was ineffective or that you somehow failed because your anxiety returned—perhaps as soon as you said, "Amen." Happens all the time to me. I take my persistent anxiety as a signal that I need more time before the Father, reviewing all the details of my problem, telling Him how much it plagues me, and sometimes even admitting that I'm afraid He won't handle it soon enough. Having a deep, persistent concern for a problem is not the same as worry. Worry is choosing to fret and churn instead of turning it completely over to God.

Most people whom I consider to be men and women of prayer go before God because their hearts are heavy. They tell me that nothing but continual conversation with Him brings them relief. So if you tend to worry a lot, here's a better plan: pray a lot. For such relief to become a reality, you will have to exercise the discipline of surrender as you rely on Him to solve the problem . . . in His way and in His time. Effective, results-getting prayer includes the thought, *Lord, this is Your problem to fix. You take control. Let me know what You want me to do if I'm to be involved in the solution. By leaving it with You, I will consider it solved.* It's at that point you discipline your mind not to worry, not to continue seeking answers or trying to find resolution. You solved the problem by

> *Worry is wrestling with anxiety on your own rather than releasing it to the Father.*

giving it to God. Your major responsibility now is to wait for His leading. When He wants you to act, He will make it clear. He has dozens of ways to do that, so there's no need for me to open that door. As you wait before Him, He will direct your thoughts to the next step you should take. If there is nothing He leads you to do, do nothing more. He will take it from there.

Because we are weak creatures of habit, our anxiety will quite likely return and we will have to return to prayer and release it all again. That's normal. In fact, if we could rid ourselves of all anxiety with a thirty-second prayer, 1 Thessalonians 5:17 wouldn't make much sense: "pray without ceasing."

Start your day with prayer and continue praying off and on throughout the day. Pray as you drive. Pray at work. Pray before your lunch break. Pray when you get that difficult phone call. Pray when you are disappointed by something. Pray when surprises come. Pray when you triumph. Pray in the midst of painful news. Pray without ceasing—*literally*. Your heavenly Father, being touched deeply over your struggles, loves it when you come to Him asking for help. He is right there, ready to step in. Invite Him to do just that!

LET HIS PEACE FILL YOU

Prayer is classic proof that we don't master spiritual disciplines easily. Developing the discipline of prayer while breaking the habit of worry will call for great mental effort. It will take time for you to master this new way of thinking. Stay with it. After persistent, continual conversation with the Father, mixed well with waiting for Him to work, you will receive what has been promised you. After doing your part, God will do His. Count on it!

"And the peace of God, which surpasses all comprehension, will guard your hearts and your minds in Christ Jesus" (Philippians 4:7). Inexplicable peace will replace inner churning. Tranquility that seems to come from nowhere will envelop your mind. It will begin to take over other parts of your life.

In *The Spirit of the Disciplines*, Dallas Willard describes how this happens:

> Praying with frequency gives us the readiness to pray again as needed from moment to moment. The more we pray, the more we think to pray, and as we see the results of prayer—the responses of our Father to our requests—our

confidence in God's power spills over into other areas of our life. Out of her vast experiences with prayer in the harrowing life of a missionary wife and mother, Rosalind Goforth explains: "Perhaps the most blessed element in this asking and getting from God lies in the strengthening of faith which comes when a definite request has been granted. What is more helpful and inspiring than a ringing testimony of what God has done?"[5]

COMMON PERILS AND UNCOMMON PROMISES

We began this chapter by addressing what prayer is and isn't. A good way to end it is with a few thoughts on what we can and cannot expect from a life of continual conversation with God. First some common misconceptions and mistakes that I have seen among well-meaning Christians; then a few promises from God to encourage you.

The Peril of Irresponsibility: Substituting Prayer for Responsible Action

Make no mistake here.

Imagine a seminary student, preparing for a lifetime of teaching and preaching the Word of God, getting ready for an exam. As the date approaches, he begins to pray, *Lord, help me score well on the exam.* Every day he gets on his face before God and pleads for the ability to do well, but he never once cracks a book. He is faithful to pray, but he fails to prepare. In situations like that the Lord will do at least this during the test: He will help the student bring to mind all that he studied!

> *Prayer is never a substitute for human responsibility.*

Very often God has granted us the privilege of contributing to the answer to our own prayers. So don't merely pray about losing weight, exercise! Don't merely hope that someone helps meet the needs of the impoverished, give! By all means, pray for your friends who do not know Christ, but tell them about the free gift of salvation! Take your concerns about your children before the Lord, but don't forget to listen to them! Divine intervention and human involvement often work hand in hand.

The Peril of Misperception: Picturing God as Merely Superhuman

I remember thinking as a little boy that God is eight hundred years old, looks like a great-great-granddad, has a long, white beard, and is very powerful but essentially is like a kind, old man. Ridiculous! What's worse, do you know what that does to prayer? It shackles God with all the limits of humanity.

Your view of God will shape every aspect of your spiritual life, especially how you pray. It will determine what you pray for, the peace (or lack of such) you will glean from the discipline, and greatly impact what you expect God to accomplish. The truth is, He is limitless in power, and His capabilities are far beyond our imagination. Do your prayers reflect an awesome, sovereign God or merely a kind, old man?

The Peril of Overcommitment: Postponing Prayer Due to a Busy Schedule

When you're too busy, prayer gets squeezed out of the schedule.

J. Sidlow Baxter once shared a page from his own pastoral diary with a group of pastors who had inquired about the discipline of prayer. He began telling how in 1928 he entered the ministry determined he would be the "most Methodist-Baptist" of pastors, a real man of prayer. However, it was not long before his increasing pastoral responsibilities and administrative duties and the subtle subterfuges of pastoral life began to crowd prayer out. Moreover, he began to get used to it, making excuses for himself.

Then one morning it all came to a head as he stood over his work-strewn desk and looked at his watch. The voice of the Spirit was calling him to pray. At the same time another velvety voice was telling him to be practical and get his letters answered, and that he ought to face up to the fact that he was not one of the "spiritual sort"—only a few people could be like that. "That last remark," says Baxter, "hurt like a dagger blade. I could not bear to think it was true." He was horrified by his ability to rationalize away the very ground of his ministerial vitality and power.[6]

Prayer is an investment. The time you dedicate to prayer isn't lost; it will return dividends far greater than what a few moments spent on a task ever could.

The Peril of Oversimplification: Reducing Prayer to Shallow Formulas

God isn't a vending machine. Yet, too often we come to Him hungry and ready to trade our sacrifices for whatever will fill our need. Popular televangelist figures would have us believe that we're still hungry because we didn't pray correctly. We weren't specific in our asking. We didn't demonstrate faith with a sacrifice. We didn't pray with enough belief. We didn't claim promises or use the right words or have the right attitude or . . . or . . . or . . . They would have us think that without the right formula, God will not act on our behalf—that He withholds His goodness until we approach Him using the right ritual.

God is a true and very real being, not an impersonal force. Prayer is a vital part of our relationship with Him. The faith we exercise in prayer is not in seeing specific results for specific requests, but an expression of trust in our almighty, loving Father who cares for us and knows, better than we, what we need.

Martin Luther used to have "table talk" lectures with his students. During one of those sessions, this is what he told them about prayer:

> To be sure, all of the churches across the land are filled with people praying and singing, but why is it that there is so little improvement, so few results from so many prayers? The reason is none other than the one which James speaks of when he says, "You ask and do not receive because you ask amiss" (James 4:3). For where this faith and confidence is not in prayer, the prayer is dead.
>
> From this it follows that the one who prays correctly never doubts that the prayer will be answered, even if the very thing for which one prays is not given. For we are to lay our need before God in prayer but not prescribe to God a measure, manner, time or place. We must leave that to God, for he may wish to give it to us in another, perhaps better, way than we think is best. Frequently we do not know what to pray as St. Paul says in Romans 8, and we know that God's ways are above all that we can ever understand as he says in Ephesians 3. Therefore, we should have no doubt that our prayer is acceptable and heard, and we must leave to God the measure, manner, time and place, for God will surely do what is right.[7]

So much for the bad news. Enough of perils! Here's the good news.

THREE PROMISES TO HELP YOU PRAY.

God Promises that He Will Hear and Answer Regardless of the Time

And how bold and free we then become in his presence, freely asking according to his will, sure that he's listening. And if we're confident that he's listening, we know that what we've asked for is as good as ours. (1 John 5:14–15 MSG)

God is never too busy, never sleeps, never has His mind so occupied with running the universe that He will not hear you. And yet, never forget that an answer to prayer doesn't mean that He will solve our problems the way we want them solved. He will hear our requests and respond with solutions— sometimes surprising ones—that not only address our concerns but deepen our faith in His wisdom and strengthen our confidence in His sovereignty.

God Promises His Presence Regardless of the Outcome

God wants good things for every son and daughter, and He wants to bless us, but never at the expense of our holiness. He may choose to deny our request for one blessing if the refusal paves the way for a greater one. Paul, no doubt, was terribly disappointed and frustrated when God refused a reasonable request:

Because of the extravagance of those revelations, and so I wouldn't get a big head, I was given the gift of a handicap to keep me in constant touch with my limitations. Satan's angel did his best to get me down; what he in fact did was push me to my knees. No danger then of walking around high and mighty! At first I didn't think of it as a gift, and begged God to remove it. Three times I did that, and then he told me,

"My grace is enough; it's all you need.

My strength comes into its own in your weakness."

Once I heard that, I was glad to let it happen. I quit focusing on the handicap and began appreciating the gift. It was a case of Christ's strength moving in on my weakness. Now I take limitations in stride, and with good cheer, these limitations that cut me down to size—abuse, accidents, opposition, bad breaks. I just let Christ take over! And so the weaker I get, the stronger I become. (2 Corinthians 12:7–10 MSG)

In time he discovered that God had given him something greater than relief from pain. He denied what Paul wanted in favor of what Paul needed—a greater sense of God's presence. Paul shared this painful story with his Christian disciples in Corinth to assure them that God will do the same for all believers.

God Promises Inner Peace and Relief Regardless of the Chaos and Complication

Remember the outcome God promised as a result of continual prayer?

Before you know it, a sense of God's wholeness, everything coming together for good, will come and settle you down. It's wonderful what happens when Christ displaces worry at the center of your life. (Philippians 4:7 MSG)

What does the Lord provide in place of worry? A transcendent peace. A tranquility that others can't understand. They'll look at you, calm in the middle of a raging storm that life has rained down on you, and say, "How can you possibly smile at a time like this?" And your answer will be, "I have no idea—except to say that my hope is in the Lord. God is good, He is in control, and I will be fine in the end." Few thoughts bring greater comfort.

God's goal for us is intimacy with Him. I have discovered, however, that the cultivation of intimacy can get complicated. That happens when our will gets in the way of seeking His. Richard J. Foster put it well:

Nothing is more central to the spiritual life than prayer, for prayer ushers us into perpetual communion with the heart of God. And there are many things to learn about this life of constant conversation with the Holy One.

But we must beware of making things too complicated. Like children coming to their parents, so we come to God. There is awe to be sure, but there is also intimacy. We bring our heart cries to a loving Father. Like the mother hen who gathers her chicks under her wings, so our God cares for us, protects us, comforts us (Matt. 23:37).

So no matter how much we study the labyrinthine realities of prayer, let us forever come as children to a loving Abba who delights to give and to forgive.[8]

Our primary goal in calling out to God throughout a life of prayer is not to make our daily existence easier or more enjoyable for ourselves—although, from a certain point of view, it will. The goal can be summed up in four words: intimacy with the Almighty. Seek that first, and you will have everything you've longed for in life, including all the things you never knew you needed.

HUMILITY: BOWING LOW

Humility must always be the portion of any man who receives acclaim
earned in the blood of his followers and the sacrifices of his friends.

—DWIGHT D. EISENHOWER

The late Dr. Paul Brand was one of the twentieth century's greatest,
most respected physicians because of his selfless care for those who
suffer from leprosy. His love for India's least of the least led him to make
discoveries that centuries had overlooked and to pioneer surgical techniques that surgeons use today in orthopedic reconstruction. He was a brilliant physician, medical teacher, writer, speaker, and champion for discarded
people. Dr. Brand coauthored with Phillip Yancey some of the most compelling books I have ever read, among them *Fearfully and Wonderfully Made*
and *The Gift of Pain*. Here's what Yancey had to say about him:

> Meeting Dr. Brand, I realized that I had misconstrued humility as a negative
> self-image. Paul Brand obviously knew his gifts: he had finished first through-
> out his academic career and had attended many awards banquets honoring
> his accomplishments. Yet he recognized his gifts as just that, gifts from a lov-
> ing Creator, and used them in a Christlike way of service.
>
> When I first met him, Brand was still adjusting to life in the United States.
> Everyday luxuries made him nervous, and he longed for a simple life close to
> the soil. He knew presidents, kings, and celebrities, yet he rarely mentioned

them. He talked openly about his failures and always tried to deflect credit for his successes to his associates. Most impressive to me, the wisest and most brilliant man I have ever met devoted much of his life to some of the lowest people on the planet: members of the Untouchable caste in India afflicted with leprosy.[1]

No, humility isn't a result of having a poor self-image. True humility comes from a place of strength and inner security. Humble people are fully aware of their gifts, their training, their experience, and all the attributes that make them successful at whatever they do. That security—that honest, healthy self-assessment—results in more than a humble constitution; it translates into actions that can be observed, actions that we will want to emulate.

HUMILITY IS NOT MERELY A VIRTUE; IT'S A DISCIPLINE

While humility is indeed a quality of one's character, we're not born with it. Humility is not a disposition some are fortunate to have, while others are simply predisposed to egomania. Humility is a character quality that needs to be cultivated. Good parenting can help a child learn humility and remain humble as he or she matures. Frequently, life's painful circumstances grind the sharp edges of pride and smooth the abrasive corners of arrogance. But more often—whether humble people recognize it or not—humility is a discipline, it is a character quality we must learn. Remember the command? "Humble yourselves therefore under the mighty hand of God . . ." (1 Peter 5:6 KJV).

As we focus our thoughts on this crucial Christian discipline, let's begin by clarifying four important issues.

First, although humility is a Christlike virtue, it is neither understood nor admired by most Western cultures. Most models of strong leadership consider it rather strange for a prominent leader to show humility. Bending the knee to help others or to admit weakness is to make oneself vulnerable to those who would displace him. Leaders usually view themselves as being there to be served, except for short periods of time when it's noble to condescend and serve others—but not for too long. They must be careful not to associate too closely with those lower on the ladder or they will compromise their own positions. They might lose the respect of their subordinates *and* their superiors if they accept too much responsibility for a poor decision.

Not so in the culture of Christ! Humility is not something a person merely has; it's what we are called to *do*.

Second, we appreciate humility in others but rarely want it for ourselves. The price is too high. Humility is not what gets us ahead, and—let's be completely honest—we like humble people around us because they don't threaten our position. They're safe people with that quaint little virtue that keeps them on the sidelines during the scramble to the top of the hill. We can afford to be humble after we're king. Even Christ's disciples weren't immune, as seen in the following scripture. Note the Lord's response:

> [The disciples and Jesus] came to Capernaum; and when He was in the house, He began to question them, "What were you discussing on the way?" But they kept silent, for on the way they had discussed with one another which of them was the greatest. Sitting down, He called the twelve and said to them, "If anyone wants to be first, he shall be last of all and servant of all." (Mark 9:33–35)

If we see humility as a discipline, not merely a virtue, we better understand the task before us. It has more to do with what we seek than what we become. If we take responsibility for what we seek, God will determine what we will be.

Third, humility is not the result of having low self-esteem. There are some who would have us focus our full attention on our own unworthiness, our pitiable estate and wormlike qualities, justifying such a mind-set by adding that we amount to nothing apart from Christ. I don't argue with the truth of any of those perspectives, but they don't nurture humility. That's not how Jesus came by His. When He was on earth, He had no sense of inferiority. He never struggled with insecurity. How could He? He was God!

Fourth, as a discipline we can measure our success in humility. As a virtue we cannot. As soon as we think we're humble, we're not! Samuel Taylor Coleridge and Robert Southey wrote in 1799, "And the devil did grin, for his darling sin is pride that apes humility." I have found that genuinely humble people have a natural inattention concerning their humility. They don't even think of themselves as humble. As a matter of fact, they rarely think of themselves at all. Humble people are too occupied with the well-being of others to guard their own interests or notice their own self-importance. J. Steven Wilkins wrote in his fine work, *Call of Duty: The Sterling Nobility of Robert E. Lee*:

> The degree to which [Lee] was indifferent to his own honor is astonishing. After the war, Lee often received distinguished visitors from the North into his home in Lexington. Assuming that the Lees, like many prominent families in the North, had household servants, the guests, after retiring to bed would often leave their boots and shoes outside their bedroom doors to be cleaned and "blacked." Many a night it was the general who stayed up after all others had retired and—in order not to embarrass his guests—collected the boots and cleaned and polished them himself.[2]

THREE LESSONS IN HUMILITY

Have I convinced you? We can only pursue humility as an action, a behavior, not as a quality of character. And yet, if we exercise the discipline long enough, it will inevitably dominate our nature without our knowing what happened. We will become oblivious to it. Unfortunately, the transformation in our character won't happen automatically or easily or quickly. So what does the exercise of this discipline look like? Scripture provides at least three good examples to study. Each one illustrates a key principle.

Humility Starts at the Bottom

I wish being around humble people would automatically make us humble. The disciples provide adequate proof that it doesn't. Mark 10:35–45 describes an incident involving James and John, two brothers. The situation will make most parents nod and smile. By the way, this is the same John who wrote the book of Revelation, the gospel of John, and the three letters that bear his name. This episode, of course, took place before he grew into maturity—still a disciple, still young, and still looking out for John:

James and John, the two sons of Zebedee, came up to Jesus, saying, "Teacher, we want You to do for us whatever we ask of You." And He said to them, "What do you want Me to do for you?" They said to Him, "Grant that we may sit, one on Your right and one on Your left, in Your glory." But Jesus said to them, "You do not know what you are asking. Are you able to drink the cup that I drink, or to be baptized with the baptism with which I am baptized?" They said to Him, "We are able." And Jesus said to them, "The cup that I drink you shall drink; and you shall be baptized with the baptism with which I am baptized. But to sit on My right or on My left, this is not Mine to give; but it is for those for whom it has been prepared." Hearing this, the ten began to feel indignant with James and John. Calling them to Himself, Jesus said to them, "You know that those who are recognized as rulers of the Gentiles lord it over them; and their great men exercise authority over them. But it is not this way among you, but whoever wishes to become great among you shall be your servant; and whoever wishes to be first among you shall be slave of all. For even the Son of Man did not come to be served, but to serve, and to give His life a ransom for many." (Mark 10:35–45)

These two sound like a couple of kids with their daddy, don't they? "Dad, we want to ask you a favor, and we want you to say yes. We want you to do whatever we ask, okay? Promise?" And don't miss what they wanted. They hoped that when Jesus eventually defeated the Romans and was crowned king of Israel, He would put His loyal followers in key positions of power. In a royal court the chair to the right of the king was reserved as the highest place of honor and authority. The next in line sat to his left. James and John didn't want to remove Jesus from His rightful place on the throne, but they had no desire to serve anyone else!

Most Christians can identify with that kind of raw ambition. We're happy to follow and obey Jesus, but we are loath to submit to a fellow human being who might abuse his or her authority. It's hard enough to submit to Jesus, who's perfect. Giving up our comfort or position for the sake of another sinner is far more difficult.

I find it interesting that Jesus didn't rebuke James and John's lust for power. I love His response to their request, His classic way of cutting to the chase. Abruptly He responded, "You don't know what you're asking." The seats next to Jesus in the kingdom of God aren't filled on a first-come, first-served basis. Certainly the most ambitious don't get the nod. In the kingdom, suffering brings reward, and positions of authority come at the expense of selfless sacrifice.

But they still didn't connect the dots. When He asked them, "Are you able to do this?" their naive reply betrayed their ignorance. "We're able," they answered, probably thinking that He was asking them to fight at His side in the battle to claim the throne of Israel. Jesus granted at least part of their request. He promised that they would share in His unjust punishment and agonizing death for the sake of others.

The response of the other ten disciples is predictable. The Greek term Mark used to describe their emotion tells us they were all incensed, out-raged; we would say, "ticked off." The other disciples had every reason to be angry, but I wonder at what specifically. Angry at the audacity of James and John for being so brazen about their ambition? Or angry because the two had taken a more direct route to what each of them secretly wanted for himself? Perhaps both. I think especially the latter.

Jesus took the opportunity to do a little mentoring. He used the occasion to contrast the kingdoms the disciples had seen on earth and the kingdom He would bring. In the world's culture, leadership is defined by high-ranking positions and the exercise of authority, power, and dominion over other people. The words "exercise authority" that Mark used refers to a forced subduing of one person by someone more powerful. This is not someone merely taking charge; this is aggressive domination. That's the picture of authority in the first-century Roman world—and ours to a great extent.

Jesus barely took a breath after contrasting the two kingdoms and added, "Not so among you." The "not so" part of the Greek sentence appears first to make it emphatic. Not so in kingdom life! There's no status. There's no privileged rank. The lowly don't pamper the privileged. Quite the opposite in Jesus' kingdom. Once He got their attention, He spelled out the details:

> Whoever wishes to become great among you shall be your servant; and who-ever wishes to be first among you shall be slave of all. For even the Son of Man did not come to be served, but to serve, and to give His life a ransom for many. (Mark 10:43–45)

Notice the verbs "to serve" and "to give." In effect the Lord said to His disciples, "In my kingdom, godliness starts at the bottom." What was true then is true now. You want to be like Christ? Find the least desired position, the task no one else wants, the worst seat in the house, and claim it. Make it yours.

William Barclay writes, "The basic trouble in the human situation is that men wish to do as little as possible and to get as much as possible. It is only when they are filled with the desire to put into life more than they take out, that life for themselves and for others will be happy and prosperous."[3] The kingdom is built on the foundation of selflessness with Jesus as the cornerstone. The world doesn't need more prima donnas. The world longs to find servants—authentic, humble-hearted servants. Let's not litter the landscape with more pride.

The sobering conclusion to this vignette in Mark 10 is that not one of the twelve disciples had a clue. All twelve failed to understand, after everything they had recently seen and heard. They went on with their day without so much as a glimpse of the entirely new way of thinking that Jesus had just presented and had been modeling ever since they met Him. Obviously humility is not something that comes merely by associating with humble people.

At the risk of being overbearing, let me urge you not to be so callous as to miss the point: "If anyone wishes to come after Me, he must deny himself, and take up his cross and follow Me" (Mark 8:34). Talk about saying it straight!

Humility Grows Out of Gratitude

Mark wrote of an event that occurred in the lives of the disciples where their lack of humility prompted a selfish lust for power. Paul encouraged the Philippian Christians to answer Jesus' call to selflessness so they would enjoy unity—a quality no congregation can enjoy without members who consistently pursue the discipline of humility. The disciples in the church at first-century Philippi lacked humility of mind—that habitual selflessness that comes by consistently putting others ahead of self.

Philippians 2:3–11 forms two segments of Paul's exhortation on humility: a command and a perspective to help his readers obey it. In verses 3–4, Paul commands humility while describing what the discipline would look like among the believers:

Do nothing from selfishness or empty conceit, but with humility of mind regard one another as more important than yourselves; do not merely look out for your own personal interests, but also for the interests of others.

What difference does the discipline of humility make in a community? I can think of at least four important results. First, Christians remove selfishness as a motivation. Second, they become less conceited. Third, believers think of others as more important than themselves. Fourth, they deliberately and consistently attend to the needs of others.

In verses 5–11 the apostle provides a perspective that should spark feelings of gratitude. I think he used this example of Jesus' selfless sacrifice to drive us to our knees:

Have this attitude in yourselves which was also in Christ Jesus, who, although He existed in the form of God, did not regard equality with God a thing to be grasped, but emptied Himself, taking the form of a bond-servant, and being made in the likeness of men. Being found in appearance as a man, He humbled Himself by becoming obedient to the point of death, even death on a cross. For this reason also, God highly exalted Him, and bestowed on Him the name which is above every name, so that at the name of Jesus every knee will bow, of those who are in heaven and on earth and under the earth, and that every tongue will confess that Jesus Christ is Lord, to the glory of God the Father.

As you read that passage, did you notice the downward trend?

Christ Jesus existed in the form of God,
    did not clutch His equality with God,
        emptied Himself,
            took the form of a slave,
                became a man,
                    humbled Himself,
                        and became obedient to death,
                            even a cross kind of death.

What begins in the glories of heaven ends with the worst kind of death—the cruelest, most shameful mode of execution ever devised by humankind: crucifixion. Paul reminds us that Jesus chose this voluntary downgrading so that He might one day lift us up.

What is it that prompts humility within me? What do I need to think or to do that will allow me to think less of myself and more of others? A full appreciation for the sacrifice that Christ made for me will do that. Everything I have, everything I am, every good thing I enjoy would not be possible were it not for Him. The more I understand the price He paid, the less room I have for pride. The more I comprehend how Christ humbled Himself and served me, the more I'm able to put my needs below those of others. I exist because of the price another has paid.

On May 29, 2004, veterans of World War II gathered in Washington, D.C. for the dedication of the memorial to the men and women who served in that great conflict. When so many of the veterans were interviewed, several Medal of Honor winners were among them. I heard a consistent theme emerge from those who had earned our nation's highest military honor. It wasn't pride. I detected no spirit of entitlement or expectation of special treatment. There was no bitterness or cynicism over how long it took our country to build that monument. Neither did I see lingering anguish, although many cried over the names of the dead heroes. Throughout the four-day dedication and celebration, I witnessed enormous gratitude—and especially humility. Why? Because they naturally go together.

Dwight Eisenhower said it best shortly after Germany's surrender in 1945: "Humility must always be the portion of any man who receives acclaim earned in the blood of his followers and the sacrifices of his friends."[4] Time and again, I heard veterans say, "I'm not the hero" as they recalled the names of the men who died at their side.

A heart filled with gratitude cannot be anything but humble.

Humility Is an Act of Faith

Peter, like James and John, learned humility the hard way. As an expert on the subject, he knew that humility is an exercise in trust. He closed his letter to persecuted Christians with advice to their spiritual shepherds, urging them to avoid "lording over" God's people. They were instead to teach humility by example. Then he broadened his scope to include everyone, especially younger believers:

> All of you, clothe yourselves with humility toward one another, for God is opposed to the proud, but gives grace to the humble. Therefore humble yourselves under the mighty hand of God, that He may exalt you at the proper time, casting all your anxiety on Him, because He cares for you. (1 Peter 5:5–7)

I encourage you to pause here before reading on. Reread those words several times. Take a few moments to ponder what Peter wrote. He expressed four distinct thoughts, each of which could stand on its own. But he combined the four here for a reason. Why? Look at them one by one.

All of you, clothe yourselves with humility toward one another. First, I find Peter's expression "clothe yourselves with humility" intriguing. The verb he used comes from a noun referring to a white scarf or apron typically worn by slaves. He may have been thinking of the last meal he had with Jesus when He taught His disciples a lesson in humility by example:

> [Jesus] got up from supper, and laid aside His garments; and taking a towel, He girded Himself. Then He poured water into the basin, and began to wash the disciples' feet and to wipe them with the towel with which He was girded. (John 13:4–5)

God is opposed to the proud, but gives grace to the humble. Next, Peter quoted Proverbs 3:34 as he drove his second point home. The arrogant find themselves at odds with God, while the humble enjoy His blessings. Putting on humility as we relate to others enhances our relationship with God.

Humble yourselves under the mighty hand of God, that He may exalt you at the proper time. The Greek phrase translated "humble yourselves under the mighty hand of God" is probably better rendered, "let yourselves be humbled under the mighty hand of God." In the Old Testament, the phrase "mighty hand of God" is used most often with two symbols in mind: God's hand of discipline and His hand of deliverance. Peter's third point? Submit to His discipline so you may receive His eventual blessing. Remember what we learned earlier? In God's kingdom plan, suffering brings reward.

Cast all your anxiety on Him, because He cares for you. Of all the statements, this fourth one seems the most out of place. But here Peter addresses the core issue, the foundational problem to lack of humility, the source of self-inter-est: anxiety, the worry that if we don't watch out for ourselves, *nobody* will.

Humility—the discipline of putting others ahead of self—is, at its core, a matter of faith. If we genuinely believe that "He cares for us," then we need never worry about serving our own interests. We can afford to focus our entire attention on meeting the needs of others because we have every con-fidence that God will spare nothing of His infinite resources to meet ours. In the meantime, allowing ourselves to be humbled by the mighty hand of God brings anxiety. It is here that the discipline of prayer will help. As Peter said, "Cast all your anxiety on Him."

I like how Thomas à Kempis put it centuries ago. Paraphrasing, he said that it is the humble man whom God protects and liberates; it is the humble whom He loves and consoles. To the humble He turns and upon them bestows great grace, that after their humiliation He may raise them up to glory. He reveals His secrets to the humble, and with kind invitation bids them come to Him. Thus, the humble man enjoys peace in the midst of many vexations, because his trust is in God, not in the world.

SIT, STAND, BOW

In thinking of how to offer counsel on how to exercise the discipline of humility, I want you to imagine three postures. The first is from Mark 10, the second from Philippians 2, and the third from 1 Peter 5.

The story in Mark 10 teaches us: *we need to sit on promoting ourselves.* If we're really gifted, the people who want to use our talent will find us. If we're meant to be discovered and used in a significant way, God will bring it about, just as He did with Joseph. Sold into obscurity and doomed to rot in one of Egypt's deep, dark dungeons, God raised him to immense power in order to preserve Israel. Joseph's humility and integrity allowed God to have His way.

Sit on the temptation to promote yourself. Trust God to promote you when He determines that the time is appropriate. When He calls you, then rely on His calling and obey His Word.

Second, from Philippians 2 we learn: *we need to stand up for others.* We can encourage others to be humble by being sensitive to them in their needs. Look for opportunities to meet the needs of others, especially those whom many would consider the least deserving. (You know the one. He or she quite possibly popped into your mind as you read that last sentence.) Think of the least liked or most obnoxious person, or that person who has made a royal mess of life. Stand up for him or her. How can you become a servant to that person? Think of something simple that you can do soon. Don't put it off—do it. Then keep doing it.

Third, from 1 Peter 5 we learn: *we need to bow low before our God.* Accept His disciplines; don't resist them. Acknowledge His deliverances, which came from Him. Give Him all the praise, and when you begin to feel anxious under the weight of His mighty hand, drop to your knees and pray.

Douglas Southall Freeman ends his four-volume work on Robert E. Lee with a touching scene. General Lee was wrinkled and gray and stooped over—very close to death—when a young mother came to see him with her infant cradled in her arms. When Lee reached out for her baby, she responded by placing the infant in Lee's still-strong arms. The great general looked deeply into the child's eyes and then slowly turned to the mother and said, "Teach him he must deny himself."

The path to greatness in the kingdom of God will lead you through the valley of selflessness. Christlike humility will emerge on its own.

SURRENDER: RELEASING OUR GRIP

When grace changes the heart, submission out of fear changes to
submission out of love, and true humility is born.[1]

—WILLIAM HENDRIKSEN

Ron Ritchie is one of a kind, a real character. I met him while I was at
Dallas Seminary, and we became good friends. Shortly after I finished
my four years at Dallas Seminary, I served as assistant pastor at Grace Bible
Church in North Dallas while Ron had another year to complete. I was glad
to have him as a friend for my first year in ministry. He had a great way of
putting life into its most basic terms, which was, no doubt, one result of
having to work his way through school as a custodian. (Many seminarians
have had their theology seasoned by hard labor.)

Ron gave me a perspective on ministry that I have returned to repeatedly
over the years, especially when it seemed overly difficult or complicated. He
often said, "Three-fourths of ministry is just showing up."

THE FAITHFUL SHOW UP

First Corinthians 4:2 says, "It is required of stewards that one be found
trustworthy." Being trustworthy often means little more than showing up,
simply being ready and available, in season and out of season. Paul tells us

it is required of a steward that he be found *faithful*—not necessarily fruitful or full of charisma or excited or brimming with optimism, but faithful. When Satan, the world, and your own hurt feelings say, "Stay home; it ain't worth it!" God has a better plan: just show up. That's what the faithful do. They keep showing up.

In the summer of 1995, Baltimore shortstop Cal Ripken Jr. brought the sports world to its feet by breaking a record that many people thought would stand forever—a record set by the legendary Lou Gehrig back in 1939. It was no great display of strength, speed, or accuracy. Just plain, old-fashioned faithfulness. On September 6, 1995, Ripken showed up again, just as he had 2,130 consecutive times before.

When Ripkin walked on the field to begin game 2,131, the ballpark thundered for twenty-two uninterrupted minutes as the crowd stood and applauded. Cal stood, too, in classic, Ripken style, turning slowly in a circle as he looked around the stadium. Then he did something wonderful. He walked over to his family and embraced each one of them. The victory was theirs too.

What a great moment in sports history. No championship trophy, no dramatic final-seconds triumph. This was simply a gracious public declaration to honor a man who faithfully did his job year after year. Cal Ripken Jr. showed up.

Before the Faithful Show Up, They Let Go

> Therefore, since we have so great a cloud of witnesses surrounding us, let us also lay aside every encumbrance and the sin which so easily entangles us, and let us run with endurance the race that is set before us. (Hebrews 12:1)

According to the author of Hebrews, we, just like Cal Ripken Jr., are surrounded by an eternal, invisible stadium full of witnesses—spectators to witness either our victory or defeat. The "therefore" points to chapter 11, which tells us that the stands aren't filled with sports fans applauding us for being faithful, but with unseen people who have gone on ahead—saints of old throughout the Old and New Testaments, early church history, and all the way up to our own century. Since we are surrounded by witnesses in this great arena called Christianity, since we have surrounding us such a great cloud of souls who have gone on before, "let us lay aside every encumbrance and the sin which so easily entangles us, and let us run with endurance the race that is set before us."

Take note that the race is "set before us." As is true of anyone who runs a race, the track is not set by the runner. The path for the race is prearranged. Competitors are disqualified if they leave their assigned lane or wander from the prescribed course.

Next, it's worth noting that before we run the race, we are told to get rid of every encumbrance. The Greek word *onkos* means, literally, "weight" or "mass." Ancient authors frequently used this word picture to represent anything that might be a burden. It could be anything, such as excess fat or bulky clothes. Competitors in the original Olympics sacrificed their pride to gain the slightest edge by running completely nude!

I think the author of Hebrews deliberately left its meaning vague here. In the word picture he paints of a runner, the encumbrance is anything that slows him down and keeps him from running his fastest.

Pause for a moment. Don't leave the scene without asking yourself, "What is my encumbrance?"

We are also instructed to set aside "the sin." The Greek carefully and conspicuously includes the definite article, pointing to a particular sin, not a group of sins or all sin in general.

The King James calls it the sin that so easily "besets" us. Some take that to mean a "besetting sin" is unique to each person. One individual's besetting sin may be greed, while the besetting sin for another may be sloth. I may be frequently overcome by gluttony while jealousy may dominate you. It could be envy or lust, pride or gossip.

I don't think that's the best explanation for the author's use of the definite article. It's best to interpret the use of "the" within the context of chapters 11 and 12. Like a pin in the hinge that holds a door to its jamb, "the" links chapter 12 to chapter 11, which is full of people who truly believed God—men and women of great faith. "The sin" in Hebrews 12:1 is, most likely, *unbelief.*

Hebrews 11 has been called the Westminster Abbey of the people of God, a memorial to believers in this great hall of faith. With them in his mind, the author writes, "Now, you are surrounded by a cloud of witnesses like those people I just told you about, and I challenge you to run the race God has prescribed for you. But first—before doing anything—lay aside *the* sin. Lay aside unbelief."

After careful observation of this verse, I am convinced of this: the author of Hebrews cannot conceive our successfully running life's race without first deciding to trust God—*really* relying on Him. And that kind of trust begins by surrendering to Him.

Our Goal Revisited

Before moving on, let's recall the finish line. It's marked out by Philippians 3:10:

> [For my determined purpose is] that I may know Him, that I may progressively become more deeply and intimately acquainted with Him, perceiving and recognizing and understanding [the wonders of His Person] more strongly and more clearly, and that I may in that same way come to know the power outflowing from His resurrection [which it exerts over believers]; and that I may so share His sufferings as to be continually transformed [in spirit into His likeness even] to His death. (Philippians 3:10 AMP)

Let's face it: most of us can talk a good fight when it comes to surrender. But I will freely confess, it is a battle royal to this day in my own life. Letting go, laying aside *the* sin: unbelief. Not so much a lack of trust in God as having such a love for my way as to miss His. We often fail to go God's way because we're so captivated by our own. I mean, we've been at this a long time. We've got this thing called life down pat, right? That's part of becoming an adult, isn't it? In truth, at the core of such thinking is a four-letter word that resists all thought of surrender: *self.*

No one understood that better than the Puritans. The following comes from a Puritan prayer titled "Man a Nothing." It's written anonymously because the words don't belong to anyone honest enough to claim them:

When thou wouldst guide me I control myself,
When thou wouldst be sovereign I rule myself.
When thou wouldst take care of me I suffice myself.
When I should depend on thy providings I supply myself,
When I should submit to thy providence I follow my will,
When I should study, love, honour, trust thee, I serve myself;
I fault and correct thy laws to suit myself,
Instead of thee I look to man's approbation,
and am by nature an idolater.
Lord, it is my chief design to bring my heart back to thee.
Convince me that I cannot be my own god, or make myself happy,
nor my own Christ to restore my joy,
nor my own Spirit to teach, guide, rule me.
Help me to see that grace does this by providential affliction,
for when my credit is god thou dost cast me lower,
when riches are my idol thou dost wing them away,
when pleasure is my all thou dost turn it into bitterness.
Take away my roving eye, curious ear, greedy appetite, lustful heart;
Show me that none of these things
can heal a wounded conscience,
or support a tottering frame,
or uphold a departing spirit.
Then take me to the cross and leave me there.[2]

SELF-INTEREST IS THE MORTAL ENEMY OF SURRENDER

So how do we surrender? How do we begin to release our grip and truly rely on God? The author of Hebrews, writing God-breathed words, gives us practical answers in the next two verses. They call for two actions. Both are antidotes to the poison that kills belief—self-interest:

Study Christ.
and
Compare yourself to Christ.

Study Christ

Hebrews 12:2 states, "fixing our eyes on Jesus, the author and perfecter of faith, who for the joy set before Him endured the cross, despising the shame, and has sat down at the right hand of the throne of God."

Read those words again, only slower this time. Picture the words in your mind. We start to practice the discipline of surrender when we focus our eyes on the person of Christ. The word picture of a race is retained in this verse. Did you notice? We might be tempted to think that Jesus is just the finish line and that we should only keep our eyes on Him as a runner would focus on the tape. But I think the author is urging us to also think of Jesus as the *example*.

He not only designed the course of the race; He ran it. In fact, He ran it perfectly. As the first verse says of us, He too had a course set before Him. Furthermore, running it necessarily involved surrender. As our example, Jesus modeled trust in the Father. He came to the planet that He had made and lived His entire life misunderstood, misrepresented, misquoted, mistreated, and finally crucified. Yet He committed no sin. From Bethlehem's manger to Golgotha's cross, Jesus exemplified a life of surrender.

The Greek term *aphora* at the beginning of verse 2 means to look exclusively at something and study it intently while consciously looking away from distractions. And the implication is imitation. Great athletes study the films of former greats to discover their techniques, to uncover any secrets to success that might offer even the slightest competitive edge. We are encouraged to go to the film vault and peer intently at one scene after another as we study Christ. "Look exclusively and thoughtfully at the One who not only designed the course but ran it flawlessly. Then run exactly as He ran." As He lived, we are to live. As He decided, we are to decide. As He obeyed, we are to obey. As He pleased the Father, we are to please the Father. As He surrendered, we are to surrender.

Here's the good news: when we live surrendered lives before Him, becoming like Him leads to the ever-increasing reality. We don't have to pray for it. We don't have to strive to accomplish it. Focusing intently on Christ naturally results in a lifestyle of greater and greater selflessness. As you read earlier, practicing the discipline of surrender begins with selflessness.

Paul wrote to his Christian friends in Philippi while he was under house arrest in Rome, hoping to convince them to imitate Christ's selflessness. In Philippians 2:3–5, he gave them four commands: the first and the third are negative; the second and the fourth are positive. He then held up Christ as the ultimate example. He modeled the discipline of surrender to such a degree that sacrifice was inevitable. Here are the commands:

1. Do nothing from selfishness or empty conceit (v. 3).
2. With humility of mind regard one another as more important than yourselves (v. 3).
3. Do not merely look out for your own personal interests (v. 4).
4. [Look out] also for the interests of others (v. 4).

Did you notice? The second command leads off with four significant words: "with humility of mind." In Matthew 11:29 Jesus called Himself "gentle and humble in heart," using the same root word, *tapeinos*, meaning lowly or of low social standing. Someone who accepts his place at the bottom of the social order has no self-serving expectations. He leaves no room for selfishness.

You want to be like Christ? Begin by thinking of yourself as lowly. Deliberately work toward becoming unselfish. For one full day, let go of anything that serves your own interest to the exclusion of others. On that same day, fix your attention on Jesus by surrendering in complete selflessness. By doing this you will follow a divinely ordained plan that is not your preference.

Don't miss the precise wording of the third command. I'm glad the editors of the New American Standard Bible included "merely" in their translation. You can't live so entirely selflessly that you never look out for your own interests. No one—not even God—expects you to become the local doormat. Obviously, failing to seek adequate food, shelter, clothing, and other necessities would be foolish. Keep all of this in balance. It's a question of priorities and emphasis. "Not merely your own personal interests, but also for the interests of others."

Eugene Peterson's *The Message* paraphrases this nicely in modern terms: "Don't push your way to the front; don't sweet-talk your way to the top. Put yourself aside, and help others get ahead. Don't be obsessed with getting your own advantage. Forget yourselves long enough to lend a helping hand" (Philippians 2:3–4 MSG).

Following the four commands, Paul points to Jesus as the perfect illustration of selflessness. Let's look at Philippians 2 again. Read the following very carefully, preferably aloud:

> Have this attitude in yourselves which was also in Christ Jesus, who, although He existed in the form of God, did not regard equality with God a thing to be grasped, but emptied Himself, taking the form of a bond-servant, and being made in the likeness of men. Being found in appearance as a man, He humbled Himself by becoming obedient to the point of death, even death on a cross. For this reason also, God highly exalted Him, and bestowed on Him the name which is above every name, so that at the name of Jesus every knee will bow, of those who are in heaven and on earth and under the earth, and that every tongue will confess that Jesus Christ is Lord, to the glory of God the Father. (Philippians 2:5–11)

Jesus "did not regard equality with God a thing to be grasped." Though Jesus deserved all the respect, all the worship, all the adoration, all the fear due Him as God, He let it all go. He released His grip on all of it.

Further, "He emptied Himself." While retaining every aspect of His deity, Jesus relinquished the independent use of His divine attributes during His earthly sojourn. Before the Son became a flesh-and-blood man, He had absolute autonomy as God, being coequal, coeternal, and coexistent with the Father. When He became a man, He voluntarily gave up the independent use of His divine attributes; and while on this earth, He submitted to the Father. He waited on the Father for His will, for His timing. He followed the Father's guidance as to where He would go and what He would do and what He would say and when He would do those things. He relinquished the voluntary use of His divine prerogatives. He gave up what was rightfully His for the sake of others—including you and me.

Moreover, He took "the form of a bond-servant" and was made "in the likeness of men." He did this so that He could suffer "a cross-kind of death" (the Greek sentence suggests such a rendering). The excruciating, humiliating anguish of a common criminal became His kind of death. And in death He personified surrender.

The Son of Man gave up His will for the Father's. As a result, the Father glorified Him.

Is it any wonder, then, that the author of Hebrews encourages us to fix our eyes on Jesus, to focus our gaze on Him, to study Christ? Focusing intently on Christ naturally results in a lifestyle of increasingly greater selflessness.

Compare Yourself to Christ

Hebrews 12:3 prescribes a second action that will help us overcome the self-interest that undermines the discipline of surrender: "For consider Him who has endured such hostility by sinners against Himself, so that you will not grow weary and lose heart."

"Consider Him" in verse 3 and "study Him" in verse 2 sound the same, but they are not. The English terms used by most translations fail to emphasize the distinction that appears so clearly in the Greek. The term used in verse 3 in the original language is *analogizomai*, an accounting term. You do this every time you balance your checkbook. You compare your figures against those of the bank, and because banks rarely make an error, you usually adjust your totals to match the statement. It's a careful, logical analysis involving comparison.

"Study" carries the idea of fixing your attention exclusively on Christ for the sake of understanding; "compare" calls for you to measure yourself against His experience and His example.

The next time you're feeling sorry for yourself, pause long enough to compare your situation to His. The next time you're unfairly criticized, again, compare; weigh your trouble against what He endured. The next time you have to surrender something comfortable or something familiar for a greater good, compare what you are surrendering to what He surrendered. The next time you're asked to adjust to a plan, compare your adjustment to His adjustment.

Keep Jesus as your standard. All other human examples are driven by a survival instinct, an internal compulsion to preserve and nurture self. Only Christ modeled godly selflessness throughout His entire life. While others seek to preserve their own lives, He came to lay His down.

What's the benefit? Look again at the verse. "[Compare, then imitate]

Him who has endured such hostility by sinners against Himself." Why? "So that you will not grow weary and lose heart."

Ever notice how much energy it takes to keep a tight grip on something? Let go. You won't grow weary; you won't get worn out if you release your grip. Some of you reading this today already know what you're holding on to. Your emotions are in turmoil because you cannot avoid the inevitable. You've been clutching it far too long, and, sooner or later, your grip will fail and it will be lost anyway. It's a problem too great for you to solve, a responsibility too heavy for you to shoulder, or perhaps even a blessing that has come to dominate your every waking thought. Rather than have it ripped from your weary, cramped fingers, choose to release it into God's care. You're not simply letting it drop; that's giving in to defeat. You're releasing it to One greater than yourself and trusting—believing—that He is both able and willing to care for it better than you.

Let me warn you again. Surrender is tough at the start, especially if you are a selfish kind of person, a little spoiled, a little pampered, a little overly indulged. Your old self will whine and fight for survival! Surrendering is not for the pampered. God honors those who pay the price to be like Him: selfless. That's why surrendering plays such a dominant role in putting self in its place.

THINGS TO SURRENDER

Before turning to some areas of life for specific application, pause for a moment to ponder Proverbs 3:5–8. We too easily take the wisdom of Solomon for granted. Sometimes his familiar advice can appear trite if we're not careful. Given all that we have discussed, his words of wisdom fit well here. Read these lines slowly several times:

> Trust in the Lord with all your heart,
> And do not lean on your own understanding.
> In all your ways acknowledge Him,
> And He will make your paths straight.
> Do not be wise in your own eyes;
> Fear the Lord and turn away from evil.

It will be healing to your body,
And refreshment to your bones.

Surrender Your Possessions

Now is a perfect time for you to put your possessions into proper perspective. If you're married, do this with your partner. Make a list of any material possessions that you know are near and dear to your heart. Then go before the Lord with your list. Release them one by one—by name—to Him. Declare Him the owner of each item. As you surrender your possessions to Him, you will find a sense of freedom and relief from materialism and greed like you've never known before. You may be surprised by how much you idolized those possessions without realizing it. If you find your heart especially close to a particular item, you might consider making it a literal gift to God. Give it to someone who needs it more than you and therefore could put it to better use. The sacrifice will sting initially—sacrifices always do!—but in time you might be surprised to discover the Lord trusting you with more than you originally had.

I don't mean to suggest that poverty is somehow more spiritual than wealth. It is not. In fact, God's purpose in giving Israel the Promised Land was to bless them with such material abundance that the nations would take notice and inquire about Him. However, it is also true that if you don't hold the possessions you own loosely, they will own you. And so, enjoy them . . . but refuse to idolize them!

Surrender Your Position

Release your grip on the top rungs of your career and/or social ladder. Stop wrapping your ego around your role. This is especially difficult for pastors. Too many identify themselves so closely with their ministry that it bears their name. Should the Lord move them to something else, a large part of them dies. The same is often true of executives and successful business owners. I have seen this happen to mothers as well. Deliberately refuse to allow any position or title to determine who you are. *Let it go!*

Release the title, release the position, release the benefits, the perks, your own importance or power, whatever goes with it. Place it all before your God. Find your security, your identity, and your contentment in Him.

Surrender Your Plans

Come now, you who say, "Today or tomorrow we will go to such and such a city, and spend a year there and engage in business and make a profit." Yet you do not know what your life will be like tomorrow. You are just a vapor that appears for a little while and then vanishes away. Instead, you ought to say, "If the Lord wills, we will live and also do this or that." But as it is, you boast in your arrogance; all such boasting is evil. (James 4:13–16)

I am convinced that wise planning is good. But plans, like material possessions, must always be held loosely. Yes—always! Plan wisely, but be ready for God to rearrange things and take you along paths that may feel dangerous to you. Don't sweat it; He knows what He's doing. And He isn't obligated to inform you . . . or request permission to upset your neat little agenda!

Surrender Your People

Hold the people you love loosely. I'm thinking especially of your children, your parents, your friends who mean so much to you. Accept the fact that nothing this side of heaven is permanent, including relationships. If they don't end, they will certainly change. Enjoy the time you have with your loved ones, but avoid the temptation to cling.

This is especially difficult with your children. Believe me, after releasing four of my own, I know. If you haven't already, go before the Lord and commit each one by name to Him. Thank Him for allowing you to nourish those precious lives, ask His guidance to do the job well, and give each one to Him for whatever He wills. Then prepare yourself for the day when you must release them into the world and His care. I should warn you, He may very well choose to take one of them before you're ready. So releasing each one now will make the premature parting more bearable.

Older parents understand that all too well. Part of the thrill of guiding children into adulthood is the release. But it's also a parent's greatest act of surrender. Still, you have to let them go. Start now.

Surprises Await You

Finally, I want to share two observations from my personal experience and my experience as a pastor. I am so confident in the truth of these that I dare call them principles. If I may go one step further, I suggest you memorize both of these statements:

Surrender results in surprises we would never otherwise experience.

and

The greater the struggle to surrender, the greater the surprise.

I urge you. Release your grip. Surrender it all to God, including your anxiety. If you still have your emotions wrapped around some issue involving a possession, a job or role, a particular expectation for the future, or a relationship, you aren't fully relying on God. As long as you fail to surrender to Him, you're holding on to anxiety. Stop. Let go. You're delaying the surprise God has waiting for you.

Peter Marshall, the late chaplain of the United States Senate, concluded a message on anxiety titled "Sin in the Present Tense" with this prayer. I leave it with you to make it your prayer today.

Forgive us, O God, for the doubting suspicion with which we regard the heart of God.

We have faith in checks and banks, in trains and airplanes, in cooks, and in strangers who drive us in cabs. Forgive us for our stupidity, that we have faith in people whom we do not know and are so reluctant to have faith in Thee who knowest us altogether.

We are always striving to find a complicated way through life when Thou hast a plan, and we refuse to walk in it. So many of our troubles we bring on ourselves. How silly we are.

Wilt Thou give to us that faith that we can deposit in the bank of Thy love, so that we may receive the dividends and interest that Thou art so willing to give us. We ask it all in the lovely name of Jesus Christ, our Savior.[3]

SELF-CONTROL: HOLDING BACK

Never miss a good chance to shut up.

—WILL ROGERS

Many years ago I was sitting up late one night, relaxing in our family room and watching *SportsCenter*. The thought occurred to me, *That half gallon of ice cream is just going to get old sitting over there in the freezer, and that would be a waste. I think I'll just have a few bites.* So I took the half gallon container of Rocky Road out of the freezer (no need to dirty a clean dish!) and sat down with a spoon. I ate it all. In fact, I emptied it before *SportsCenter* was over. Are you ready? There's more. I microwaved the last part and drank the little bits that get caught around the seams of the container. Like I said, I hate wasting ice cream.

Suddenly, I realized that the kids were sure to notice that the ice cream was gone. They would never have noticed a missing ten-pound roast or half a turkey, but no one could get away with eating more than his fair share of ice cream. So I quietly sneaked out to my car, drove to the store, bought a new half gallon—Rocky Road, of course—and carefully placed it right where the other one was. I was in the clear except for one tiny detail. I forgot that one of our kids had eaten a little bit out of the top of the other one. Busted! They let me know, in no uncertain terms, that they knew exactly what I had done. The whole family got in on that one.

THE UNIVERSAL CIVIL WAR

I've eaten too much, interfered where I had no business meddling, and spoken when I should have remained silent. Those are pretty common problems, aren't they? Universal, in fact. We have all exceeded the bounds of wisdom by failing to restrain ourselves. We all suffer from the same ailment: lack of self-control.

I would be a lot harder on myself were it not for Romans 7:14–25. I derive a lot of comfort from what the apostle Paul writes of his own experience. This man was an undisputed spiritual giant, called on by God to write God-breathed words and to lead thousands of believers on the journey to Christlikeness. Best of all, Paul led by example! He lived in submission to Christ no matter what. He was beaten, stoned, starved, shipwrecked, imprisoned, called a devil on one day and a god on another, and ultimately martyred for his faithfulness to the gospel. We might be tempted to think that he lived as close to perfection as the Lord Himself, were it not for his own admission.

Paul's candid confession in Romans 7 sounds exactly like yours or mine: "For what I am doing, I do not understand; for I am not practicing what I would like to do, but I am doing the very thing I hate" (Romans 7:15).

Look at that! The apostle Paul is openly declaring that he can't always follow the very commands he writes under inspiration. He's not saying that, theoretically, he sometimes behaves differently than he knows to be right. He's saying, "This is life as I live it. This is the unending struggle of life as I experience it. I don't understand this about myself. I decide one way, and then I wind up acting another."

Check out what he said a little later. It gets worse: "For I know that nothing good dwells in me, that is, in my flesh; for the willing is present in me, but the doing of the good is not" (Romans 7:18).

How honest is that? Isn't that true for all of us? I can't count the times I have asked myself, "Why? Why did I do something so foolish?" Paul's analysis exposing the root cause comes back, loud and clear. I especially like Eugene Peterson's paraphrase:

Something has gone wrong deep within me and gets the better of me every time. It happens so regularly that it's predictable. The moment I decide to do good, sin is there to trip me up. I truly delight in God's commands, but it's pretty obvious that not all of me joins in that delight. Parts of me covertly rebel, and just when I least expect it, they take charge. (Romans 7:20–23 MSG)

That's me. That's you. That's Paul. That's everyone. Fritz Ridenour, in his book *How to Be a Christian without Being Religious*, calls us a "walking civil war." And I heartily agree! Can you admit it? Or do you try to convince everyone that you have some kind of consistent Spirit-walk going down the straight and narrow? Don't waste your time.

As we begin to address this universal problem, our inability to master the discipline of self-control, it is essential that we understand the consequences. Let me paraphrase Proverbs 25:28 in today's terms. *When we fail to control our desires—when we allow our natural inclinations to control us—we are like a bank vault with a screen door.* Failure to exercise the discipline of self-control is an open invitation for Satan to rob us of all the good things we receive from God.

KNOW YOUR ENEMY

Once we accept that everyone wages his or her own civil war and acknowledge the grave consequences of defeat, we are ready to begin our plan of attack with an honest assessment of the problem. Chinese general Sun Tzu wrote in *The Art of War*, "If you know the enemy and know yourself, you need not fear the results of a hundred battles."[1] According to Romans 7–8 and Galatians 5, the problem can be boiled down to one five-letter word—*flesh*:

The flesh sets its desire against the Spirit, and the Spirit against the flesh; for these are in opposition to one another, so that you may not do the things that you please. But if you are led by the Spirit, you are not under the Law. Now the deeds of the flesh are evident, which are: immorality, impurity, sensuality, idolatry, sorcery, enmities, strife, jealousy, outbursts of anger, disputes, dissensions, factions, envying, drunkenness, carousing, and things like these, of which I forewarn you, just as I have forewarned you, that those who practice such things will not inherit the kingdom of God. (Galatians 5:17–21)

Because so many throughout history have misconstrued Paul's meaning of the word *flesh*, we must define it clearly and accurately. We cannot hope to win the war against this enemy if we don't understand the term as Paul intended.

Yet believers also have an old nature—a habitual, sinful way of thinking—that Paul called "the flesh." Let me put it straight. The flesh is a self-serving, nonbelieving, godless mind-set that lives by animal instinct. Its natural stance is facing away from God. Its innate priority is self-preservation. The lens through which the flesh sees the world is "eat or be eaten." It's the pattern of living that you inherited when you were born, that the world taught you as you matured. To make matters worse, it comes as natural to you as breathing. The Holy Spirit notwithstanding, the flesh remains within us, never improving, always ready to be satisfied.

Many have mistaken Paul's meaning and have come to the conclusion that our physical body is innately evil. Some have even gone further, saying that our spirit—the nonmaterial part of our being—is good. This belief comes from the influence of ancient philosophy and is neither Christian nor biblical. In Genesis, God created the human body and called it good. But when Adam and Eve chose evil instead of obedience to God, they fell into sin completely—body and spirit, material and immaterial. Every part of their humanity became a slave to sin. So when Paul uses the word *flesh*, he doesn't refer only to the material, physical part of a person. He means the entire person's inclination in his or her former, before-Christ state—a condition that had them living in allegiance to the corrupted world, just like Adam and Eve after their fall into sin.

Here's how that influences our discussion. When you believed in Christ, your inner self was re-created. Everything changed for you, whether you were aware of it or not. But old habits die hard, and the flesh knows sin like you know how to ride a bicycle. It never forgets. Can you untrain your body so that you can no longer ride a bike? That's why the flesh can never conquer itself or choose not to sin when given a chance—and the world gives it numerous opportunities to ride again.

Our Flesh Versus His Spirit

The flesh is most at home in the realm of wrong. I hardly need to remind you that we live in a world filled with twisted truth and distorted ethics. When you mix a flawed world with a failed nature, you've got the right combination for defeat.

On the other hand, if you are a believer in Jesus Christ, you also have the Spirit of God living in you. According to Galatians 5:16, the only hope we have against slavish obedience to the flesh is the Spirit. His re-creative work in us gives us the opportunity to let Him have His way instead. Paul writes, "But I say, walk by the Spirit, and you will not carry out the desire of the flesh."

What a profound statement! That's the foundation of living this thing we call the Christian life. The Spirit and our flesh are completely opposed to each other. While walking in the Spirit we cannot possibly carry out the desires of the flesh. So we're either operating from the realm of the Spirit and under His control, or we're operating in the realm of the flesh and under its control.

It's helpful to remember those things Paul identifies as "the deeds of the flesh." The following words describe those fleshly deeds in a way that captures the raw realities of sin:

> . . . repetitive, loveless, cheap sex; a stinking accumulation of mental and emotional garbage; frenzied and joyless grabs for happiness; trinket gods; magic-show religion; paranoid loneliness; cutthroat competition; all-consuming-yet-never-satisfied wants; a brutal temper; an impotence to love or be loved; divided homes and divided lives; small-minded and lopsided pursuits; the vicious habit of depersonalizing everyone into a rival; uncontrolled and uncontrollable addictions; ugly parodies of community. I could go on. (Galatians 5:19–21 MSG)

Downright ugly, isn't it? What's worse is that the list is selective, not exhaustive. Face it, that's you and that's me. If the flesh wins too many battles in your own, personal civil war, then you become nothing more than a walking dead person. A generation ago we had a name for those who lived in that condition: carnal Christians. Flesh-driven believers. Our bodies are a precious gift from God, so they are by no means evil. But given the opportunity, our bodily drives will rule us.

THE GOOD NEWS

If I ended the chapter with our battle with the flesh, we'd be in a heap of trouble. Fortunately, God has followed up this bad news with some very good news. God is personally at work in all of His people. He's given us the power and the presence of His Holy Spirit. As corrupting as sin has been, His Spirit is all the more cleansing. Where the flesh leads only to a foul harvest of sin, the Spirit produces an abundance of sweet fruit:

> But the fruit of the Spirit is love, joy, peace, patience, kindness, goodness, faithfulness, gentleness, self-control; against such things there is no law. (Galatians 5:22–23)

Talk about an attractive list! Go back and read again those nine qualities the Spirit of God produces within us. When the Holy Spirit takes up residence in the believer, these are what He begins to produce in us and through us. I'm sure that this list of nine qualities, like the other list of the "deeds of the flesh," isn't exhaustive but selective. Take note of the last quality Paul named: self-control.

SELF-CONTROL LEADS TO GREATER FREEDOM

As we cultivate the discipline of self-control, you and I can experience victory over the very things we despise in ourselves. The new nature trumps the old nature as we allow the Spirit of God to rule our minds and our hearts. As a result, life soon begins to improve because the restraining power of the Holy Spirit overcomes the tempting urges of the flesh. He brings strength we do not have in ourselves.

Enkrateia is the Greek word translated "self-control." The stem is the term *kratos*, meaning "strength" or "might." Often *kratos* is translated "dominion."

The prefix personalizes the word, in a manner of speaking. So *enkrateia* is the ability to have dominion over one's impulses or desires.

For the person without Christ, the desires dictate and he or she obeys. Those in Christ, living under the authority of His Spirit and ruled by Him, are able to defy this once-powerful dictator. As a result, we experience a transforming change that others notice.

As for the tongue, we exercise verbal restraint. Where our diet is concerned, we exercise restraint at the dinner table. (And I leave the ice cream in the freezer!) Pertaining to the temper, we exercise emotional restraint. As it relates to our thoughts, we exercise mental restraint. In terms of sexual lust, we exercise moral restraint. All of us have areas that tempt us more than others, so we must give ourselves over to the Spirit's authority. He steps in and empowers us to hold back before we take steps to satisfy our impulse or our desire.

Let's get practical. I have found that a three-second pause can make all the difference. Just as an impulse hits me, I decide to wait just three seconds before taking any action. During that pause, I do a quick assessment of what the consequences might be. Would this action be something that I would be embarrassed about later? Not all impulses are bad; some are good. Those three seconds have kept me out of a lot of hot water over the years.

Sometimes I know that I shouldn't act, so I pray, "Right now, Lord, in this very moment, I'm struggling. Spirit of God, control my tongue. Stop my mind from dwelling on that thought. Don't let that impulse have its way." Obviously all of that happens in an instant, and I rarely say those words out loud. But I am frequently amazed by how effectively the Lord provides self-control when I need it. As I release the struggle to Him, He takes over. Every time.

This mastery of self is an incredibly difficult discipline, but it's the path to freedom. Maxie Dunham put it well:

> The purpose of self-control is that we may be fit for God, fit for ourselves, and fit to be servants of others. . . . It is not a rigid, religious practice—discipline for discipline's sake. It is not dull drudgery aimed at exterminating laughter and joy. It is the doorway to true joy, true liberation from the stifling slavery of self-interest and fear.[2]

WINNING THE WAR

Now that we know the enemy, what can we do to defeat it? If we are to win, self-control plays a major role in the victory. We read Paul's candid confession earlier as he described his private "civil war" between the flesh and the Spirit. Let's observe another admission Paul makes. With intensity, he writes of the importance of discipline:

> Do you not know that those who run in a race all run, but only one receives the prize? Run in such a way that you may win. Everyone who competes in the games *exercises self-control* in all things. They then do it to receive a perishable wreath, but we an imperishable. Therefore I run in such a way, as not without aim; I box in such a way, as not beating the air; but *I discipline my body and make it my slave,* so that, after I have preached to others, I myself will not be disqualified. (1 Corinthians 9:24–27, emphasis added)

RUN WITH PURPOSE AND HAVE A STRATEGY

Don't merely run, but, as Paul puts it, "Run in such a way that you may win." Paul's hope is that we will run with purpose. He desires for all of us to become winners, not merely runners.

So, what's the secret? How do winners compete? "Everyone who competes in the games exercises self-control in all things" (v. 25). It's always required the same secret: discipline. Those who run to win exercise restraint over their impulses and emotions and desires. Olympic hopefuls are this very day watching their diet, getting sufficient sleep, and training their bodies in just the right way for just the right amount of time. They are not fudging on anything that might hedge their performance on the track, on the bike, in the pool, or in the ring. And they measure the consequences of every impulse to judge whether it will assist them or hinder them from fulfilling the purpose of competition: winning the gold.

Look carefully at Paul's personal testimony: "Therefore I run in such a way, as not without aim; I box in such a way, as not beating the air" (v. 26). He says, in effect, "My focus is Christ. Christ only, Christ alone. He's the goal and the prize for which I run. And I'm not shadow boxing. I have a very real opponent; I battle the adversary."

SHOW YOUR BODY WHO'S BOSS

I love how down to earth Paul gets with his next word picture: "I discipline my body and make it my slave" (v. 27). The Greek word translated "discipline" here literally means "to strike under the eye." It is the word for beating the face black and blue. But that's not to say we're to abuse our bodies for the sake of discipline. Some people take that to extremes, literally and repeatedly punching their bodies as a means of keeping themselves under control. Even in Paul's day the word was a figure of speech. It was one of those humorous, extreme word pictures we sometimes use to describe our actions. My grand-daughter is a runner. She might say, "Bubba, I'm gonna have to kill myself to get ready for that cross-country meet."

The purpose of this discipline over the body is, as the literal Greek would put it, "to enslave it." That includes saying no to its whining wish that we indulge its every whim. The point of disciplined self-control is to make the body serve us rather than the other way around. That makes all the sense in the world if you've ever encountered an addict. His body cries out for a substance that is so satisfying its craving becomes goal number one. Every thought, every decision, every action, every motivation becomes the tool of his body's desires. He is enslaved to it. Paul not only demanded that we exercise the discipline of self-control; he also modeled it.

MEETING OUR IMPULSES HEAD-ON

I need to clarify the difference between temptation and indulgence. Not every stray thought, no matter how graphic or angry or ugly it may be, makes you guilty. And let's face it: we live in a world where sensual images constantly assault us from the least likely places.

A couple of years ago I was on an annual retreat with our church leader. After a busy afternoon of work, most of us men decided to relax and watch a championship playoff game between the Lakers and the Pistons. The Lakers weren't playing very well, so the network kept switching back and forth from the game to coach Phil Jackson. As the gap in the score widened, he was getting more and more perturbed.

Just over Phil Jackson's shoulder was a woman wearing a low-cut blouse and, well . . . let's just say she filled it to overflowing. There was more of her than blouse. Whenever the cameraman showed the coach, he made sure to frame the shot to include the woman. Not her face, mind you. Just what he, and most red-blooded men in America, would find most interesting. Not surprisingly the network showed the coach *a lot* during the latter part of the game. With each shot of Jackson, we saw less of the coach and more of the sports fan behind him—though never her face.

I noticed that the pastors grew more and more silent, and after a little while it was as quiet as a room full of nuns. Finally I blurted out, "Kinda hard to keep looking at Phil Jackson, isn't it?" The guys burst into laughter, and every ounce of tension fled away. I don't think anyone there was guilty of lust, though that's exactly how it can start. In an unguarded, unexpected moment, something grabs our attention, and without appropriate boundaries and an honest acknowledgment of the temptation, we can yield. We can dwell on the image, nurture it into a fantasy, and even in the middle of a room full of pastors, allow the impulse to drag us into lust. But simply noticing an enticing image doesn't qualify as a lack of self-control. What happens in the next five seconds may or may not, depending on what we choose to do.

Paul obviously had the same penchant for lack of self-control as the rest of us. He says, "I discipline my body and make it my slave, so that, after I have preached to others, I myself will not be disqualified" (v. 27). I wish that full-time ministry made the battle against the flesh easier, but it doesn't. And even when a man is writing God-breathed words, he still has to suit up and face the enemy in a civil war that never skips a day.

FIRST STEPS TO LIVING ABOVE THE FLESH

Now, if we can't win this fight, then Scripture is mocking us by dangling a hope that will never be realized. And to put it bluntly, Paul is a liar. But fortunately, we're in a winnable war. Paul isn't lying. Our study of these passages leads to four truths, four perspectives that will arm us for the conflict.

First, appreciating the nature of the battle is essential. It's a universal war that began all the way back in the Garden of Eden and includes every one of us. Our flesh craves satisfaction in the very things that God hates. And until we stand with the Savior in heaven, the age-old civil war rages on! Yes, we will experience the attack of Satan from the outside, but we have an enemy within that we must never forget. The flesh never takes a holiday.

Second, we are powerless to win the war against the flesh without the Spirit of God. By conscious submission, we engage the Holy Spirit in the first moments of each decision. Our ability to do that will grow as we continue practicing the spiritual disciplines. All of them prepare us for battle. All of them give us greater intimacy with the Almighty, who lives within us. The result is predictable: when faced with temptation, He fights the battle on our behalf.

Third, developing this discipline is a personal matter. We can depend upon no one else to develop our own discipline of self-control. Paul says, "*I* box, *I* run, *I* discipline *my* body." This is something only we can do in the Lord's strength. If someone else has to restrain us, it's not self-control!

As a pastor, I've seen a lot of people marry with the hope that his or her partner's strength will prop up their own weakness. The opposite is more often the case. Marriage isn't a magic pill. A godly marriage can be the instrument of God's working to make us holier, but marriage by itself makes nobody strong. Developing the discipline of self-control cannot be the responsibility of a husband or wife.

Fourth, ignoring the consequences invites disaster. Lack of self-control will invariably lead to embarrassment for us and those we love. With issues of self-control, we're usually dealing with things that we know are wrong or will have negative fallout. And they usually involve something habitual, which means that the people we hurt are probably growing weary. What's worse, it negatively affects our spiritual life.

In verse 27, Paul uses a word that most translations render "disqualified." It's in keeping with the word picture of the athletic competition, but "disqualified" can lead us to some wrong conclusions about the spiritual consequences. Salvation and the assurance of heaven are not the issues in Paul's mind here. You will not lose your salvation if you fail to control yourself. However, you quite possibly can be put out of the race by God's disciplinary action. I have seen, on more than one occasion, a believer sidelined by God for the good of the family, the church, and the individual.

The word that Paul uses can also mean "worthless, of no account, useless," or in the context of a race, a last-place loser. We're in the race called life, and God calls us to run it with purpose, to restrain our impulses so as not to be too flabby to run well. And His desire is that we enjoy victory and not have to go through life labeled a loser because we defeated ourselves.

You want to be like Christ? Refuse to surrender to the flesh, surrender instead to the Spirit, and let Him live His life through you.

PART THREE

How You Should Live
Now That You're New

DEVELOPING A GODLY MORAL COMPASS

We don't have prophets today, at least not in the strict sense of the word. Before and during the time when the Bible was being written, prophets received revelation from God and delivered it to the people. People knew that when a genuine prophet spoke, the message was as good as from the lips of God Himself. The truthfulness of the message authenticated the messenger. If a person claimed to speak from God and gave information that proved to be false, he or she was taken to the edge of town, cast into a ditch, and stoned to death. So, generally speaking, the word of a prophet was considered reliable . . . at least when the people cared to hear from God.

Micah was one of those trustworthy prophets who lived and ministered in Judah around 700 BC. Scholars group him among those they call the "minor prophets" because their writings are significantly shorter than those of the "major prophets," such as Isaiah, Jeremiah, and Ezekiel.

After Solomon's reign ended around 931 BC, civil war divided his kingdom into two nations, Israel to the north and Judah in the south. As Judah wavered in its faithfulness to God under the ambiguous morality of its kings, Israel consistently pursued evil. And by 722 BC, after repeated warnings by a multitude of faithful prophets, God's patience reached the end of its tether and He allowed the Assyrian Empire to invade and conquer Israel.

As Micah began to write, the awful spectacle of Israel's destruction was still fresh in his mind. He feared for his people, who had begun to behave as their brothers up north had. He saw compromise in the corruption of the priests, the selfishness of the ruling class, and the outright fabrication on the part of false prophets.

His people needed a word from God.

WHAT THE LORD DOES NOT EXPECT

Against the chorus of false prophets, Micah stood alone to deliver God's message to Judah. In the sixth chapter of his book, Micah alternately records the words of God and then responds on behalf of Judah. Speaking for God, he asks the nation Judah:

> My people, what have I done to you,
> And how have I wearied you? Answer Me.
> Indeed, I brought you up from the land of Egypt
> And ransomed you from the house of slavery,
> And I sent before you Moses, Aaron and Miriam. (vv. 3–4)

Then in response, Micah represents the words of Judah before the Lord:

> With what shall I come to the LORD
> And bow myself before the God on high?
> Shall I come to Him with burnt offerings,
> With yearling calves?
> Does the LORD take delight in thousands of rams,
> In ten thousand rivers of oil?
> Shall I present my firstborn for my
>   rebellious acts,
> The fruit of my body for the sin of my soul? (vv. 6–7)

Take note of how the people of Judah think they must approach God. They're bargaining. They're treating the Lord like the capricious gods of Egypt, Canaan, and the idolatrous, brutal Assyrians. All false religions have at least one thing in common: they attempt to win divine favor through deeds of service or sacrifice. The people of Judah began with expressions of worship prescribed by Hebrew law and then expanded them to ridiculous proportions.

Shall I bring an olah? That's the Hebrew word for a burnt offering of an entire animal, from nose to tail—hide, hooves, and all. *Shall I bring an expensive animal and burn all of it before the Lord? How about several?* Then they suppose that if the Lord is pleased with that sacrifice, certainly He would be ecstatic over a massive offering. *Would He be pleased if I offered whole herds of livestock? What if I topped it off with multiple barrels of expensive olive oil? Or even better, ten thousand rivers of oil! Is that what He wants from us?*

Their bargaining doesn't stop there. *What if I sacrifice my precious firstborn child on the altar? Will God then be pleased?*

Their bartering for the Lord's favor moved from regular worship to exaggerated reverence, to hyperbole, then blasphemy. That's the problem with works-based religion. You can never sacrifice enough, work hard enough, pray long enough, or bow low enough to earn God's pleasure. And the tragic irony of Judah's cosmic bribery is that the Lord valued nothing they offered.

The Lord doesn't expect us to barter for His favor. His love isn't for sale.

If, on the other hand, you desire to honor the Lord because you love Him, Micah offers an uncomplicated approach. God looks beneath and beyond all outward expressions of religious devotion to examine our character. What honors the Lord is a heart that beats in the same rhythm as His, a spirit that values the same qualities that define Him. He wants people who do what is right, who love kindness, and who walk humbly with Him. Do as Micah instructs, and you will not only honor the Lord you love, you will live life well.

GOD EXPECTS US TO DO WHAT IS RIGHT

"Do what is right." In this postmodern era, that statement requires clarification before we can proceed. Postmodernism has so blurred the line between right and wrong that people have a difficult time discerning what kind of behavior is good, appropriate, and expected; what behavior is fundamentally wrong; and which choices are morally neutral. Most adults shy away from declaring their beliefs as hard and fast rules of conduct. Thanks to the postmodern worldview, it's considered foolish to declare that truth exists and boorish to suggest that one can have it.

I can say with genuine certainty and with absolutely no arrogance, *I have a direct line to absolute truth.* I didn't uncover it. I didn't create it. I wasn't the first to see it or even recognize it. I merely accept God's Word as authentic revelation from the Author of truth. The sixty-six books of the Bible provide us with God's directives and principles. He took the time to have His Word written down and preserved through the centuries so that we may know Him and obey His will. The Bible reflects His character, and by reading it we may discover what values and choices give Him the most pleasure. Therefore, to do what is right is to conform one's life to the directives and principles found in the sixty-six books of the Bible.

THE COST OF OBEDIENCE

Roughly 750 years after Micah's prophecy, two of Jesus' disciples wrestled with a deadly dilemma. After Jesus was crucified, buried, resurrected, and had ascended to heaven, His followers began to share the good news with everyone they met. And to prove the truth of their message, Peter and John healed a man who was paralyzed from birth, the same kind of miracle Jesus had performed numerous times before. But, despite this irrefutable proof, Israel's religious officials were determined to silence the message of salvation through Christ and destroy anyone who preached it.

> As they were speaking to the people, the priests and the captain of the temple guard and the Sadducees came up to them, being greatly disturbed because they were teaching the people and proclaiming in Jesus the resurrection from the dead. And they laid hands on them and put them in jail until the next day, for it was already evening. But many of those who had heard the message believed; and the number of the men came to be about five thousand. On the next day, their rulers and elders and scribes were gathered together in Jerusalem; and Annas the high priest was there, and Caiaphas and John and Alexander, and all who were of high-priestly descent. When they had placed them in the center, they began to inquire, "By what power, or in what name, have you done this?" (Acts 4:1–7)

To appreciate the pressure Peter and John faced, imagine two American, high school educated, working-class Joes hauled before a joint session of Congress and the Supreme Court without the benefit of legal representation.

Standing in the foreboding presence of such intelligence and political power, the two simple fishermen heard the following demands: make a legal case for the actions you have taken. Explain why we shouldn't hand you over to the Romans and let them nail you to a cross.

The question, "By what power, or in what name, have you done this?" refers to their proclaiming the resurrection of Jesus. This wasn't a genuine question; it was a charge. The Sadducees already knew the answer. Peter knew this and courageously chose to preface his answer with a charge of his own.

> Then Peter, filled with the Holy Spirit, said to them, "Rulers and elders of the people, if we are on trial today for a benefit done to a sick man, as to how this man has been made well, let it be known to all of you and to all the people of Israel, that by the name of Jesus Christ the Nazarene, whom you crucified, whom God raised from the dead—by this name this man stands here before you in good health. [Jesus] is the stone which was rejected by you, the builders, but which became the chief corner stone. And there is salvation in no one else; for there is no other name under heaven that has been given among men by which we must be saved." (Acts 4:8–12)

Note two phrases in particular: "filled with the Holy Spirit" and "whom you crucified." To be filled with the Holy Spirit means to be controlled by the Spirit of God. And when you are under the full control of the Holy Spirit, immoral choices are impossible. In fact, when you submit yourself to the dominating control of the Holy Spirit, you are transformed from within, empowered to think clearly and act confidently. Peter boldly and shrewdly turned the Sadducees' accusation of insurrection around to show that they— not he and John—were the treasonous ones.

So there stood Peter and John before the most powerful men in Israel, using this earlier memory to turn the accusation around. But in case anyone wasn't paying attention, Peter made his countercharge crystal clear. He said, in effect, "The King you killed is alive again, He is God, and you must come to Him—and no other—for salvation."

Can you hear the stunned silence that followed Peter's speech? These high-powered, religious authorities did their best to intimidate the two apostles into silence. But observe their response.

Now as [the rulers, elders, scribes, Annas, Caiaphas, John, Alexander, and all who were of high priestly ancestry] observed the confidence of Peter and John and understood that they were uneducated and untrained men, they were amazed, and began to recognize them as having been with Jesus. And seeing the man who had been healed standing with them, they had nothing to say in reply. (Acts 4:13–14)

Careful observation of this passage reveals no fewer than three qualities that distinguish a godly person when he or she chooses to do what is right. And each quality points to a principle we can apply to help us behave more like these two steadfast men.

First, observe the confidence of Peter and John. This is not arrogance. An arrogant person cannot walk humbly with God. The two men spoke with confidence because they found security in the Lord, not themselves.

Second, consider the authority of Peter and John. They were not formally trained in higher education to debate theology and philosophy as the Sadducees were. The apostles stood on Christ's authority, not their own. They possessed a direct line to absolute truth: Jesus Christ, the Living Word of God.

Third, see the effectiveness of Peter and John. Doing what is right—conforming one's conduct to the principles of Scripture and submitting to the control of the Holy Spirit—produces results. The undeniable effect of the apostles' obedience stood beside them: a formerly paralyzed man brought to perfect health.

Peter and John exemplify the first quality of a life well lived according to Micah 6:8. The quality of justice is the consistent, unwavering decision to do what is right. And when you choose to do what is right, you can walk and speak with complete confidence. Your thoughts and actions proceed from a clear understanding of truth. Though perhaps misunderstood, maligned, or even persecuted, you can walk with steadfast peace, knowing that the Lord understands, approves, and rewards those who remain faithful.

Peter and John knew what was right. Their respect for the religious leaders didn't blind them to their duty before the Lord. Jesus had said, "Go . . . make disciples . . . teaching them to observe all that I commanded you" (Matthew 28:19–20), and "You shall be My witnesses" (Acts 1:8). This gave them the courage to obey God rather than people. And, in this case, their enemies had no choice but to honor their dedication. Peter and John's followers—the rest of the disciples and the thousands of believers who had proclaimed the resurrection of Jesus Christ—shouted and sang and prayed in celebration.

> And when they had prayed, the place where they had gathered together was shaken, and they were all filled with the Holy Spirit and began to speak the word of God with boldness. (Acts 4:31)

The obedience Peter and John sowed that day returned an abundant harvest. Obedience encouraged more obedience. And "abundant grace was upon them all" (Acts 4:33).

At this point, I would love to end with the fairy-tale words "and they preached happily ever after." But, as is usually the case in this fallen world of ours, no good deed shall go unpunished. As obedience—doing what is right—grows, opposition will develop in direct proportion. The news of Peter and John's earlier healing of the paralyzed man spread, which brought multitudes to Jerusalem, hoping to have the miracle repeated. And, before long, the apostles found themselves facing an increasingly agitated body of religious leaders.

> And all the more believers in the Lord, multitudes of men and women, were constantly added to their number, to such an extent that they even carried the sick out into the streets and laid them on cots and pallets, so that when Peter came by at least his shadow might fall on any one of them. Also the people from the cities in the vicinity of Jerusalem were coming together, bringing people who were sick or afflicted with unclean spirits, and they were all being healed.
>
> But the high priest rose up, along with all his associates (that is the sect of the Sadducees), and they were filled with jealousy. They laid hands on the apostles and put them in a public jail. (Acts 5:14–18).

The foolish, two-dimensional thinking of the religious elite led them to believe that the followers of Jesus would respond to coercion, that they would be discouraged by the loss of personal freedom and creature comforts. But Peter and John's ethics extended beyond the approval of people and above the earthly plane to include the vertical dimension. They were miraculously released from prison, and instead of fleeing the city, they returned to the temple to resume their proclamation of Christ's resurrection. When they were again brought before the religious council and challenged to stop their preaching, the apostles responded with words we would all do well to memorize: "We must obey God rather than men" (Acts 5:29).

To do what is right is to side with the truth of God. And never doubt it, the truth of God will always prevail. Evil may cause setbacks, and it may hamper the steady march of God's plan, but it is ultimately powerless to stop it. To do what is right is to join the winning side of the fight, though the battle will not be without pain or struggle.

The men of the council took the advice of Gamaliel, the respected teacher, and released the apostles. But they couldn't deny their bloodlust. Before letting the followers of Jesus go free, they subjected them to the same kind of scourging their Master endured. If you saw the film *The Passion of the Christ*, you saw a graphic portrayal of this brutal Roman punishment. Victims were beaten within an inch of their lives and very often died from their wounds. Recovery could take months. Nevertheless . . .

> They went on their way from the presence of the Council, rejoicing that they had been considered worthy to suffer shame for His name. And every day, in the temple and from house to house, they kept right on teaching and preaching Jesus as the Christ. (Acts 5:41–42)

Meaning? They kept doing what was right!

DOING WHAT IS RIGHT IN THE TWENTY-FIRST CENTURY

Within just a few generations, much of the Roman world had been saturated with the gospel. Less than three hundred years later Christianity became the official religion of the empire. While, admittedly, that may not have been the best thing to happen to the church, it nonetheless demonstrates the powerful effect of people doing what is right.

And it's this kind of commitment that the Lord expects of those who call themselves Christian. He has a plan, and He calls us to become a part of it. Three timeless, practical principles will help us do just that.

We Must Know What Is Right.

Obviously, we cannot *do* what is right if we don't *know* what is right. Unfortunately, our culture is awash with information and opinions and philosophies and ideologies—all in the context of a postmodern worldview that doubts the very existence of definable truth.

I am also concerned by what I see as a growing trend in evangelical churches—the notion that God reveals truth directly to our hearts in spoken and unspoken messages, that we can receive instructions from the Lord. I often hear people say things like, "I wasn't sure what to do about that job offer until the Lord spoke to my heart and told me what to do," or "I haven't made a decision yet; I'm waiting to hear from God on that."

Let me be clear. In the past, the Lord spoke to people directly—via visual and audible manifestations of Himself, in dreams and visions, even in silence—and His purpose was to have them convey those supernaturally communicated messages to others or write them down for future generations. We have a record of those messages preserved in the sixty-six books of the Bible. Once the Bible was complete, the Lord stopped supernaturally speaking to people directly. He replaced this method with a greater, more intimate one.

In the old covenant, God issued orders that He expected to be fulfilled to the letter. But in the new covenant, He has stopped issuing orders. Instead, He sent His Holy Spirit to transform the heart of the believer, to renew his or her mind to think as the Father thinks. He no longer shouts to the faithful, in effect, "Drop and give Me twenty pushups!" Now He reforms the character of His people so that they will say within, "I want to give You fifty!" In a process called sanctification, God transforms the character of the believer to match that of His Son, creating agents who think like He thinks, behave as He desires, and make choices that reflect His values and accomplish His will.

Therefore, as you seek to do what is right, don't look for God's voice within saying, "Turn left. Take this job, not that one. Read your Bible. Eat less fat." Instead, make use of the resources God has made available to you. Let me mention just three.

1. *Let God reveal to you what is right from His Word.* Read your Bible to become increasingly intimate with His character. Set aside the newspapers and turn off the television; make time to get into God's inspired, reliable Word. Discover timeless facts and principles directly from the Author of truth. Allow the reading of Scripture to prompt new perspectives and trigger new insights.

2. *Trust the transforming power of the Holy Spirit to lead you toward what is right.* As the Holy Spirit does His work of gradual transformation, listen to your inner convictions. They are not the voice of God. They are the thoughts of a mind changed to think like the Lord Himself. Your old character and values will be exchanged for the Lord's so that you begin to think with the mind of Christ. This is far better than some people's idea of the new covenant in which God merely barks orders from within the heart rather than issuing commands on tablets of stone.

3. *Heed the wisdom of those who follow Christ and who do what is right.* God gave us His Word, He gave us His Spirit, and He gave us one another. Paul the apostle wrote, "Be imitators of me, just as I also am of Christ" (1 Corinthians 11:1), and "Now you followed my teaching, conduct, purpose, faith, patience, love, perseverance, persecutions, and sufferings" (2 Timothy 3:10–11). I urge you to find a seasoned follower of Jesus and let his or her experience become a guide for your own journey.

We Must Expect Resistance.

When we choose to do what is right and meet with resistance, a common reaction is to wonder, *Where did I go wrong? Did I displease God?* The answer is, quite simply, no. The bold choice to do something that honors the Lord or reflects His character will be punished by a world that is opposed to His way. Peter and John received a flogging for their faithfulness, a punishment normally reserved for criminals.

You may lose popularity. You might be denied opportunities you rightfully deserve. You might be persecuted for taking a stand for truth, for defending the innocent, or for refusing to look the other way while others do wrong. Don't expect to be rewarded. Expect resistance. Don't be surprised when (not if) you face difficulties as a result of doing what is right.

We Must Remember That God Will Superintend His Plan.

Walking the path that the prophet Micah marked for us will never be easy. When the going gets tough, remind yourself that you are not alone. It would have been easy for Peter and John, sitting in their jail cells, to wonder if the Lord had forgotten them. They were faithful to proclaim the message they had been given, they were busy carrying out Jesus' commission to make disciples, and jail time was the thanks they received. But instead of becoming bitter, they rejoiced!

What kept them hopeful despite the imprisonment and the floggings was the trust they had placed in the Lord. He warned that they would drink of the same cup that He was to drink, but that ultimate victory was certain. His resurrection secured the eventual triumph of His kingdom, which gave the apostles courage to stand strong in the face of severe persecution. They knew God was in control. That meant they were fighting for the winning side. It is remarkable how invincible such knowledge can make you feel.

When you find yourself being punished for doing what is right, you have joined the ranks of a very distinguished league. You and I have a great "cloud of witnesses surrounding us" (Hebrews 12:1). We are following in the steps of faithful men and women who extended the kingdom of God and made the world a better place, and did so at great personal cost. Fearlessly do as they did. Trust that God is right in all His ways, and take courage that you, too, fight for the winning side.

DEALING WITH FAILURE, SUFFERING, TEMPTATION, AND GUILT

Joseph Parker, a great preacher of yesteryear, once said to a group of aspiring young ministers, "Preach to the suffering and you will never lack a congregation. There is a broken heart in every pew."

Truly, suffering is the common thread in all our garments.

This has been true since the beginning, when sin entered the world and Adam and Eve were driven from the garden. It shouldn't surprise us, therefore, that when the apostle Peter wrote his first letter to fellow believers scattered throughout much of Asia Minor he focused on the one subject that drew all of them together. Suffering. These people were being singed by the same flames of persecution that would take the apostle's life in just a few years. Their circumstances were the bleakest imaginable. Yet Peter didn't try to pump them up with positive thinking. Instead, he gently reached his hand to their chins and lifted their faces skyward—so they could see beyond their circumstances to their celestial calling.

> Peter, an apostle of Jesus Christ, to those who reside as aliens, scattered throughout Pontius, Galatia, Cappadocia, Asia, and Bithynia, who are chosen according to the foreknowledge of God the Father, by the sanctifying work of the Spirit, that you may obey Jesus Christ and be sprinkled with His blood: May grace and peace be yours in fullest measure. (1 Peter 1:1–2)

The men and women Peter wrote to knew what it was like to be away from home, not by choice but by force. Persecuted for their faith, they had been pushed out into a world that was not only unfamiliar but hostile.

While most of us are not afflicted by horrible persecution for our faith, we do know what it means to face various forms of suffering, pain, disappointment, and grief. Fortunately, in the letter of 1 Peter we can find comfort and consolation for our own brand of suffering. Just as this treasured document spoke to the believers scattered in Pontius or Galatia or Cappadocia or Asia, so it speaks to us in Texas and California, Arizona and Oklahoma, Minnesota and Maine.

The first good news Peter gives us is the knowledge that we are "chosen by God." We aren't just thrown on this earth like dice tossed across a table. We are sovereignly and lovingly placed here for a purpose, having been chosen by God. His choosing us was according to His foreknowledge, by the sanctifying work of the Spirit, that we may obey Jesus Christ, having been sprinkled with His blood. Powerful words!

God has given us a purpose for our existence, a reason to go on, even though that existence includes tough times. Living through suffering, we become sanctified—in other words, set apart for the glory of God. We gain perspective. We grow deeper. We grow up!

Can you imagine going through such times without Jesus Christ? I can't. But frankly, that's what most people do. They face those frightening fears and sleepless nights in the hospital without Christ. They struggle with a wayward teenager without Christ. Alone, they endure the awful words from a mate, "I don't want to live with you any longer. I want my freedom. I don't love you anymore. I'm gone." And they go through it all without Christ.

Yet if we will only believe and ask, a full measure of God's grace and peace is available to any of us. By the wonderful, prevailing mercy of God, we can find purpose in the scattering and sadness of our lives. We can not only deal with suffering but rejoice through it. Though our pain and our disappointment and the details of our suffering may differ, there is an abundance of God's grace and peace is available to each one of us.

These truths form the skeleton of strong doctrine. But unless the truths are fleshed out, they remain hard and bony and difficult to embrace. Knowing this, Peter reminds his readers of all they have to cling to so that they can actually rejoice in times of suffering, drawing on God's grace and peace in fullest measure.

REJOICING THROUGH HARD TIMES

As I read and ponder Peter's letter to persecuted and struggling Christians in the first century, I find six reasons why believers in any age, no matter how difficult, can rejoice through hard times and experience hope beyond suffering.

We Have a Living Hope

Blessed be the God and Father of our Lord Jesus Christ, who according to His great mercy has caused us to be born again to a living hope through the resurrection of Jesus Christ from the dead. (1 Peter 1:3)

"Who can mind the journey," asks the late, great Bible teacher James M. Gray, "when the road leads home?"

How can we concern ourselves that much over what happens on this temporary planet when we know that it is all leading us to our eternal destination? Peter calls that our "living hope," and he reminds us that it is based on the resurrection of Jesus Christ. If God brought His Son through the most painful trials and back from the pit of death itself, certainly He can bring us through whatever we face in this world, no matter how deep that pit might seem at the time.

Do you realize how scarce hope is to those without Christ? One cynical writer, H. L. Mencken, an American newspaperman during the early half of the twentieth century, referred to hope as "a pathological belief in the occurrence of the impossible."

So if you want to smile through your tears, if you want to rejoice through times of suffering, just keep reminding yourself that, as a Christian, what you're going through isn't the end of the story—it's simply the rough journey that leads to the right destination.

We Have a Permanent Inheritance

Blessed be the God and Father of our Lord Jesus Christ, who according to His great mercy has caused us . . . to obtain an inheritance which is imperishable and undefiled and will not fade away, reserved in heaven for you. (1 Peter 1:3–4)

We also can rejoice through suffering because we have a permanent inheritance—a secure home in heaven. And our place there is reserved under the safekeeping, under the constant, omnipotent surveillance of Almighty God. Nothing can destroy it, defile it, diminish it, or displace it. Isn't that a great relief?

We Have a Divine Protection

[We] . . . are protected by the power of God, through faith for a salvation ready to be revealed in the last time. (1 Peter 1:5)

Under heaven's lock and key, we are protected by the most efficient security system available—the power of God. There is no way we will be lost in the process of suffering. No disorder, no disease, not even death itself can weaken or threaten God's ultimate protection over our lives. No matter what the calamity, no matter what the disappointment or depth of pain, no matter what kind of destruction occurs in our bodies at the time of death, our souls are divinely protected.

"God stands between you and all that menaces your hope or threatens your eternal welfare," James Moffatt wrote. "The protection here is entirely and directly the work of God."

Two words will help you cope when you run low on hope: *accept* and *trust*.

Accept the mystery of hardship, suffering, misfortune, or mistreatment. Don't try to understand it or explain it. Accept it. Then, deliberately *trust* God to protect you by His power from this very moment to the dawning of eternity.

We Have a Developing Faith

In this you greatly rejoice, even though now for a little while, if necessary, you have been distressed by various trials, that the proof of your faith, being more precious than gold which is perishable, even though tested by fire, may be found to result in praise and glory and honor at the revelation of Jesus Christ. (1 Peter 1:6–7)

Here is the first of several references to rejoicing in Peter's letter. The words "even though" indicate that the joy is unconditional. It does not depend on the circumstances surrounding us. And don't overlook the fact that this joy comes in spite of our suffering, not because of it, as some who glorify suffering would have us believe. We don't rejoice because times are hard; we rejoice in spite of the fact that they are hard.

These verses also reveal three significant things about trials.

First, *trials are often necessary*, proving the genuineness of our faith and at the same time teaching us humility. Trials reveal our own helplessness. They put us on our face before God.

Second, *trials are distressing*, teaching us compassion so that we never make light of another's test or cruelly force others to smile while enduring it.

When someone else is hurting, express your sympathy and weep with them. Put your arm around them. Don't reel off a lot of verses. Don't try to make the hurting person pray with you or sing with you if he or she is not ready to do that. Feel what that person is feeling. Walk quietly and compassionately in his or her shoes.

Third, *trials come in various forms*. The word *various* comes from an interesting Greek term, *poikolos*, which means "variegated" or "many colored." We also get the term "polka dot" from it. Trials come in a variety of forms and colors. They are different, just as we are different. Something that would hardly affect you might knock the slats out from under me—and vice versa. But God offers special grace to match every shade of sorrow.

Paul had a thorn in the flesh, and he prayed three times for God to remove it. "No," said God, "I'm not taking it away." Finally, Paul said, "I've learned to trust in You, Lord. I've learned to live with it." It was then God said, "My grace is sufficient for that thorn." He matched the color of the test with the color of grace. The purpose of these fiery ordeals is that we may come forth as purified gold, a shining likeness of the Lord Jesus Christ Himself. That glinting likeness is what ultimately gives glory and praise and honor to our Savior.

We Have an Unseen Savior

And though you have not seen Him, you love Him, and though you do not see Him now, but believe in Him, you greatly rejoice with joy inexpressible and full of glory. (1 Peter 1:8)

Keep in mind that the context of this verse is suffering. So we know that Peter is not serving up an inconsequential, theological hors d'oeuvre. He's giving us solid meat we can sink our teeth into. He's telling us that our Savior is standing alongside us in that furnace. He is there even though we can't see Him.

You don't have to see someone to love that person. The blind mother has never seen her children, but she loves them. You don't have to see someone to believe in him or her. Believers today have never seen a physical manifestation of the Savior—we have not visibly seen Him walking among us—but we love Him nevertheless. In times of trial we sense He is there, and that causes us to "greatly rejoice" with inexpressible joy.

REJOICING, NOT RESENTMENT

When we are suffering, only Christ's perspective can replace our resentment with rejoicing. I've seen it happen in hospital rooms. I've seen it happen in families. I've seen it happen in my own life.

Our whole perspective changes when we catch a glimpse of the purpose of Christ in it all. Take that away, and it's nothing more than a bitter, terrible experience.

Suffering comes in many forms and degrees, but His grace is always there to carry us beyond it. I've lived long enough and endured a sufficient number of trials to say without hesitation that only Christ's perspective can replace our resentment with rejoicing. Jesus is the central piece of suffering's puzzle. If we fit Him into place, the rest of the puzzle—no matter how complex and enigmatic—begins to make sense.

Only Christ's salvation can change us from spectators to participants in the unfolding drama of redemption. The scenes will be demanding. Some may be tragic. But only then will we understand the role that suffering plays in our lives. Only then will we be able to tap into hope beyond our suffering.

TEMPTATION:
STAYING CLEAN IN A CORRUPT SOCIETY

Wouldn't it be wonderful if God would save us and then, within a matter of seconds, take us on to glory? Wouldn't that be a great relief? We would never have any temptations. We would never have to battle with the flesh. We would never even have the possibility of messing up our lives. We could just be whisked off to glory—saved, sanctified, galvanized, glorified! Trouble is, I have a sneaking suspicion that many, if not most, would wait until fifteen minutes before takeoff time to give their lives to Christ and then catch the jet for glory.

Think about that. "I'm not asking You to take them out from among the midst of a crooked and perverse generation," Jesus said. "But I do ask You to guard them, to protect them." Jesus doesn't ask the Father to isolate His disciples from the world but to insulate them, "to keep them from the evil one."

He has left us in the world on purpose and for His purpose. Just before Jesus' arrest and death on the cross, He said:

> "I have given them Your word; and the world has hated them, because they are not of the world, even as I am not of the world. I do not ask You to take them out of the world, but to keep them from the evil one." (John 17:14–15)

In a world where the majority are going the wrong way, we are left as lights—stoplights, directional lights, illuminating lights—as living examples, as strong testimonies of the right way. We are spiritual salmon swimming upstream.

The physical world upon which we have our feet planted is visible. It can be measured. It can be felt. It has color and odor and texture. It's tangible, obvious. What is not so obvious is the system that permeates and operates within lives on this earth. It is a world system manipulated by the pervasive hand of Satan and his demons, who pull the strings to achieve the adversary's wicked ends. If we are ever to extricate ourselves from those strings, we must be able to detect them and understand where they lead.

> Do not love the world, nor the things in the world. If anyone loves the world, the love of the Father is not in him. For all that is in the world [the cosmos], the lust of the flesh and the lust of the eyes and the boastful pride of life, is not from the Father, but is from the world. And the world is passing away, also its lusts; but the one who does the will of God lives forever. (1 John 2:15–17)

So what is this system? What is its philosophy? What is the frame of reference of the *cosmos*—its thinking, its drives, its goals?

The first thing we need to know is that it is a system that operates apart from and at odds with God. It is designed to appeal to us, to attract us, to seduce us with its sequined garb of fame, fortune, power, and pleasure. God's ways are often uncomfortable, but the world system is designed to make us comfortable, to give us pleasure, to gain our favor, and ultimately to win our support. The philosophy of the world system is totally at odds with the philosophy of God.

Greek grammarian Kenneth Wuest wrote:

> *Kosmos* refers to an ordered system . . . of which Satan is the head, his fallen angels and demons are his emissaries, and the unsaved of the human race are his subjects. . . . Much in this world-system is religious, cultured, refined, and intellectual. But it is anti-God and anti-Christ.[1]

Pay close attention to the commercials on television and observe what they're advertising and how virtually every word, picture, and sound is designed to pull you in, to make you dissatisfied with what you have and what you look like and who you are. The great goal is to make you want whatever it is that is being sold.

But it's not just on television. The world system, the cosmos philosophy, is everywhere. It's going on all the time, even when you can't see it, and especially when you're not thinking about it. It's whistling its appeal: "Come on. Come on. You'll love it. This is so much fun. It'll make you look so good. It'll make you feel so good." It motivates us by appealing to our pride and to that which pleases us, all the while cleverly seducing us away from God.

And over all this realm, don't forget, Satan is prince.

A CHALLENGE TO BE DIFFERENT

The pull of the world is every bit as strong and subtle as gravity. So invisible, yet so irresistible. So relentlessly there. Never absent or passive.

Unless we realize how strong and how subtle the world's influence really is, we won't understand the passion behind Peter's words.

Living in Holiness

> Therefore, prepare your minds for action, keep sober in spirit, fix your hope completely on the grace to be brought to you at the revelation of Jesus Christ. As obedient children, do not be conformed to the former lusts which were yours in your ignorance, but like the Holy One who called you, be holy yourselves also in all your behavior; because it is written, "You shall be holy, for I am holy." (1 Peter 1:13–16)

Reading these statements, we can't help but catch something of Peter's assertive spirit. He seems to be saying that this is no time to kick back; this isn't a day to be passive. In fact, I think Peter really bears down with his pen at this point. Look at the forcefulness of his phrases: "prepare your minds for action . . . keep sober . . . fix your hope." He spits them out in staccato form. Today we might say, "Straighten up!" "Get serious!" And then the clincher command from God, saying, in essence: "Be holy like I am."

How easy it is to allow the world, the cosmos, to suck you into its system. If you do, if you conform, then you are adopting the kind of lifestyle that was yours when you were in ignorance, when you didn't know there was another way to live. That was back when the cosmos was your comfort zone.

Have you been in Christ so long that you have forgotten what it was like to be without Him? Remember, He has called us to follow in His footsteps—to be *holy* "like the Holy One who called you, be holy yourselves also in all your behavior; because it is written, 'You shall be holy, for I am holy.'" We have a Father who is holy, and as His children, we're to be like Him.

But what does it mean to be *holy*? That's always a tough question to answer. Stripped down to its basics, the term *holy* means "set apart" in some special and exclusive way. Perhaps it will help if we think of it in another context. In holy matrimony, for example, a man and a woman are set apart, leaving all others as they bond exclusively to each other.

Church ordinances or sacraments, such as baptism and communion, are often called holy. In Holy Communion, for example, the bread and wine are set apart from common use and set aside to God alone. The same meaning lies behind the word *sanctify* in 1 Peter 3:15: "But sanctify Christ as Lord in your hearts." I love that. We are to "set Him apart" as Lord in our hearts.

What a successful way to deal with the cosmos! To begin the morning by saying, "Lord, I set apart my mind for You today. I set apart my passion. I set apart my eyes. I set apart my ears. I set apart my motives. I set apart my discipline. Today I set apart every limb of my body and each area of my life unto You as Lord over my life." When we start our day like that, chances are good that temptation's winks will not be nearly as alluring.

Walking in Fear

And if you address as Father the One who impartially judges according to each one's work, conduct yourselves in fear during the time of your stay on earth. (1 Peter 1:17)

Another secret of living a godly life in the midst of a godless world involves the way we conduct ourselves hour by hour through the day. Peter says we are to do it "in fear." We don't hear much about the fear of God today, and when we do, some may think only of images of a fire-and-brimstone preacher pounding a pulpit. We need a better perspective. Perhaps the word *reverence* gives us a clearer picture of what Peter means here. In fact, the New International Version translates this phrase "live your lives as strangers here in reverent fear." The point is, if we're going to address God as Father, then we should conduct ourselves on earth in a way that reflects our reverence for Him as our Father.

Also, if you're going to address Him as your Father, if you're going to have a one-on-one relationship with Him in fellowship and in prayer, then conduct yourself as one who knows that you will someday have to account to Him for your life. Why? Well, in case you didn't know, "each one of us shall give an account of himself to God" (Romans 14:12). When we die, we will be brought before the judgment seat of Christ where we will independently account for our lives before God. He will see us as our lives pass in review, and He will reward us accordingly. It's not a judgment to see if we get into heaven. That's taken care of when you invite Jesus into your life as God and Savior. We will all give an account of the deeds we have done in this life, and God will "test the quality of each man's work" (1 Corinthians 3:13). That thought, alone, will instill a big, healthy dose of the fear of God in us!

This Christian life is a tough fight. Earlier in this century, Donald Grey Barnhouse, a well-known minister and radio preacher, wrote an entire book on this subject, *The Invisible War*. This conflict is not a war fought with Uzis or tanks or smart bombs or ground-to-air missiles. The land mines, ambushes, and traps set by our enemy are much subtler than that—and even deadlier, for they aim at the soul. And they are everywhere.

But with the pride and pleasures of the cosmos so alluring, how can weaklings like us run the race without being disqualified and forfeiting our reward? How can we win the battle over an enemy we can't see? The solution to that problem rests within our minds.

Focusing Your Mind

. . . knowing that you were not redeemed with perishable things like silver or gold from your futile way of life inherited from your forefathers, but with precious blood, as of a lamb unblemished and spotless, the blood of Christ. For He was foreknown before the foundation of the world, but has appeared in these last times for the sake of you who through Him are believers in God, who raised Him from the dead and gave Him glory, so that your faith and hope are in God. (1 Peter 1:18–20)

I'm convinced that the battle with this world is a battle within the mind. Our minds are major targets of the enemy's appeal. When the world pulls back its bowstring, our minds are the bull's-eyes. Any arrows we allow to become impaled in our minds will ultimately poison our thoughts. And if we tolerate this long enough, we'll end up acting out what we think.

The most grievous and destructive sins are rarely the result of impulse. The insightful British pastor and writer, F. B. Meyer, wisely said, "No man suddenly becomes base." Just as no marriage suddenly fractures, just as no tree suddenly rots, and just as no church suddenly splits, no person suddenly falls. Long before a decisive temptation and subsequent moral tumble ruins a person's life, his or her mind had been toying with the idea. "Harmless fantasy" gave way to wishful thinking, and wishful thinking eroded the conscience. Gradually, imperceptibly, evil came to be seen as good.

Christ delivered us from slavery—slavery to a "futile way of life," which includes the mind. Whether we knew it or not, we were trapped in a lifestyle that had only empty pleasures and dead-end desires to offer. We were in bondage to our impulses spawned from our sinful nature. In such a condition, we were hopelessly unable to help ourselves. The only way for us to be emancipated from that slavery was to have someone redeem us. That ransom price was paid by Christ, not with gold or silver, but with His precious blood. In doing so, He broke the chains that bound us to this world. He opened the door and said, "Now you're free to live for Me and serve Me." That single emancipation proclamation made possible a life of hope beyond temptation.

TECHNIQUES TO REMEMBER

When we're in the comfortable conclave of Christian fellowship, it's relatively easy to be holy, to conduct our lives in the fear of God, and to focus our minds on the Savior (at least externally). But when we're out in the world, when we're in the minority, it's different, isn't it?

If you want to stay clean, even when you're walking alone in the dark, low-ceilinged coal mine of the corrupt and secular culture, you need to remember a few practical things—four come to mind.

First, pay close attention to what you look at. This takes us back to verse 13, where we are told to gird our minds for action, keep sober in spirit, and fix our hope completely on the grace that's revealed in Jesus Christ.

Our eyes seem to be the closest connection to our minds. Through our eyes we bring in information and visual images. Through our eyes we feed our imaginations. Through our eyes we focus on things that are alluring and attractive and, don't kid yourself, extremely pleasurable for a while . . . for a while. Remember, the Bible says that Moses, by faith, gave up the "passing pleasures of sin" to walk with the people of God (Hebrews 11:24–26). The cosmos offers pleasures, no doubt about it, but they are passing.

> If then you have been raised up with Christ, keep seeking the things above, where Christ is, seated at the right hand of God. Set your mind on things above, not on the things that are on earth. (Colossians 3:1–2)

Second, give greater thought to the consequences of sin rather than to its pleasures. One of the characteristics of the cosmos is that nobody ever mentions the ugly underside of pleasurable sins. If you're thinking about having an affair, if you are getting caught in that lustful trap, I strongly suggest that you walk through the consequences in your mind. Stroll slowly . . . ponder details. Think through the effects of that act in your life and in the lives of others whom your life touches.

In a *Leadership* magazine article titled "Consequences of a Moral Tumble," Randy Alcorn says that whenever he is feeling "particularly vulnerable to sexual temptation," he finds it helpful to review the effects such action could have. Here is his list:

- Grieving the Lord who redeemed me.
- Dragging His sacred name into the mud.
- One day having to look Jesus, the Righteous Judge, in the face and give an account of my actions.
- Following in the footsteps of these people whose immorality forfeited their ministries and caused me to shudder: (list names).
- Inflicting untold hurt on [my partner], my best friend, and loyal wife.
- Losing [my wife's] respect and trust.
- Hurting my beloved [children].
- Destroying my example and credibility with my children, and nullifying both present and future efforts to teach them to obey God ("Why listen to a man who betrayed Mom and us?").
- If my blindness should continue or my wife be unable to forgive, perhaps losing my wife and my children forever.
- Causing shame to my family ("Why isn't Daddy a pastor anymore?").
- Losing self-respect.
- Creating a form of guilt awfully hard to shake. Even though God would forgive me, would I forgive myself?
- Forming memories and flashbacks that could plague future intimacy with my wife.
- Wasting years of ministry training and experience for a long time, maybe permanently.
- Forfeiting the effect of years of witnessing to my father and reinforcing his distrust for ministers that has only begun to soften

by my example but that would harden, perhaps permanently, because of my immorality.

- Undermining the faithful example and hard work of other Christians in our community.
- Bringing great pleasure to Satan, the enemy of God and all that is good.
- Possibly bearing the physical consequences of such diseases as gonorrhea, syphilis, chlamydia, herpes, and AIDS; perhaps infecting [my wife] or, in the case of AIDS, even causing her death.
- Possibly causing pregnancy, with the personal and financial implications, including a lifelong reminder of my sin.
- Bringing shame and hurt to these fellow pastors and elders: (list names).
- Causing shame and hurt to these friends, especially those I've led to Christ and discipled: (list names).
- Invoking shame and lifelong embarrassment upon myself.[2]

And that's just a partial list of the consequences! It doesn't even begin to factor in the consequences for the other person in the affair and the number of people affected by his or her sin.

Take a realistic look at the other side of a moral tumble. For a change, force yourself to give greater thought to the painful consequences than to the passing pleasures of sin.

Third, begin each day by renewing your sense of reverence for God. Start each new day by talking to the Lord, even if that early-morning talk has to be brief.

"Lord, I'm here. I'm Yours. I want You to know that I'm Yours. Also I want to affirm that I reverence You. I give You my day. I will encounter strong seductive forces that will allure me. Since I am frail and fragile, I really need Your help."

If you know of some challenges you'll be facing that day, rehearse the areas of need. If you know a real test is coming, talk to the Lord about it. Then trade off with Him. Hand over your fragility and receive His strength in return. Reverence Him as the source of your power.

Fourth, periodically during each day focus fully on Christ. In his book *Spiritual Stamina*, Stuart Briscoe cites a good example of this:

> It's fun watching young men in love. It can be even more fun when the romance is long distance.
>
> You can predict what will happen. There'll be hours of late-night, heart-pounding telephone conversations. The postal service will be overrun with love notes crossing each other in the mail. Pillows will be soaked with tears.
>
> But the most telling symptom is the glazed, faraway look in Romeo's eyes. I'm sure you've seen it. You ask the man a question and you get a blank stare. He's not at home. He's elsewhere. He's in another land. He's with his sweetheart.
>
> You might say his heart is set on things afar, where Juliet is seated right by the telephone.[3]

That's being focused fully on another person. I challenge you to do this with your Lord. Deliberately set aside a few minutes every day when your eyes glaze over, when you don't realize where you are, when a telephone ring means nothing because you are focusing fully on Christ. Imagine Him as He walks with His disciples, touching those who were sick, praying for them in John 17, going to the cross, sitting with His disciples at the seashore and having broiled fish for breakfast. Then imagine Him as He is thinking about you, praying for you, standing with you, living in you.

These four techniques will help you stay clean in a corrupt society—to be in the world but not of it.

GUILT:
BECOMING LIVING STONES

Here are some letters that children have written to God. The tone and innocence will probably be only vaguely familiar to most adults.

Dear Lord,
    Thank you for the nice day today. You even fooled the TV weatherman.
    Hank (age 7)

Dear Lord,

I need a raise in my allowance. Could you have one of your angels tell my father?

Thank you.

David (age 7)

Dear God,

Charles my cat got run over. And if you made it happen you have to tell me why.

Harvey[4]

Wouldn't it be interesting to compile an assortment of adult letters to God? Undoubtedly the childhood innocence would be lost. The words would be guarded, sophisticated. Fear and feelings of worthlessness would underscore the halting sentences. Shame, guilt, and regret would punctuate the paragraphs. We have lost much, haven't we, on the road to adulthood?

We can learn a great deal from children about simple faith and simple hope. Yet we have had years to experience those truths. We can look back at the many times God has taken our brokenness and made something beautiful of our lives. Our greatest failures, our deepest sorrows, have offered opportunities for the operation of His mercy and grace. How can we forget that?

GOD'S APPRAISAL OF US

The Bible is filled with reminders of how much God cares for us, His plans for our welfare, and what our relationship with Him should be. Take, for example, the familiar words of the psalmist. Though an adult, he writes of God with free-flowing delight.

> Bless the LORD, O my soul;
> And all that is within me, bless His holy name.
> Bless the LORD, O my soul,
> And forget none of His benefits;
> Who pardons all your iniquities;
> Who heals all your diseases;

> Who redeems your life from the pit;
> Who crowns you with lovingkindness and compassion;
> Who satisfies your years with good things,
> So that your youth is renewed like the eagle. . . .
> For as high as the heavens are above the earth,
> So great is His lovingkindness toward those who fear Him.
> As far as the east is from the west,
> So far has He removed our transgressions from us.
> Just as a father has compassion on his children,
> So the LORD has compassion on those who fear Him.
> For He Himself knows our frame;
> He is mindful that we are but dust. (Psalm 103:1–5, 11–14)

What a list! What a relief! Our Lord understands our limits. He realizes our struggles. He knows how much pressure we can take. He knows what measures of grace and mercy and strength we'll require. He knows how we're put together.

Frankly, His expectations are not nearly as unrealistic as ours. When we don't live up to the agenda we have set, we feel like He is going to dump a truckload of judgment on us. But that will not happen. So why do we fear it could? Because we forget that He "knows our frame; He is mindful that we are but dust."

After the fall of Jerusalem, the prophet Jeremiah reminded himself of God's hope-filled plans.

> This I recall to my mind,
> Therefore I have hope.
> The LORD's lovingkindnesses indeed never cease,
> For His compassions never fail.
> They are new every morning;
> Great is Thy faithfulness.
> "The LORD is my portion," says my soul,
> "Therefore I have hope in Him."
> The LORD is good to those who wait for Him,
> To the person who seeks Him.

> It is good that he waits silently
> For the salvation of the LORD. (Lamentations 3:21–26)

Right now you may be waiting for something from the Lord. Matter of fact, most people I meet are in some sort of holding pattern. (I certainly am!) They have something on the horizon that they're trusting God for. (I certainly do!) And their hope is not misplaced. He is good to those who wait for Him. He is good to those who seek Him. We have nothing to fear. And we certainly have no reason for living each day crushed by guilt or shame.

He has redeemed us, given us an inheritance, and shown us forgiveness. The most succinct summary of God's appraisal of our relationship as His children can be found in Romans 8:31–32. Many years ago I memorized the concluding paragraph in Romans 8, which begins with these two verses. I cannot number the times I have had my hope renewed by quoting these words to myself.

> What then shall we say to these things? If God is for us, who is against us? He who did not spare His own Son, but delivered Him up for us all, how will He not also with Him freely give us all things?

Contrary to popular opinion, God doesn't sit in heaven with His jaws clenched, His arms folded in disapproval, and a deep frown on His brow. He is not ticked off at His children for all the times we trip over our tiny feet and fall flat on our diapers. He is a loving Father, and we are precious in His sight, the delight of His heart. After all, He "has qualified us to share in the inheritance of the saints in Light" (Colossians 1:12). Think of it! He's put us in His inheritance!

Remember that the next time you think God is coming down on you. You have reason to give thanks. You don't have to qualify yourself for His kingdom. His grace has rescued you. He has already qualified you by accomplishing a great deliverance in your life. That brings to mind another verse I love to quote:

> For He rescued us from the domain of darkness, and transferred us to the kingdom of His beloved Son, in whom we have redemption, the forgiveness of sins. (Colossians 1:13–14)

He has literally transferred us from the dark domain of the enemy of our souls into the light of the kingdom of His Son. He considers us there with Him, surrounded by love, receiving the same treatment He gives His Son.

God is not only "for us," according to Romans 8, He is constantly giving great gifts to us.

> Every good thing bestowed and every perfect gift is from above, coming down from the Father of lights, with whom there is no variation, or shifting shadow. (James 1:17)

Literally, that last phrase means "shadow of turning." In other words, there is no alteration or modification in His giving, regardless of how often we may turn away. No shifting shadow on our part causes Him to become moody and hold back His gifts to us. Talk about grace!

God is for us. I want you to remember that.

God is for us. Say those four words to yourself.

God is for us.

Remember that tomorrow morning when you don't feel like He is for you. Remember that when you have failed. Remember that when you have sinned and guilt slams you to the mat.

God is for you. Make it personal: *God is for me!*

WE ARE LIVING STONES IN A SPIRITUAL HOUSE

The metaphor woven through the fabric of this passage is that of a building, Christ being the cornerstone and we, His children, being the living stones that make up the building. (The apostle Paul uses this same image in Ephesians 2:19–22.)

Each time someone trusts Christ as Savior, another stone is quarried out of the pit of sin and fitted into the spiritual house He's building through the work of the Holy Spirit. And carefully overseeing the construction is Christ, who is the hands-on contractor of this eternal edifice.

We are His living stones, being built up as a spiritual house.

Think of it this way. There's a major construction project going on through time as Jesus Christ builds His family. It's called the *ekklesia*, the "church," those who are called out from the mass of humanity to become a special part of God's forever family. And you, as a Christian—a follower of Christ— have been picked, chosen, and called out to be one of them.

He has quarried you from the pit of your sin. And now He is chiseling away, shaping you and ultimately sliding you into place. You are a part of His building project.

All kinds of prophets of doom wonder about the condition of God's building. They see it as condemned property, worn out, dilapidated, and derelict rather than as a magnificent edifice that is being constructed on schedule. The truth is, God is the master architect, and every stone is being placed exactly where He designed it to fit. The project is right on schedule. Never forget, even on those blue days, we are living stones in a spiritual house. But there's more. . . .

WE ARE A PEOPLE
WHO HAVE RECEIVED MERCY

Have you lived so long in the family of God that your memory has become blurred? Have you forgotten what it was like when you weren't?

> . . . for you once were not a people, but now you are the people of God; you had not received mercy, but now you have received mercy. (1 Peter 2:10)

As a result of God's mercy, we have become a people who are uniquely and exclusively cared for by God. The fact that we are the recipients of His mercy makes all the difference in the world as to how we respond to difficult times. He watches over us with enormous interest. Why? Because of His immense mercy, freely demonstrated in spite of our not deserving it. What guilt-relieving, encouraging news!

Of all the twelve disciples, none could have been more grateful than Peter . . . or, if he had allowed it, none more guilt-ridden. Called to serve his Savior, strong-hearted, determined, zealous, even a little cocky on occasion, the man had known the heights of ecstasy but also knew the aching agony of defeat.

Though warned by the Master, Peter announced before His peers, "Even though all may fall away . . . I will never fall away" (Matthew 26:33). And later . . . "Lord, with You I am ready to go both to prison and to death!" (Luke 22:33). Yet only a few hours later he denied even knowing Jesus—three times!

What bitter tears Peter wept when the weight of his denials crushed his spirit. But our Lord refused to leave him there, wallowing in hopeless discouragement and depression. He found the broken man and forgave him —and used him mightily as a leader in the early church. What grace . . . what mercy!

Charles Wesley beautifully captures the theology of such mercy in the second stanza of his magnificent hymn "And Can It Be?"

> He left His Father's throne above,
> So free, so infinite His grace!
> Emptied Himself of all but love,
> And bled for Adam's helpless race!
> 'Tis mercy all, immense and free,
> For, O my God, it found out me.

OUR LIVES ARE BEING WATCHED

Beloved, I urge you as aliens and strangers to abstain from fleshly lusts which war against the soul. Keep your behavior excellent among the Gentiles, so that in the thing in which they slander you as evildoers, they may on account of your good deeds, as they observe them, glorify God in the day of visitation. (1 Peter 2:11–12)

Peter begins his practical summary of this section with the words, "Beloved, I urge you." He feels passionate about this—and there's a warning here. Peter is telling us that in light of all that we are as God's children, in light of our roles as living stones in a building that will never be destroyed, and in light of our being these things he's described—a royal priesthood, a chosen race, a holy nation, a people for His own possession, those who have received mercy, we are to live in a certain way. Our earthly behavior is to square with our divinely provided benefits. To live the kind of life God requires, Peter offers four suggestions.

First, live a clean life. Don't think for a moment that it makes no difference to unbelievers how Christians live. We live out our faith before a watching world. That's why Peter urges us to abstain from fleshly lusts, "in order to get their attention" and to prove that what we believe really works.

Second, leave no room for slander. When the ancient Greek philosopher Plato was told that a certain man had begun making slanderous charges against him, Plato's response was, "I will live in such a way that no one will believe what he says."[5]

The most convincing defense is the silent integrity of our character, not how vociferously we deny the charges.

Third, do good deeds among unbelievers. What makes the story of the Good Samaritan so compelling? The merciful deeds were done on behalf of a total stranger. That is how we win the right to be heard—not by a slick mass-advertising campaign, but by our compassionate and unselfish actions.

Notice that Peter says, "on account of your good deeds," not your good words. The unsaved are watching our lives. When our good deeds are indisputable the unbeliever says, "There must be something to it." Chances are good that at that point the person will hear what we have to say.

Fourth, never forget—we are being watched. The world is watching us to see if what we say we believe is true in our lives. Warren Wiersbe tells a brief but powerful story that illustrates this beautifully.

In the summer of 1805, a number of Indian chiefs and warriors met in council at Buffalo Creek, New York, to hear a presentation of the Christian message by a Mr. Cram from the Boston Missionary Society. After the sermon, a response was given by Red Jacket, one of the leading chiefs. Among other things, the chief said . . .

"Brother, we are told that you have been preaching to the white people in this place. These people are our neighbors. We are acquainted with them. We will wait a little while and see what effect your preaching has upon them. If we find it does them good, makes them honest and less disposed to cheat Indians, we will then consider again what you have said."[6]

Whew! That's laying it on the line. I wonder how many people are looking at us and saying to themselves, "I hear what he's saying. Now I'm going to watch how he lives. I'll see if what he says is what he does."

LET'S NOT FORGET—GOD IS FOR US

Allow me to remind you of that oft-repeated line from Romans 8. "God is for us." In devoted love He chose us. In great grace He stooped to accept us into His family. In immense mercy He still finds us wandering, forgives our foolish ways, and (as He did with Peter) frees us to serve Him even though we don't deserve such treatment.

So . . . away with guilt! If you need a little extra boost to make that happen, read Eugene Peterson's paraphrase of Romans 8:31–33. Read it slowly, preferably *aloud*. As a good friend of mine once put it, "If this don't light your fire, you got wet wood!"

So, what do you think? With God on our side like this, how can we lose? If God didn't hesitate to put everything on the line for us, embracing our condition and exposing himself to the worst by sending his own Son, is there anything else he wouldn't gladly and freely do for us? And who would dare tangle with God by messing with one of God's chosen? Who would dare even to point a finger? The One who died for us—who was raised to life for us!—is in the presence of God at this very moment sticking up for us. Do you think anyone is going to be able to drive a wedge between us and Christ's love for us? There is no way! Not trouble, not hard times, not hatred, not hunger, not homelessness, not bullying threats, not backstabbing, not even the worst sins listed in Scripture:

They kill us in cold blood because they hate you.
We're sitting ducks; they pick us off one by one.

None of this fazes us because Jesus loves us. I'm absolutely convinced that nothing—nothing living or dead, angelic or demonic, today or tomorrow, high or low, thinkable or unthinkable—absolutely *nothing* can get between us and God's love because of the way that Jesus our Master has embraced us. (Romans 8:31–39 MSG)

Let me close this chapter with a prayer:

Father ... dear gracious Father, all of us have experienced failure. It has left us broken and disappointed in ourselves. To make matters worse, there are times when a flashback of those failures returns to haunt us.

Renew our hope as we read and reflect on the words of Peter, with whom we so easily identify. Remind us that, just as You used him after he had failed repeatedly, You will also use us, by Your grace. And thank You, again, for Your grace.

Father give us grace to match our trials. Give us a sense of hope and purpose beyond our suffering. Give us assurance that we're not alone, that Your plan has not been aborted though our suffering intensifies. Let us never forget that every jolt on this rugged journey from earth to heaven is a reminder we're on the right road.

Lord, since You don't save us and then suddenly take us home to glory, hear our prayer this day as we ask You to bring our attention to those things that will assist us in staying clean in a corrupt world. Give us an intense distaste for things that displease You and an increased pleasure in things that bring You honor and magnify Your truth.

And, Father, lift us out of the mire of our own self-condemnation. All too frequently we are our own worst enemy. We focus on our failures rather than on Your rescues ... on our wrongs rather than on Your commitment to making us right ... on our puny efforts rather than on Your powerful plans for our good. Even our attempts at being devoted to You can become so self-centered. Turn our attention back to You.

Remind us of our exalted position in Your Son.

Refresh us with frequent flashbacks—"God is for us."

Lord, renew our spirits with the realization that we're Your possession.

Then, with those joyful thoughts to spur us on, may we rise above failures, find joy in the midst of suffering, grow strong despite temptation, and slay the dragons of guilt within us so we might enjoy more deeply than ever Your ultimate embrace.

Through Christ I pray.

Amen.

13

OVERCOMING SHAME
AND DOUBT

When it comes to public shame, few people think of Jesus. If I were to ask you to list the names of twenty people you feel are deserving of shame, you'd probably not include the name Jesus Christ. I'm certainly not suggesting that He is deserving of shame, but we easily forget He experienced it.

The sinless Son of God took all our sins on Himself when He died on the cross. It was there He endured the shame of the world. Every wicked deed done by humanity, He took on Himself when He suffered and died in our place. The horror of Auschwitz, the evils of Stalin and Pol Pot and Saddam Hussein, the atrocities of Rwanda, the silent slaughter of tens of millions of aborted children, the maximum depth of each of our sinful thoughts, and the full extent of our reckless actions—all were piled on Christ at the cross. His death personified shame.

In his volume, *The Execution of Jesus*, William Riley Wilson writes, "Not only was the cross the most painful of deaths, it was also considered the most debasing. The condemned man was stripped naked and left exposed in his agony, and often the Romans even denied burial to the victim, allowing his body to hang on the cross until it disintegrated. It is understandable that, according to Jewish law, anyone who was crucified was considered cursed."[1]

To be cursed is to suffer shame. Twelfth-century monk Bernard of Clairvaux described it this way:

O sacred Head, now wounded,
With grief and shame weighed down,
Now scornfully surrounded
With thorns thine only crown;
How pale art Thou with anguish,
With sore abuse and scorn,
How does that visage languish,
Which once was bright as morn![2]

PUBLIC SHAME EXPLORED AND EXAMINED

The old monk understood that there is often agony and cruelty connected with shame. Shame runs deeper than guilt. Guilt typically remains a private affair. We learn to keep those inner indictments to ourselves, safely out of public view. But the tough stuff of shame follows you wherever you go like a bad rap sheet. Shame straps you to your torturous past, putting everything on display. Private shame—the shame that comes from years of physical or sexual abuse, or the lonely suffering that emerges from disabilities such as speech impediments, anxiety or eating disorders, a prison sentence or time spent in a mental institution or a rehab clinic—pushes victims to the corners of the room, into the shadows of society. Shame becomes a relentless, accusing voice that whispers, "You are worthless! You don't mean anything to anyone! You're totally unworthy! You will never amount to anything! You blew it! You're finished!"

Shame penetrates deeper than embarrassment; it cuts wider than disappointment. Being the lowest form of self-hatred, shame has driven many people slumping under its burden to retreat into a sort of living death. Unfortunately, shame can't simply be sloughed off. There remains a lingering disgrace that holds us tightly in its grip.

But that bottomless despair does not have to be our lot indefinitely. The scars need not be permanent. Christ desires to meet us in those dark corners and lift us to safety by redeeming our dignity and worth. His grace is greater than our shame. Where sin abounds, grace superabounds! He becomes for us our personal shame-bearer who walks with us through those harsh, agonizing days when we feel most alone and afraid. How can He do that? Remember,

He's been there. He has felt the aches of indignity and humiliation. In fact, there's no limit to the depth of shame He can see us through, because there's no limit to the grace He can supply.

Travel back with me to a first-century scene. Jesus confronts a broken and humiliated woman ensnared in the most shameful of circumstances. We are allowed to watch as He rescues her from the jagged edge of shame's powerful jaws.

AN ADULTERESS AND HER ACCUSERS

A nameless woman takes center stage in one of the most poignant scenes in all the New Testament. There, in the midst of her sin, she encounters Jesus, the Savior of the world. She had assumed that her deeds done in the dark would never be known in the light. Hers was a shameful, secret sin. Then one day she comes face-to-face with Jesus, the spotless Lamb of God, whose penetrating gaze looks squarely on her disgrace.

We are indebted to one of Jesus' original disciples, John, for including this narrative as part of his record of Christ's ministry to the broken people of Judah. Read carefully as he describes this unusually delicate scene.

Early in the morning [Jesus] came again into the temple, and all the people were coming to Him; and He sat down and began to teach them. The scribes and the Pharisees brought a woman caught in adultery, and having set her in the center of the court, they said to Him, "Teacher, this woman has been caught in adultery, in the very act. Now in the Law Moses commanded us to stone such women; what then do You say?" They were saying this, testing Him, so that they might have grounds for accusing Him. But Jesus stooped down, and with His finger wrote on the ground. But when they persisted in asking Him, He straightened up, and said to them, "He who is without sin among you, let him be the first to throw a stone at her." Again He stooped down and wrote on the ground. And when they heard it, they began to go out one by one, beginning with the older ones, and He was left alone, and the woman, where she was, in the center of the court. Straightening up, Jesus said to her, "Woman, where are they? Did no one condemn you?" And she said, "No one, Lord." And Jesus said, "I do not condemn you, either. Go. From now on sin no more." (John 8:1–11)

You have just read one of the most remarkable dramas in the entire Bible. We can only imagine what it would have been like to have been a bug on the wall of that temple watching it unfold.

It all began early in the morning when Jerusalem lay damp with dew. Several people joined in what we would call today a small-group Bible study, to be taught by the One who taught as no other. They had come to hear the words of the thirtysomething teacher from Nazareth. He was young, but He had wisdom beyond His years.

Suddenly a regimen of stern-faced scribes and Pharisees interrupted Jesus, dragging a disheveled woman across the pavement and into the great hall. The people must have gasped in disbelief at the spectacle. Jesus rose to His feet and faced the self-righteous brigade of clerics and their humiliated prisoner in tow. They were the grace-killing legalists of Israel, all spit-shined and polished for another day's work of judging and criticizing others. They had come to make a public example of someone who didn't belong in their midst. Not a man, but a woman. But not just any woman—a lady of the night who had just been in bed with a man who wasn't her husband. They had actually caught her in the act.

The woman—never named by John or anyone else in the story—must have stood trembling like an abused dog, muzzled by fear. Her head was bowed, her hair disheveled, her clothing torn. Shame was written across her face. Her accusers planned to use her to trap Jesus. They loathed Him and His teaching and especially His growing popularity. They hated His grace most of all. Their goal was to get Him killed, whatever it took. What they were doing on this morning was all part of a diabolical plan to rid themselves and the land of the menacing prophet from Nazareth.

The religious leaders abruptly addressed Jesus. "Teacher, this woman has been caught in adultery, in the very act. Now, in the Law Moses commanded us to stone such women; what then do You say?" Interestingly, they invoked the name of Moses before they leveled the charge.

That was part of the trap. They'd haul this pitiful woman in front of Jesus and a crowd of wide-eyed people, claim the authority of Moses, and then ask sneering, "What then do You say?" British author William Barclay writes:

The Scribes and Pharisees were out to get some charge on which they could discredit Jesus; and here they thought they had impaled Him inescapably on the horns of a dilemma. When a difficult legal question arose, the natural and routine thing was to take it to a rabbi for a decision. So the Scribes and Pharisees approached Jesus as a rabbi.[3]

The Mishnah, Judaism's handbook of religious tradition, minced no words. It mandated that a man caught in adultery was to be strangled and placed knee-deep in dung, with a towel wrapped around his neck so the rope wouldn't break his skin. A woman caught in the act of adultery faced public stoning. Moses had written in the law that if the act occurred in a city, both the man and woman were to be stoned. Was this particular woman guilty? Absolutely. They apparently caught her in the very act of sexual intercourse. The Greek word translated "caught" literally means "to seize" or "to overcome," suggesting that her accusers themselves found her in the very act of adultery and apprehended her while still in bed with her partner. But what about the man? Had he escaped? Likely not, since the religious leaders would have easily outnumbered him. My suspicions prompt me to suggest that he was a coconspirator (maybe one of them!), who had been put up to the lurid tryst beforehand. A conspiracy is not out of the question, knowing the wickedness of the accusers' hearts. The trembling woman in disarray, humiliated in front of the morning Bible study group, was nothing more than half a small piece of bait used to capture bigger game. They had Jesus in their sights. They cared nothing about the woman or her future. At that moment she meant nothing to them or to anyone else for that matter—no one except Jesus.

The unflappable young Teacher stood silently and stared, studying the entire scene. He read their motive like an open book. He sensed their deliberate attempt to catch Him unprepared and snare Him with His own words.

Consider quickly the options. Had Jesus immediately agreed to the stoning, they could have accused Him of hypocrisy. A man who had been teaching the importance of compassion and forgiveness would not allow such a harsh penalty. In addition, had Jesus made that call, He could have been charged with treason. Only a Roman official could determine the verdict of death on an individual. Jesus would have had no legal authority to have her stoned to death.

On the other hand, had He simply demanded she be forgiven and set free, they would have pounced on Him for condoning sin and ignoring the law of Moses.

Choosing neither option, according to John's narrative, "Jesus stooped down and with His finger wrote on the ground." The only time in all Scripture where we're told Jesus wrote anything is here in this scene. But what did He write? There are some who believe Jesus simply scribbled in the dust as He was collecting His thoughts. Yet the Greek word translated "wrote" suggests something more.

I believe John was an eyewitness. Writing now toward the end of the first century, he recorded that Jesus wrote in the sand. The Greek term John uses, which the English renders as "wrote," is *katagraphō*. The last half of that word, *graphō*, is the verb "to write." The Greek prefix *kata* can mean "against." In other words, I'm suggesting that John intended to show that Jesus wrote something in the sand that would have been incriminating to the religious leaders. Could it be that Jesus stooped and began to write out the sins of the woman's accusers in letters large enough for them and others to read? We cannot say for sure. But if it did, can you imagine their surprise?

WHO OR WHAT CONDEMNS YOU?

The silence was broken by the words Jesus spoke: "He who is without sin among you, let him be the first to throw a stone at her" (v. 7). In fact, the text literally reads, "The sinless one of you, first, on her, let him cast a stone." That's awkward in English, but emphatic in Greek. In so many words, Jesus said, "The first one whom I invite to throw a stone is the sinless one! Be sure you have no sins against you. And then you're qualified to bring shame, accusation, and even death on this woman. Only make sure your hearts are pure and sinless."

An aching, awkward silence followed Christ's stinging reply. A mute void swept across the once snarling pack of junkyard dogs.

Jesus, after dismissing the accusers, looked directly into the eyes of a woman full of shame, openly exposed and condemned by her accusers. And if that were not enough, there she stood before the righteous Judge of the universe, guilty of adultery, having broken God's holy law. As she met the gaze of the spotless Savior, we need to realize there has not been in the history of time a more remarkable and striking contrast of character: a woman . . . a man; a sinner . . . the sinless Son of God; the shameful adulteress . . . the Holy One of heaven. Imagine it! Two more different people never stood so close.

It is that which makes the final exchange between them so profound. It is here that grace eclipses shame: "Straightening up, Jesus said to her, 'Woman, where are they? Did no one condemn you?' She said, 'No one, Lord.' And Jesus said, 'I do not condemn you, either. Go. From now on sin no more'" (vv. 10–11).

The only person on earth qualified to condemn the woman refused to do so. Instead, He freed her. Could it be that for the first time in her life she stopped condemning herself too? That's what Jesus does for us in the humiliating blast of shame—He delivers us from self-condemnation as He sets us free. Free at last!

To All Weighed Down by Shame

Two thoughts linger as we close this chapter on overcoming shame. Here are two simple statements that I'm hoping will help you in your struggle to put your painful memories and shameful thoughts behind you.

First, those most unqualified to condemn you, will. Count on it. Those with hearts heavier than the stones in their hands will be the first to throw them. Stay away from modern-day Pharisees, who love few things more than exposing your sin and rubbing your nose in shame. Make certain you keep plenty of distance between you and those who would self-righteously throw stones at you.

Second, the One most qualified to condemn you, won't. You can count on this as well. Stay close to Him. Because by staying close to Him you will discover that you can recover more quickly. Draw near and confess your sin to the One who is qualified to condemn but doesn't. And like the woman, you'll be able to go on with your life enjoying a new freedom and purpose for living.

If you're reading this and feeling the weight of your own shameful past or stubborn sinful ways, I invite you to come to the Savior. He's the only One perfectly qualified to judge you and condemn you, but because of what His death accomplished, He is ready to forgive and to set you free. His invitation to freedom requires your response. It isn't automatic. Being delivered from shame's shackles necessitates your coming to the precipice of the cross and acknowledging your need for Jesus. He will be there to cleanse you and make you whole.

> Are you tired? Worn out? Burned out on religion? Come to me. Get away with me and you'll recover your life. I'll show you how to take a real rest. Walk with me and work with me—watch how I do it. Learn the unforced rhythms of grace. I won't lay anything heavy or ill-fitting on you. Keep company with me and you'll learn to live freely and lightly. (Matthew 11:28–30 MSG)

The "unforced rhythms of grace" will truly and completely set you free. So what are you waiting for?

DOUBT AND FAITH—OIL AND WATER?

Can we have lingering doubts and remain a person of faith? Strong and capable people on both sides disagree.

The great reformer Martin Luther had absolutely no place in his theology for doubt. He scored few things more scathingly than what he termed that "monster of uncertainty," a "gospel of despair." [4] But Alfred Lord Tennyson, on the other hand, wrote, "There lives more faith in honest doubt, believe me, than in half the creeds." [5]

Down through the centuries the church has had representatives on both sides. On the one hand, there have always been the Jonathan Edwardses, the George Whitefields, the Dwight L. Moodys, whose strong pulpits have rung with such assurance you would wonder as you read their sermons if they at any time ever entertained a doubt. On the other hand, God has given His church C. S. Lewis, Flannery O'Connor, Blaise Pascal, and more recently, Philip Yancey, who have encouraged us to question.

Is it possible for faith and doubt to coexist? You may find yourself occupying a place in the ranks of the doubters of this world. If so, this chapter is written especially with you in mind. To exacerbate matters, you may live among people who have never once questioned their faith. Their piety makes you feel isolated, even a little weird—out of place. Perhaps your doubts have sunk you to the depth of despair. You too have cried, "Lord, I believe. Help me in my unbelief."

Daniel Taylor, in his book *The Myth of Certainty*, doesn't choose to use the term "doubting Christians." He refers to the doubters among us as "reflective Christians." Frankly, that works for me. There's not much dignity in doubt, but there is a touch of dignity in reflection. Taylor offers a variety of questions that represent the common struggles of a reflective Christian. Here's a sampling:

- Does one minute it seem perfectly natural and unquestionable that God exists and cares for the world, and the next moment uncommonly naive?
- Have you sometimes felt like walking out of a church service because it seemed contrived and empty?
- How confident are you that you know God's desires regarding the specific political, social, and moral issues which face our society?[6]

According to Daniel Taylor, a nonreflective person asks, "What could be worse than unanswered questions?" To him, the reflective person would consider *unquestioned answers* his or her struggle. A reflective Christian is one who is thinking deeply, questioning often. When we doubt, our minds are at work.

When are those times I allow my intellect to challenge my beliefs? When do I question? When do I reflect? And candidly, when do I doubt? Likely, it's at those same crossroads of doubt and faith common to most of us. When we encounter a sudden, unexpected calamity. When we pray for a specific outcome and the exact opposite occurs. When we lose a valued staff member or coworker or when our dearest friend moves away to another state. When we live right and suffer miserably for it. When we take a course at school that makes more sense than what our church believes. Ouch!

When life takes us through unexpected twists and tragic turns, we're often overwhelmed by the tough stuff of doubt.

Thankfully the Bible does not leave us awash in our questions. A familiar story in John's gospel shows us that the answer to much of our doubting is a Person. His name is Jesus and—as He did for one struggling disciple—He helps us in our unbelief . . . transforming those lingering questions into more stabilized faith.

A REFLECTIVE THOMAS

Remember Doubting Thomas? Of course you do. Talk about a bad rap that stuck! My heart goes out to the poor guy. I'd rather think of him, thanks to Daniel Taylor's analysis, as Reflective Thomas. He's the one honest disciple who didn't check his brain at the synagogue door. He had faith in his doubts when his questions weren't answered. He had the guts to question the crowd, to raise his hand and press for answers that made better sense. I call that kind of honesty not only reassuring but valiant. I would love to see the ranks of Christianity filled with more courageous believers willing to declare openly the struggles they have, to weep when they're hurting, to admit their doubts rather than deny them.

In the Face of an Uncertain Future

John 14 shows that Thomas had his doubts about the future too. They had come to Jerusalem. It was there Jesus stood in the darkening shadow of the cross. He slipped away to a second-story flat in the busy city where He and the Twelve would gather for their final meal. Jesus had broken the news to them that His death was near. Separation from them was certain. As He scanned the room for their reactions, He read fear and doubt in their eyes. That's when He spoke what are perhaps some of His most tender words as He attempted to calm their worried minds and steel their shaken resolve.

> "Do not let your heart be troubled; believe in God, believe also in Me. In My Father's house are many dwelling places; if it were not so, I would have told you; for I go to prepare a place for you. If I go and prepare a place for you, I will come again and receive you to Myself, that where I am, there you may be also. And you know the way where I am going." (John 14:1–4)

Jesus hardly finished His words before Thomas blurted out, "Lord, we do not know where You are going, how do we know the way?" (v. 5). I love his unguarded honesty! The rest of the men were thinking the same thing, but only Thomas had the guts to say so. He wasn't arguing, and he wasn't trying to stop the plan. He was stating the truth. He didn't have a clue where Jesus would be going, so he questioned Jesus' comment, " . . . you know the way." The fact is he didn't. None of them knew. That's why he asked, "How do we know the way?"

"Jesus said to him, 'I am the way, and the truth, and the life; no one comes to the Father but through Me. If you had known Me, you would have known My Father also; from now on you know Him, and have seen Him'" (vv. 6–7).

Now think this through. Had Thomas not expressed his doubts in the form of that question, it's possible Jesus might never have uttered those remarkable words . . . words, in fact, that have brought both hope and comfort to the world since that day. So, good question, Thomas. Good for you. Without a hint of rebuke, Jesus graciously worked with Thomas and respected his doubts. He understood his confusion. His fear. His grief.

When my father died at the age of eighty-seven, he had lived with us for four years before we found it necessary to admit him to a very fine, clean place where he lived awhile longer. He was kept under the watchful care of my sister and me during his final days in the hospital. I grieved silently. Yet when it came to my duties as a pastor of a growing, dynamic church, it was like someone threw a switch and I pressed on in my responsibilities.

I preached Dad's funeral to a small gathering of family and friends. I spoke somberly and appropriately about the promises of God and the hope we have beyond the grave. I buried my father's frail body with grace and poise, as all good ministers do. I never missed a beat. I've done that duty hundreds of times throughout my many years in the ministry. I could do much of it with my eyes closed . . . but always with tenderness and compassion.

My sister, Luci, and I got back on the plane to return home. During a quiet moment, she asked, "Babe, do you believe every single thing you said today?" It made me think . . . deeply.

"No," I said, almost sighing under my breath. "There are things that the jury's still out on in my mind."

"That's not what I'm asking," she said back to me gently. "I know you believe a lot of it. I just want to know if you fully believe every single thing. 'Cause if you do, we're very different."

I said, "No. There are things that I really have a hard time believing and understanding. I just can't fit everything together in my mind and in my heart." She paused, then lovingly put her hand on my arm and with tears in her eyes answered, "That's good, Babe. And that's okay." Perhaps softened by her tender expression of love and honesty, I looked at the clouds outside the window as tears began to flow for my dad and for our losing him.

I fear that too many believers think they have captured the message of Christianity and placed it in a box marked on top, "Don't ask. Don't tell." On the side it reads, "Off limits for doubts and questions."

I find airtight conclusions mainly in people who have not hurt much. They're usually people who have become tightly wired, rigid, and isolated from the real world. They're closed . . . unwilling to be vulnerable. Suddenly, a divorce comes. Or someone dies in a tragic set of circumstances or loses his job. Reality hits and a storm blows in and threatens their once tranquil existence. The emotional explosion results in more questions than answers. They discover things they didn't really know. They are in the vortex of dilemmas they cannot solve. At that point simplistic solutions are replaced with realistic reflections . . . and the deep things of God begin to emerge, eclipsing shallow answers.

That explains why Jesus doesn't rebuke Thomas and say, "Look in your notebook! We covered that in my discourse on the Mount of Olives—page 59." He said in effect, "Thomas, your questions will be settled in Me. I am the way and the truth and the life" (John 14:6).

How could He be "the Way" when they found themselves at a dead end? How could He call Himself "the Truth" when it all appeared to have been a hoax? How could He have been "the Life" when they had just been told of His impending death? For three days after Christ's death, the disciples grieved, haunted by fear, dogged by doubt. Then, when Jesus appeared to them, all that changed.

John remembers the transforming encounter:

So when it was evening on that day, the first day of the week, and when the doors were shut where the disciples were, for fear of the Jews, Jesus came and stood in their midst and said to them, "Peace be with you." And when He had said this, He showed them both His hands and His side. The disciples then rejoiced when they saw the Lord. So Jesus said to them again, "Peace be with you; as the Father has sent Me, I also send you. . . ."

But Thomas, one of the twelve, called Didymus, was not with them when Jesus came. (John 20:19–21, 24)

With hopes dashed and dreams gone, Thomas was nowhere to be found. He was lost in his doubts and disillusionment. Wherever he was, though, the remaining disciples soon found him and exclaimed, "We have seen the Lord!"

But that was not enough for our reflective friend. He wanted tangible proof. That's why Thomas said to them, "Unless I see in His hands the imprint of the nails, and put my finger into the place of the nails, and put my hand into His side, I will not believe" (v. 25).

John writes of that event:

After eight days His disciples were again inside, and Thomas with them. Jesus came, the doors having been shut, and stood in their midst and said, "Peace be with you." Then He said to Thomas, "Reach here with your finger, and see My hands; and reach here your hand and put it into My side; and do not be unbelieving, but believing." Thomas answered and said to Him, "My Lord and my God!" (vv. 26–28)

Thomas, having honestly faced his doubts, discovered a firm faith. Once convinced, he yielded. We get through the tough stuff of doubt the same way—by facing those doubts and bringing them to the Savior! Just like Thomas.

Any question asked without guile is not a skeptical question. It's an honest search. Jesus very graciously responds, "Because you have seen Me, have you believed? Blessed are they who did not see, and yet believed" (v. 29).

When You Cannot Cope

Times of doubting become schoolrooms of learning, those places where a new kind of faith is forged. It will come slowly, and that's healthy. It's being shaped on the anvil of God's mysterious plan, some of which you will not be able to explain. And that's okay.

Now the real question is how. How do we grow this new kind of faith in the tough stuff of doubt?

First, we grow by risking and failing, not always playing it safe. You can't afford to live a life of fear. You must not always play life safe. Winning over doubts means beginning to live by faith and not by sight. Walking this new journey has its risks. You cannot see around every bend or anticipate every danger. You will sometimes fail, but that isn't fatal! That's how we grow, by trusting God through the risks we take and the failures we endure. Step out. Refuse to play it safe.

Second, we keep growing by releasing and losing things valuable, not finding security in the temporal. At the heart of this technique is the principle of holding all things loosely.

Cynthia and I know a couple who have to be as close to the ideal set of parents as we've ever met. Every Christmas we get a lovely card from them. For years they were to us the picture-perfect family. Yet one day they found themselves in an inescapable abyss. Their precious daughter was admitted to a psychiatric facility after attempting suicide over an eating disorder. Our dear friends hit absolute bottom. They weren't grinning and quoting verses. They didn't run around smiling at life, quoting tired clichés like, "In spite of this, God is great, God is good." No, they nearly drowned in their doubts. They wept bitter tears. They questioned everything they ever believed.

Are they still qualified as people of faith though they wavered in the dark? Absolutely. By God's grace, in time, they released those doubts, having faced them honestly, and they refused to seek security in the temporal. Today, looking back, they're convinced those lonely days proved to be some of the best days of their lives. Their walk with the Lord is far more mature than before.

Third, we continue to grow by questioning and probing the uncertain, not mindlessly embracing the orthodox. Read that once again, aloud. We don't just blindly swallow someone else's answers. We keep our minds and our hearts engaged in the pursuit of God's truth. By searching the Scriptures. By seeking God's wisdom and understanding. That's what I mean by questioning and probing.

Fourth, we grow by admitting and struggling with our humanity, not denying our limitations and hiding our fears. And I can assure you that this author for God understands when you find yourself cornered by doubt. I've been there more times than you'd ever believe. You are definitely not alone.

DON'T DOUBT, BELIEVE

Perhaps you have just read for the first time in your life that there is room at the cross for your doubts and your questions. Maybe some well-meaning soul has pushed you into a corner and attempted to make you believe or tried to force you into feeling your questions are an offense to Christ. You need to hear anew the tender words of One who knows your doubts and fears better than you. He says, "Peace be with you. Look at My hands and feet. Look with eyes of faith and believe. You are blessed when you believe in spite of your doubts."

Sacrifice: Personal and Financial

He is no fool who gives what he cannot keep to gain what he cannot lose.

—Jim Elliot

In early January 1958, I was in a U.S. Marine staging regiment back at Camp Pendleton, preparing to ship out. I had a negative attitude toward life in general and toward God in particular. To be honest, I was borderline bitter. Why on earth would He have allowed this to happen? I was convinced I would never smile again.

Rather than hang out in the barracks that final weekend in the States, I decided to take a bus to Pasadena to visit my older brother, Orville, and his wife, Erma Jean. Our time together sped by quickly, and soon I needed to catch the bus back to Camp Pendleton. As I related earlier, just before my brother said good-bye, he handed me a book and told me, "You'll never be the same after you read this." I had no intention of even opening it. I shrugged and mumbled an insincere, "Thanks," as I got on the bus. It was a rainy, cold night. I blinked through tears of loneliness and self-pity as I sat staring out the window. I couldn't even pray. A hard rain hammered against the oversized bus window. My world had collapsed.

Then for some unexplainable reason, I decided to dig into my bag and pull out the book Orville had given me. I flipped on the tiny light above my head as my eyes gazed across the title: *Through Gates of Splendor*. I thought I recognized those words as being from one of the hymns I had sung in church. I opened the book and soon discovered that it was the true account of how five young men had been murdered—really, martyred—by a small tribe of Auca Indians in the Ecuadorian jungle.

The painfully raw and realistic pictures in the book held my attention. One was a tragic scene: the body of one of the missionaries, speared to death and left floating downriver. That did it! I was hooked. I decided that maybe it wouldn't hurt to glance over a chapter or two, if for no other reason than to get my mind off myself.

Seven hours later I finished the last page. I was on the floor back at the barracks, sitting under the only light that stayed on all night. It was just before dawn. I can remember it as if it were yesterday. All alone, I laid the book aside, put my head in my hands and sobbed audibly. Sitting there on that concrete floor, I realized I had just spent all night enraptured by the story of five brave young men whose hearts beat for Christ. Their passion was to win the hearts of that tribe of Aucas for the singular purpose of introducing each one of them to the Lord Jesus, who had died for their sins. Their ultimate hope in life was not self-centered. On the contrary, it was Christ-centered. Here were five young men fairly near my own age, whose passion for Him was intense—driven by the hope that those in that dangerous tribe might come to know and love Jesus and thereby gain the assurance of forgiveness, secure their eternal life in heaven, and discover His transforming power.

I found myself rebuked. There I was, preoccupied by self-pity because things hadn't gone as I had expected. And here were a few men who sacrificed their entire lives for a cause that made my situation pale into insignificance. The contrast was embarrassingly real! As one of the men had written so eloquently in his personal journal, "He is no fool who gives what he cannot keep to gain what he cannot lose."

I cannot describe the change that swept over me as I watched the morning sun break through the windows. My depression had slowly lifted during that night—it never returned. Beginning that morning and throughout the seventeen days aboard the troopship across the Pacific, my whole attitude toward life began a transformation. God used this example of selflessness—the sacrifice of those men—to teach me the value of caring more about others than myself. He taught me so many lessons regarding trusting instead of fearing and worrying, seeing His hand at work in difficulties instead of always asking why.

I became a changed man. In the months that followed, that change in perspective made all the difference in how I viewed life. It still does!

Candidly, I am convinced I am in the Lord's work today because I read Elisabeth Elliot's book on the darkest night of my life up to that point. God used her words to touch my soul and reach my heart with His calling to ministry, a vocation fueled by the discipline of sacrifice.

> *I realized that life doesn't revolve around me—my comfort, my desires, my dreams, my plans. Clearly, it is all about Him.*

God will occasionally ask some of His own to suffer death for the sake of Christ, but that is not the sacrifice He wants from most of us. He desires that we offer ourselves as nothing less than living sacrifices. You read that correctly. Each one of us is called to become a "living sacrifice."

Those are the words Paul used in his letter to his Christian friends in Rome. In Romans 12:1 (NLT), we find Paul on his knees before us, begging, "I plead with you." Why beg? Because what he's asking for doesn't come naturally or easily or automatically. When people sacrifice, they're usually not doing it on a whim. Sacrifice hurts. Sacrifice works against our natural inclinations to keep a tight hold on our possessions and creature comforts. And we come hardwired with the instinct to watch out for ourselves, to guard against risk, and to preserve our own lives at any cost.

The word Paul uses in Romans 12:1, rendered "sacrifice," is the Greek term *thysia*. Interestingly he uses it sparingly, just a handful of times in all of his letters. That says to me that it was not a term he tossed around loosely or lightly, so we should sit up and pay attention whenever we see it. *Thysia* is the same word we find in the book of Hebrews, referring to the Old Testament temple sacrifices, looking toward what Jesus would one day do on the cross.

In Ephesians 5:1-2, Paul calls for us to be like Christ, and he defines the kind of sacrifice we are to make of ourselves: "Therefore be imitators of God, as beloved children; and walk in love, just as Christ also loved you and gave Himself up for us, an offering and a sacrifice to God as a fragrant aroma."

> We naturally serve what we trust. Hoarding wealth is a sure sign that a person trusts his things instead of his God.

In that sentence, two significant ideas are placed side by side: offering and sacrifice, *prosphora* and *thysia*. Both picture someone giving up something. In each case the giver no longer has something that is valuable in his possession. But there is a slight distinction, a subtle difference that makes all the difference. An offering is a sacrifice with an added element: choice.

An offering is a voluntary act. Christ made a conscious choice to offer Himself as an atoning sacrifice so that He might have us. We are to make that same choice for the sake of having Him in a more intimate way. Not to earn His pleasure or blessing, but as a means of deeply coming to know Him.

The exercise of sacrifice begins small. As we consistently carry it out, it becomes habitual. To cultivate the discipline of sacrifice, we must apply it in at least three realms of our lives: personal, relational, and material.

PERSONAL SACRIFICE

In Matthew 6, we find a record of the day when Jesus delivered His Sermon on the Mount to His friends and followers. He came on rather strong when He started to discuss material wealth and things that have price tags. (It's good to remember that everything costs something.) As you read His words to them, you will not see the term *sacrifice*. Keep the word in the back of your mind, however, as you read.

"Do not store up for yourselves treasures on earth, where moth and rust destroy, and where thieves break in and steal. But store up for yourselves treasures in heaven, where neither moth nor rust destroys, and where thieves do not break in or steal; for where your treasure is, there your heart will be also.

"The eye is the lamp of the body; so then if your eye is clear, your whole body will be full of light. But if your eye is bad, your whole body will be full of darkness. If then the light that is in you is darkness, how great is the darkness!

"No one can serve two masters; for either he will hate the one and love the other, or he will be devoted to one and despise the other. You cannot serve God and wealth.

"For this reason I say to you, do not be worried about your life, as to what you will eat or what you will drink; nor for your body, as to what you will put on. Is not life more than food, and the body more than clothing? Look at the birds of the air, that they do not sow, nor reap nor gather into barns, and yet your heavenly Father feeds them. Are you not worth much more than they? And who of you by being worried can add a single hour to his life? And why are you worried about clothing? Observe how the lilies of the field grow; they do not toil nor do they spin, yet I say to you that not even Solomon in all his glory clothed himself like one of these. But if God so clothes the grass of the field, which is alive today and tomorrow is thrown into the furnace, will He not much more clothe you? You of little faith! Do not worry then, saying, 'What will we eat?' or 'What will we drink?' or 'What will we wear for clothing?' For the Gentiles eagerly seek all these things; for your heavenly Father knows that you need all these things. But seek first His kingdom and His righteousness, and all these things will be added to you." (Matthew 6:19–33)

I find at least two sermons in Jesus' words. The first one is on hoarding—the greedy grappling for more and more stuff. Complicating life with better, larger, more expensive, more extravagant things that bind us to mandatory service to maintain them. Anytime you hear a sermon on this passage, that's what the preacher usually goes for. It's a valid focus, and I will be addressing financial sacrifice later. However, any sermon based on Jesus' words that only condemns materialism is but half a sermon.

Being the master communicator, Jesus used word pictures that even a little child could understand. A little moth that can eat a garment. A bit of rust that can ultimately destroy a piece of steel. I love His sense of humor drawn from a scene in nature: "Look up in the air. Look at those birds. They don't sow. They don't reap. They don't store food in barns" (see v. 26).

Personal sacrifice begins with a choice: who will we trust to meet our needs? We naturally serve what we trust. Hoarding wealth is a sure sign that a person trusts his things instead of his God.

I mentioned my older brother, Orville, at the beginning of this chapter. He was a missionary for more than thirty years in Buenos Aires. Just before that, he had done some short-term mission work in Mexico and had come north to gather his wife, Erma Jean, and the kids for the long trip down into the heart of South America.

Before leaving, they stopped off for a quick visit with our parents. Now, you have to appreciate the kind of man my father was. Look up the word *responsible* in the dictionary, and his picture is there! To him, risks are for those who fail to plan. Responsible people leave nothing to chance. As far as he was concerned, faith is something you exercise when your three backup plans fall through and you have run out of all other options. My father was a believer, but he never understood the life of faith. Not really.

My brother, on the other hand, was stimulated by faith. He has lived his entire adult life on the raw edge of faith. To him, life doesn't get exciting until only God can get us through some specific challenge. That drove Dad nuts!

After a great supper of good ol' collard greens and cornbread, onions, and red beans, my mother and sister went into the kitchen, leaving my father at one end of the table, Orville at the other, and me sitting on one side. Then it started.

"Son, how much money do you have for your long trip?"

"Oh, Dad, don't worry about it. We're gonna be fine."

Before he could change the subject, my father pressed the issue. "Son, how much money do you have in your wallet?"

Orville smiled as he said, "I don't have any money in my wallet."

I sat silent, watching this verbal tennis match.

"How much money do you have? You're gettin' ready to go down to South America! How much money you got?"

With that, my brother dug into his pocket, pulled out a quarter, set it on its edge on his end of the table, then gave it a careful thump. It slowly rolled past me all the way to my father's end of the table and fell into his hand. Dad said, "That is all you've got?"

Orville broke into an even bigger smile and said, "Yeah. *Isn't that exciting!*"

That was not the word my father had in mind at the moment. After a heavy sigh and a very brief pause, Dad shook his head and said, "Orville, I just don't understand you."

My brother grew serious. Looking Dad in the eyes, he answered, "No, Dad, you never have."

I don't know how he actually made the trip or how he and Erma Jean took care of all their little kids, but they never went hungry. And they served in Buenos Aires and other parts of South America for more than three decades. My father was a man who emerged through the Great Depression, lived in fear of poverty his whole life, and never experienced the joy of trusting God. Regardless, the possibility of adventure made my brother smile so big that day.

The point of Jesus' sermon was not to say that having nice things is wrong. Read the passage again and look for anything that would suggest that He wanted people to be poor. Whether or not we own nice things, He wants to be sure that we aren't owned by them! As soon as something begins to feel just a little too crucial to our happiness or safety, it's time to apply the discipline of sacrifice.

When was the last time you just gave something away? I mean something very nice. Something that has meant something to you. It probably wasn't easy. Sacrifice doesn't come naturally. It's a discipline that requires faith—a trust that the Almighty will look after your needs in ways that you will never see until you allow Him the opportunity.

Dallas Willard explains it much better than I:

> The discipline of sacrifice is one in which we forsake the security of meeting our needs with what is in our hands. It is total abandonment to God, a stepping into the darkened abyss in the faith and hope that God will bear us up. . . .
>
> The cautious faith that never saws off a limb on which it is sitting never learns that unattached limbs may find strange, unaccountable ways of not falling.[1]

I wonder how much better we would know our God if we didn't make such a good living. I would be willing to wager that we don't have intimacy with the Almighty because we haven't given enough away. We don't really trust our God sufficiently. To exercise the spiritual discipline of sacrifice, start cultivating generosity.

RELATIONAL SACRIFICE

In Genesis 22, God had told Abraham that he would be the father of a great nation, a people who would inhabit the land of promise and worship the one true God. All of God's promises to Abraham rested in this one son. How easy for Isaac to become virtually everything to his father! One evening the Lord stepped into Abraham's world: "Take now your son, your only son, whom you love, Isaac, and go to the land of Moriah, and offer him there as a burnt offering on one of the mountains of which I will tell you" (Genesis 22:2).

I'm convinced that Abraham spent a restless night, if not in anguish, at least in soul-searching prayer. Let's face it, Abraham was a hero of faith, but we dare not turn him into a superhero. He was just a man. Imagine how you would feel if you were asked to take the life of your child. Just like you or me, Abraham had to evaluate his priorities and check his faith. After all, God didn't stutter. His voice was clear. Abraham had unmistakable orders from the Lord: "Sacrifice your son."

While I'm sure Abraham didn't sleep at all that night, we are told that he wasted no time obeying:

> So Abraham rose early in the morning and saddled his donkey, and took two of his young men with him and Isaac his son; and he split wood for the burnt offering, and arose and went to the place of which God had told him. On the third day Abraham raised his eyes and saw the place from a distance. Abraham said to his young men, "Stay here with the donkey, and I and the lad will go over there; and we will worship and return to you." (Genesis 22:3–5)

Don't hurry past how Abraham explained his plan to his servants. "We will go." And then? "We will worship." What a great perspective! Sacrifice is worship. Notice also, "*and* return to you." In the Hebrew, Abraham was specific in his use of the plural. He didn't say, "*We* will go worship, and *I* will return to you." We cannot know for sure what he was thinking. He knew that he would have to kill Isaac, but he also knew that God would keep His promises—the promises that rest in Isaac. Hebrews 11:17–19 clearly states that Abraham knew God could raise Isaac from the dead once he sacrificed his life on the altar. Whatever his thinking, he obeyed:

> Abraham took the wood of the burnt offering and laid it on Isaac his son, and he took in his hand the fire and the knife. So the two of them walked on together. Isaac spoke to Abraham his father and said, "My father!" And he said, "Here I am, my son." And he said, "Behold, the fire and the wood, but where is the lamb for the burnt offering?" (Genesis 22·6–7)

Isaac had been mentored in the sacrifices. He had helped his father prepare sacrifices before. He saw the torch and the firewood, but saw no animal. Abraham was so wise. Now he mentored his son in faith:

> Abraham said, "God will provide for Himself the lamb for the burnt offering, my son." So the two of them walked on together. (Genesis 22:8)

The whole story turns on trust. There's no argument, there's no further questioning, and the boy trusts his dad. Even better, the dad is confident in his God:

> Then they came to the place of which God had told him; and Abraham built the altar there and arranged the wood, and bound his son Isaac and laid him on the altar, on top of the wood. Abraham stretched out his hand and took the knife to slay his son. But the angel of the LORD called to him from heaven and said, "Abraham, Abraham!" And he said, "Here I am." He said, "Do not stretch out your hand against the lad, and do nothing to him; for now I know that you fear God, since you have not withheld your son, your only son, from Me." (Genesis 22:9–12)

God took Abraham all the way to the edge of his relationship with his son. This faithful servant said by his actions, "Lord, You're more to me than any relationship ever will be. If You tell me to put the most important person in the world to me on an altar, I'll sacrifice him."

A. W. Tozer wrote about this struggle in his fine book *The Pursuit of God*:

We're often hindered from giving up our treasures to the Lord out of fear for their safety. This is especially true when our treasures are loved ones, relatives, and friends. But we need have no such fears. Our Lord came not to destroy but to save. Everything is safe which we commit to Him, and nothing is really safe which is not so committed.[2]

FINANCIAL SACRIFICE

Personal sacrifice overcomes a love for self that may be nurtured by any number of things, material wealth being only one of them. Financial sacrifice overcomes a love for money and possessions. In my own experience this is probably the easiest of the three to address. When one adequately deals with personal sacrifice and relational sacrifice, financial sacrifices naturally follow. By the time one has worked through the issues of personal treasures and idolatrous relationships, money becomes so insignificant!

Paul's letter to the church in Philippi—a letter from an itinerant preacher to a new and growing church—is a very sweet note overflowing with joy and thanksgiving. These brothers and sisters loved Paul and believed in his ministry, and they lived to give. Overflowing with feelings of gratitude, Paul writes to them:

You yourselves also know, Philippians, that at the first preaching of the gospel, after I left Macedonia, no church shared with me in the matter of giving and receiving but you alone; for even in Thessalonica you sent a gift more than once for my needs. Not that I seek the gift itself, but I seek for the profit which increases to your account. But I have received everything in full and have an abundance; I am amply supplied, having received from Epaphroditus what you have sent, a fragrant aroma, an acceptable sacrifice, well-pleasing to God. (Philippians 4:15–18)

From verse 15, we discover that this church was *the only one* to give. Verse 16 tells us that they gave *repeatedly*. We know from verse 18 that they gave *recently* and *generously*. Paul put his finger on the word that best describes such liberal giving on the part of the Philippians: *sacrifice.*

Notice also the follow-up promise Paul set forth in verse 19: "And my God will supply all your needs according to His riches in glory in Christ Jesus."

Their part was repeated generosity. God's part was abundantly supplying their need.

The great fear in financial sacrifice is that we might run out of provisions. We're tempted to think that giving them away will only bring the poverty sooner. Fortunately, as with relationships, God will provide. He is infinite in His resources and in His creativity. He never runs dry or shy of ideas.

Unfortunately, many people, both within the church and without, honestly feel money is "filthy lucre" so we are better off not even mentioning it. I have actually heard laymen bragging that their minister has never once talked about money during the years he has been their pastor. While I have serious concerns about such silence, I understand how that could happen. I, too, tend to shy away from the subject.

WHAT MAKES US SO DREADFULLY DEFENSIVE?

Having been engaged in ministry for about four decades, I can remember times when I could almost hear the groans and feel the sighs as I announced that I'd be speaking on giving that particular Sunday. Why do we feel that way? I think it is a lot like the groans and sighs we release in mid-October when the stores drag out the plastic trees and put Santa Claus in the window. Three specific analogies come to mind.

First, *it seems terribly repetitive.* The subject of giving is seldom approached creatively, and then when it is addressed, the comments are usually overstated and punctuated with guilt-giving remarks. Most often the congregation is not instructed as much as they are exhorted and exploited. Furthermore, there is neither subtlety nor much humor employed—only large helpings of hard-core facts mixed with a pinch of panic "because giving has dropped off." It doesn't take a Ph.D. from Yale to sense the objective during the first five minutes: *Give More!* Same song, ninth verse. The repetitive cycle gets monotonous.

Second, *the whole thing has been commercialized.* Because grace has been separated from giving, greed has come in like the proverbial flood. Mr. and Mrs. Average Christian are punchy, suspicious, and resentful—sometimes for good reason. During the latter half of the twentieth century, all of us were embarrassed, weren't we? We saw shameful examples of greed employed in the name of religion. Unbelievable techniques were used to wrench money from the public's pocket, and we've gotten fed up with the gimmicks. Everybody wants more, not just religious folks. Enough is never enough.

Third, *there always seems to be a hidden agenda.* Just as merchants don't go to a lot of extra expense and trouble getting their stores ready for Christmas simply for the fun of it, neither do most ministers speak on financial stewardship because it is a fun subject. The bottom line is usually uppermost. The emphasis is seldom on the charming joy of grace-oriented giving but rather on the obligation and responsibility to give "whether you like it or not."

This is an appropriate time for me to mention a couple of things, just to set the record straight. How and why we give is of far greater significance to God than what we give. Attitude and motive are always more important than amount. Furthermore, once a person cultivates a taste for grace in giving, the amount becomes virtually immaterial. When those age-old grace killers, guilt and manipulation, are not used as leverage, the heart responds in generosity. Giving at that point becomes wonderfully addictive.

What Makes Giving So Wonderfully Addictive?

Grace can liberate you to become a model of unusual and consistent generosity, all the while filling you with inexpressible joy. No, this is not some ideal reserved for a chosen few; this is reality for all of God's people to claim.

Now is the right moment to step into the time tunnel and return to the first century. The original church in Jerusalem had fallen on hard times. Unable to pull itself out of a financial slump, thanks to the depressed economy in Judea and other Palestinian regions, those early believers were facing a bleak and barren future.

As is often the case in our own times, while one part of the world was suffering great need, another was flourishing. The Greeks in Corinth were doing quite well, which prompted Paul to urge them to give financial assistance to their fellow Christians in Jerusalem. His words to the Corinthian believers regarding this need are recorded in 2 Corinthians 8 and 9, two of the finest chapters in the entire Bible on grace giving.

At the beginning of his charge he mentions the generosity of the struggling churches in Macedonia who gave during days of affliction. In spite of their own poverty, and with great joy, they took delight in giving to those in need. On the basis of their example, Paul urges the Corinthians to follow the example they set. Those words of background information will help you understand the apostle's opening remarks:

> Now, brethren, we wish to make known to you the grace of God which has been given in the churches of Macedonia, that in a great ordeal of affliction their abundance of joy and their deep poverty overflowed in the wealth of their liberality. For I testify that according to their ability, and beyond their ability they gave of their own accord, begging us with much entreaty for the favor of participation in the support of the saints, and this, not as we had expected, but they first gave themselves to the Lord and to us by the will of God. (2 Corinthians 8:1–5)

Paul admits that he was surprised. He states that what the Macedonians gave was "not as we had expected." Of greater importance, their gifts did not originate in their purses and wallets. No, "they first gave *themselves* to the Lord" (emphasis mine), and then they gave their money. Grace giving begins in the heart. Grace-oriented generosity is the overflow of a liberated heart. This assures us that it has nothing to do with one's investment portfolio or monthly salary. Whether Macedonian or Corinthian, American or Canadian, Asian or Australian, the challenge is the same: first and foremost, we are to give ourselves to the Lord. When we do, our treasure will follow the leading of our heart.

Returning to my earlier question, what is it that makes all this so addictive?

First, *it helps us keep a healthy balance.* "But just as you abound in everything, in faith and utterance and knowledge and in all earnestness and in the love we inspired in you, see that you abound in this gracious work also" (2 Corinthians 8:7).

In many a church there is faith; there is good teaching ("utterance"), a working knowledge of the Christian life; there is zeal, spiritual passion, and a great deal of love . . . but generosity? A superabundant willingness to give? Often that is the one ingredient conspicuous by its absence. How easy to take, to be blessed, instructed, encouraged, exhorted, affirmed, and strengthened—all those things received in abundance—yet fail to balance the receiving with our giving.

Did you notice how Paul refers to financial support? He calls it "this gracious work," and he exhorts us to "abound" in it. The Christian life takes on a healthy balance when our taking in and giving out stay in step. You and I feel closer to the Savior because that is what He did—He gave. "For you know the grace of our Lord Jesus Christ, that though He was rich, yet for your sake He became poor, that you through His poverty might become rich" (2 Corinthians 8:9).

The second reason that giving is addictive is that *in giving we model the same grace of Jesus Christ.* I am impressed that the verse of Scripture doesn't say, "for you know the obligation of the Lord Jesus Christ," or, "You know the sense of duty," though that is true. It was a duty that He come to earth. But Paul doesn't write, "You know the requirement" or, "You know the sacrifice." No, he mentions only the grace. When our Lord Jesus left heaven, He didn't leave gritting His teeth and clenching His fists, shouting, "Okay . . . *Okay!*" It wasn't obligation—it was grace that motivated Him to come. It was grace within Him that brought Him to Bethlehem as a little baby. It was grace within Him that allowed His hands and feet to be pierced with nails and grace within Him to say, "Father, forgive them. They do not know what they are doing." When you give knowing there will be no gift in return, you have modeled the purest form of the grace of the Lord Jesus Christ. It will help if you think about giving in that way.

Let me mention a third reason generosity based on grace is so addictive: *You can't help but be generous when grace consumes you.* "Now this I say, he who sows sparingly shall also reap sparingly; and he who sows bountifully shall also reap bountifully" (2 Corinthians 9:6).

Here is an encouraging verse for anyone who fears that giving more will result in "running out." If I read these words correctly, the bountiful sower becomes that kind of reaper. I cannot explain the magic, the beauty, and the wonder of it all, but this much I know for sure: we cannot outgive our God.

WHAT MAKES GIVING WITH GRACE SO ATTRACTIVE?

Beginning in 2 Corinthians 9, verse 6, through the end of the chapter, I discover four things that make grace so attractive, not just at the Christmas season but all through the year. In verse 7 we are told: "Let each one do just as he has purposed in his heart."

Here is the first reason grace is so attractive: *Grace individualizes the gift.* When you give by grace, you give individually. You give proportionately to your own income. You have needs, and you have an income to meet those needs. That combination is unlike anyone else's on earth. You are an individual. When you give on that basis, your gift is an individual kind of gift. We are not all shoved into a tank, blended together, then "required" to give exactly 10 percent. (Though if everyone gave 10 percent, we would have such an enormous surplus in God's work we would not know what to do with the extra—but I'm sure we'd quickly find out.) It is much more individualized than that. Grace, remember, brings variety and spontaneity.

If you are married, how about regularly discussing your giving plans with your mate? Or if you are single and you have a job where your salary is increasing and you respect your parents and their giving habits, how about talking over with them a game plan for giving during this next year? By discussing it, you can discover ways to individualize your style of giving. Paul puts it this way: "Each *one* do *just* as he purposed in his heart."

You know our problem? Most folks don't "purpose"; they don't plan; they impulsively react. But God says, "Let each one do just as he purposed in his heart." Think of how carefully you would plan a room addition. You leave nothing to chance, making certain not to miss one detail, one electrical socket in your planning, one window placement, or one place where you will or will not use carpet. You purpose and plan exactly how you want to add on to the house. I challenge you to do the same with your giving. Give grace a chance! Start with planning, praying, and thinking it through.

Determine the amount and where your gift will go and when, and then release it with joy.

The second reason grace is so attractive: *Grace makes the action joyfully spontaneous*: "not grudgingly or under compulsion; for God loves a cheerful giver" (v. 7).

I never have been able to understand why everyone in the church looks so serious during the offering. Wouldn't it be great if, when the offering plates are passed in church next Sunday, instead of grim looks, stoic silence, and soft organ music, you hear laughter? I can just imagine: "Can you believe we're doing this?" "Put it in the plate, honey. Isn't this great? Put it in!" . . . followed by little ripples of laughter and applause across the place of worship. Wonderful! Why not? Deep within the heart there is an absence of any compulsion, only spontaneous laughter. The word *cheerful* is literally a Greek term from which we get the word *hilarious*. "God loves a *hilarious* giver."

I have said all through my ministry, and I repeat it again: If your giving isn't done with hilarity, don't bother. Giving is not for the unbeliever or for those who are grim and resentful. Such giving will not be blessed. The best kind of giving has no strings attached.

Now for a third reason grace is so attractive: *Grace enables us to link up with God's supply line.* Look at verse 8: "And God is able to make all grace abound to you, so that always having all sufficiency in everything, you may have an abundance for every good deed." When we possess an attitude of grace, we give. We give ourselves. We give from what we earn. And He, in turn, gives back in various ways, not matching gift for gift, but in an abundance of ways, He goes beyond.

A fourth reason grace is so attractive: *Grace leads to incomparable results.*

Because of the proof given by this ministry, they will glorify God for your obedience to your confession of the gospel of Christ, and for the liberality of your contribution to them and to all, while they also, by prayer on your behalf, yearn for you because of the surpassing grace of God in you. (2 Corinthians 9:13–14)

As I read these verses, I find at least three results I would call "incomparable":

1. Others give God the glory.
2. They learn, by example, to be generous.
3. The relationship transcends any gift we give.

Allow me one final bit of counsel: Once you begin to give on the basis of grace, do so *confidentially*. In plain English, keep your mouth closed. Keep the extent of your giving to yourself. Ideally, do so anonymously. And He who rewards in secret will fulfill His part of the bargain.

The "apostle of grace" concludes this lengthy section on giving by announcing, "Thanks be to God for His indescribable gift!" (v. 15). Paul had a pretty good vocabulary, but when he attempted to describe God's gift of Christ, he ran out of Greek words. He simply couldn't find a word for it, so he admits it is *indescribable*.

Elisabeth Elliot's book introduced me to the discipline of sacrifice that dark, damp night when everything seemed so bleak. I began a journey that would teach me what it meant to be a living sacrifice. In my naivete, I had assumed that being a living sacrifice meant having a willingness to lay down my life for Christ in one grand gesture, much as those five missionaries had done. As a marine, I had already considered the possibility of dying for my country. I felt sure I would die for Christ if circumstances demanded it. But her book showed me so much more. She writes in the 1958 epilogue of *Through Gates of Splendor*:

> We know that it was no accident. God performs all things according to the counsel of His own will. The real issues at stake on January 8, 1956, were very far greater than those which immediately involved five young men and their families, or this small tribe of naked "savages." Letters from many countries have told of God's dealings with hundreds of men and women, through the examples of five who believed literally that "the world passeth away, and the lust thereof: but he that doeth the will of God abideth for ever."[3]

These men didn't go on a suicide mission. Their goal was not to die. Their death was the result of living a habitual life of sacrifice to Christ. Their precious lives ended in tragedy near a river in the Ecuadorian interior in the early days of 1956. They were no fools. They were heroes of the life of faith. Their deaths taught me what it meant to live. Really live.

God will not likely expect you to surrender your life all at once as these men did. Instead, He patiently waits for you to sacrifice yourself in small amounts, one decision at a time, one day at a time, so that you might enjoy an ever-increasing intimacy with Him. And this deepening intimacy with Him will inevitably make you more like Christ.

LIVING FREE

I have never witnessed slavery, not in raw reality. I have seen where slavery was portrayed in all its cruelty, but I have never seen it firsthand. I'm glad I haven't. I know of nothing more unjust or ugly. As an American I find it amazing—perhaps a better word is confusing—to think that my forefathers were willing to fight for their own freedom and win our country's independence, yet turned around and enslaved others. The triangles of such twisted logic are not mentally congruent—free citizens owning slaves. Ultimately, it took a civil war to break that yoke.

At Abraham Lincoln's second inaugural in 1865, only weeks before he was assassinated, he spoke of how both parties "deprecated war," and yet a war had come. He continued:

> Neither party expected for the war, the magnitude, or the duration, which it has already attained.... Each looked for an easier triumph.... Both read from the same Bible, and pray to the same God, and each invokes His aid against the other.[1]

At that point the reelected sixteenth president's voice broke, his feelings showing through. And he spoke of how strange it was "that any men should dare to ask a just God's assistance in wringing their bread from the sweat of other men's faces."[2]

Ultimately, with the adoption of the Thirteenth Amendment of the United States Constitution, slavery was legally abolished. It was then that black slaves all across America were officially set free. It was on New Year's

Day 1863 when the Emancipation Proclamation was publicly stated, but it was not until December 18, 1865, that the Constitution made those convictions official. Though dead by then, Lincoln still spoke. At last his dream was realized. The word swept across Capitol Hill and down into the valleys of Virginia and the back roads of the Carolinas and even deeper into the plantations of Georgia, Alabama, Mississippi, and Louisiana. Headlines on newspapers in virtually every state trumpeted the same message: "Slavery Legally Abolished."

And yet something happened that many never would have expected. The vast majority of the slaves in the South who were legally freed continued to live as slaves. Most of them went right on living as though nothing had happened. Though free, the blacks lived virtually unchanged lives throughout the Reconstruction Period.

Shelby Foote, in his monumental three-volume work *The Civil War*, verifies this surprising anomaly:

> . . . the Negro—locked in a caste system of "race etiquette" as rigid as any he had known in formal bondage . . . every slave could repeat with equal validity, what an Alabama slave had said in 1864 when asked what he thought of the Great Emancipator whose proclamation went into effect that year. "I don't know nothing bout Abraham Lincoln," he replied, "cep they say he sot us free. And I don't know nothing bout that neither."[3]

I call that tragic. A war had been fought. A president had been assassinated. An amendment to the Constitution had now been signed into law. Once-enslaved men, women, and children were now legally emancipated. Yet amazingly, many continued living in fear and squalor. In a context of hard-earned freedom, slaves chose to remain as slaves. Cruel and brutal though many of their owners were, black men and women chose to keep serving the same old master until they died. There were a few brave exceptions, but in many parts of the country you'd never have known that slavery had been officially abolished and that they had been emancipated. That's the way the plantation owners wanted it. They maintained the age-old philosophy, "Keep 'em ignorant and you keep 'em in the field."

Now if you think that is tragic, I can tell you one far worse. It has to do with Christians living today as slaves. Even though our Great Emancipator, Christ the Lord, paid the ultimate price to overthrow slavery once for all, most Christians act as though they're still held in bondage. In fact, strange as it is, most seem to prefer the security of slavery to the risks of liberty. And our slave master, Satan, loves it so. He is delighted that so many have bought into that lie and live under the dark shadow of such ignorance. He sits like the proverbial fat cat, grinning, "Great! Go right on livin' like a slave!" even though he knows we have been liberated from his control. More than most in God's family, the adversary knows we are free, but he hates it. So he does everything in his power to keep us pinned down in shame, guilt, ignorance, and intimidation.

REVIEWING SOME BASIC THOUGHTS ON SLAVERY

Though some are well informed about these facts I want to mention regarding slavery in the spiritual realm, most aren't. Therefore, I believe a brief review of some basics is necessary. Let's begin in the "emancipation letter" of Romans.

> As it is written,
> "There is none righteous, not even one;
> There is none who understands,
> There is none who seeks for God;
> All have turned aside, together they have become useless;
> There is none who does good,
> There is not even one."
> "Their throat is an open grave,
> With their tongues they keep deceiving,"
> "The poison of asps is under their lips";
> "Whose mouth is full of cursing and bitterness";
> "Their feet are swift to shed blood,
> Destruction and misery are in their paths,
> And the path of peace have they not known."
> "There is no fear of God before their eyes."

Now we know that whatever the Law says, it speaks to those who are under the Law, so that every mouth may be closed and all the world may become accountable to God; because by the works of the Law no flesh will be justified in His sight; for through the Law comes the knowledge of sin. (Romans 3:10–20)

I find in Romans at least three analogies regarding slavery. The first analogy is grim: *All of us were born in bondage to sin.* You wonder how bad our slavery really was in our unsaved condition? Look back over those words and observe for yourself:

No one righteous
No spiritual understanding
No worthwhile achievements before God
No purity, no innocence, no peace, no hope

On top of all that, we had no escape . . . we were unable to change our enslavement to sin. In that unsaved condition the lost person truly knows nothing about liberty.

The second analogy is glorious: *A day came when Christ set us free.* There came a day when an eternal Emancipation Proclamation was made known throughout the heavens and all the way to the pit of hell—"The sinner is officially set free!" It is the announcement that originated from Christ's empty tomb on that first Easter, the day our Great Emancipator, Christ, set us free. Doctrinally, the word is *redemption.* He redeemed us.

But now apart from the Law the righteousness of God has been manifested, being witnessed by the Law and the Prophets, even the righteousness of God through faith in Jesus Christ for all those who believe; for there is no distinction. (Romans 3:21–22)

I love those last two words—"no distinction." To qualify for freedom, you don't have to be born in a certain country. You don't have to speak a certain language. Your skin doesn't have to be a certain color. You don't have to be educated or cultured or make a certain amount of money or fulfill some list of requirements. There is absolutely no distinction. Why? Because we were all slaves, slaves of our master and slaves of sin. "For all have sinned and fall short of the glory of God" (v. 23). Therefore, all sinners are "savable," if I may use that word. How? "Being justified as a gift by His grace through the redemption which is in Christ Jesus" (v. 24).

Before Christ came into our lives, we were hopelessly lost in our lust, helpless to restrain our profanity, our glandular drives, our insatiable greed, our continual selfishness, or our compulsions either to please people or to control and manipulate others. While some of those things may have brought us feelings of pleasure and periodic satisfaction, our inability to control them was not without its complications. We were slaves! We were chained to the slave block, and we had to serve the old master. There was insufficient strength within us to live any other way. By "redeeming" us, Jesus set us free. When God raised Jesus from the dead (the crucial act of triumph over Satan), He said, in effect, "No one else need ever live as a victim of sin. All who believe in Jesus Christ, My Son, will have everlasting life and will have the power to live in Me." How could it be that wicked slaves could be given such standing before God?

The third analogy I find in Romans 3 is tragic: *Many Christians still live as though they are enslaved.* When told they are free, some could easily respond like the Alabama slave: "I don't know anything about grace, except they say it set us free. And I don't know anything about that either." As a result of choosing to ignore the freedom Christ won for His own, many still live with a sin-oriented mentality. Most do, in fact.

Christians too often resemble frightened and unsure religious slaves. Sometimes it emerges in other manifestations. We rationalize around our sin; we act hypocritically; occasionally we lie and cheat and steal. Then with a shrug we say, "Well, you know, man, nobody's perfect." In effect, we are saying, "I'm still enslaved. Sin still overpowers me. I'm so ashamed. But I just can't help it." Nonsense! When will we start living like those who are free? God says to every one of us, "Where sin abounded, grace superabounded. You were once enslaved to a passion, yes, but no longer . . . Now you're free from that. You can live above it." Grace awakens, enlivens, and empowers our ability to conquer sin.

Once we truly grasp the freedom grace brings, we can spend lengthy periods of our lives without sinning or feeling ashamed. Yes we can! And why not? Why should sin gain the mastery over us? Who says we cannot help but yield to it? How unbiblical! You see, most of us are so programmed to sin that we wait for it to happen.

To tell the truth, most Christians have been better trained to expect and handle their sin than to expect and enjoy their freedom. The shame and self-imposed guilt this brings is enormous, to say nothing of the "I'm defeated" message it reinforces. We begin the day afraid of sin. We live ashamed. We go to bed with a long list, ready to confess. If it isn't very long, we fear we've overlooked several "hidden sins." Maybe we've gotten proud.

What in the world has happened to grace? Furthermore, where is the abundant life Christ offered? Are freed people supposed to live such a frightened existence? Are we emancipated or not? If so, let's live like it! That isn't heresy; it's the healthiest kind of theology imaginable.

I can assure you, your old master doesn't want you to read this or think like this. He wants you to exist in the shack of ignorance, clothed in the rags of guilt and shame, afraid of him and his whip. Like the cruel slave owner, he wants you to think you "gotta take a beatin' every now 'n' then" just so you will stay in line. Listen to me today: that is heresy! Because our Savior has set us free, the old master—the supreme grace killer—has no right whatsoever to put a whip to your back. Those days have ended, my friend. You're free. Those of us who are a part of the grace awakening refuse to live like slaves. We've been emancipated!

Understanding the Themes of Liberty

Turning a few pages further in the liberating letter of Romans, we arrive at Romans 6, one of the great chapters in all the Word of God. Having spent months studying this one chapter (and loving every minute of it!), I have come to realize it contains the Christian's Emancipation Proclamation. Here, as in no other section of Scripture, is the foundational truth of our liberty—freedom from Satan's intimidation and sin's domination. It is here all young Christians should spend their first hours in the Bible—not passages that tell us what to do once we sin (like 1 John 1:9) or how to restore our fellowship, important as those scriptures may be. No, it is here the believer discovers his or her freedom from sin's control and how to live on that victorious level above fear, guilt, shame, and defeat.

For the next few minutes, graze gently over the first fifteen verses of Romans 6. Take plenty of time; there is no hurry:

> What shall we say then? Are we to continue in sin so that grace may increase? May it never be! How shall we who died to sin still live in it? Or do you not know that all of us who have been baptized into Christ Jesus have been baptized into His death? Therefore we have been buried with Him through baptism into death, so that as Christ was raised from the dead through the glory of the Father, so we too might walk in newness of life. For if we have become united with Him in the likeness of His death, certainly we shall be also in the likeness of His resurrection, knowing this, that our old self was crucified with Him, in order that our body of sin might be done away with, so that we should no longer be slaves to sin; for he who has died is freed from sin.
>
> Now if we have died with Christ, we believe that we shall also live with Him, knowing that Christ, having been raised from the dead, is never to die again; death no longer is master over Him. For the death that He died, He died to sin once for all; but the life that He lives, He lives to God. Even so consider yourselves to be dead to sin, but alive to God in Christ Jesus.
>
> Therefore do not let sin reign in your mortal body that you should obey its lusts, and do not go on presenting the members of your body to sin as instruments of unrighteousness; but present yourselves to God as those alive from the dead, and your members as instruments of righteousness to God. For sin shall not be master over you, for you are not under law but under grace.
>
> What then? Shall we sin because we are not under law but under grace? May it never be!

Even a casual reading of these thoughts reveals two questions that get the same answer from the apostle. The questions may appear to be the same, but they are not.

> What shall we say then? Are we to continue in sin so that grace may increase? May it never be! (vv. 1–2)

What then? Shall we sin because we are not under law but under grace? May it never be! (v. 15)

These two questions introduce two themes related to liberty. The first question addresses *those who fail to claim their liberty and continue to live like slaves*—those who *nullify* grace. (That theme is developed in the opening fourteen verses of Romans 6.)

The second question is addressed to *those who take their freedom too far* (vv. 15–23). In other words, they take advantage of their liberty. They live irresponsibly. Those who do that *abuse* grace. Now, go back and read Romans 6 again and see if that doesn't make sense and help you understand the chapter better.

Paul's summary answer to the first question comes in the form of another question: "How shall we who died to sin still live in it?" (v. 2).

All it takes to appreciate that question is a brief mental trip back to our unsaved days. Many of you may recall that time with misery. Remember how you couldn't get control of your desires? Perhaps you helplessly dropped into bed night after night a victim of a habit that you couldn't conquer for the life of you. You recall the feeling that there was no hope at the end of a tunnel—no light. No matter what, you could not change, not permanently. Your slavery was an addiction at its worst. It was a prison from which no one could escape on his own. Remember how the shame increased and, at times, overwhelmed you? Others may have lived in the realm of freedom so long they've forgotten what it was like to be enslaved in the lost estate. If so, the following words will help:

> It is my earnest conviction that everyone should be in jail at least once in his life and that the imprisonment should be on suspicion rather than proof; it should last at least four months; it should seem hopeless; and preferably the prisoner should be sick half of the time. . . . Only by such imprisonment does he learn what real freedom is worth.[4]

Back to the question: "How shall we who died to sin still live in it?" Who would volunteer to be dumped in a jail for another series of months, having been there and suffered the consequences of such a setting? His point: Then why would emancipated slaves who have been freed from sin and shame return to live under that same domination any longer?

I would venture to say that many who are Christians know 1 John 1:9 from memory: "If we confess our sins, He is faithful and righteous to forgive us our sins and to cleanse us from all unrighteousness." And yet how few could quote Romans 6:13:

And do not go on presenting the members of your body to sin as instruments of unrighteousness; but present yourselves to God as those alive from the dead, and your members as instruments of righteousness to God.

We have been programmed to think, *I know I am going to sin, to fail . . . to fall short today. Since this is true, I need to be ready to find cleansing.* You have not been programmed to yield yourself unto God as those who have power over sin.

How much better to begin each day thinking victory, not defeat; to awake to grace, not shame; to encounter each temptation with thoughts like this: *Jesus, You are my Lord and Savior. I am Your child—liberated and depending on Your power. Therefore, Christ, this is Your day, to be lived for Your glory. Work through my eyes, my mouth and my thoughts and actions to carry out Your victory. And, Lord, do that all day long. When I face temptations, I will present myself to You and claim the strength You give to handle it. Sin has no authority over me any longer.*

Yes, I know there will be times when we may momentarily fail, but they will be the exceptions rather than the rule of our day. We are under new ownership. Prompted by love, we serve a new master, Christ, not the old one who mistreated us. There is something exciting about enjoying a relationship with our new Friend. But we won't until we put our "old man" in his place.

Being creatures of habit, we still prefer the security of slavery to the risks of liberty. That is why the slaves stayed on the plantation, and that's why we continue to be sin-conscious—even more than Savior-conscious. We know down deep that He lives within us, that He has redeemed us; but most are at a loss to know how to get beyond the fear-failure-shame-confession syndrome. How is it possible to break the habit of serving the old master and start enjoying the benefits of being free under the new One?

CLAIMING OUR FREEDOM
FROM SIN'S CONTROL

In this wonderful sixth chapter of Romans, Paul presents three techniques for living by grace, above sin's domination. I find each one linked to a particular term he uses:

> Know—"Or do you not know that all of us who have been baptized into Christ Jesus have been baptized into His death? . . . knowing this, that our old self was crucified with Him, that our body of sin might be done away with, that we would no longer be slaves to sin; . . . knowing that Christ, having been raised from the dead, is never to die again; death no longer is master over Him" (vv. 3, 6, 9).
>
> Consider—"Even so consider yourselves to be dead to sin, but alive to God in Christ Jesus" (v. 11).
>
> Present—"And do not go on presenting the members of your body to sin as instruments of unrighteousness; but present yourselves to God as those alive from the dead, and your members as instruments of righteousness to God" (v. 13).

In order for us to live free from sin's control, free from the old master, with the power to walk a new kind of life, we have to *know* something, we have to *consider* something, and we have to *present* something.

Candidly, Romans 6 is not easy and entertaining. Understanding it is not Saturday-morning cartoons on the tube; we will have to think. So for the next few minutes I'll do my best to make it clear and keep it interesting as we answer three questions in the balance of this chapter. What is it that you and I have to know? What is it that you and I have to consider? And what is it that you and I have to present?

Let's start with *knowing*.

> Or do you not know that all of us who have been baptized into Christ Jesus have been baptized into His death? Therefore we have been buried with Him through baptism into death, so that as Christ was raised from the dead through the glory of the Father, so we too might walk in newness of life. For if we have become

united with Him in the likeness of His death, certainly we shall be also in the likeness of His resurrection, knowing this, that our old self was crucified with Him, in order that our body of sin might be done away with, so that we would no longer be slaves to sin; for he who has died is freed from sin. (vv. 3–7)

To understand what this is all about, we have to set aside the concept of water baptism and understand that this is a reference to dry baptism. Some baptisms in the New Testament are wet, and some of them are dry. This one is in the latter category.

The word *baptizō* primarily has to do with identification. It was a term that was used in the first century for dipping a light-colored garment into a dye that was, let's say, scarlet. Once the fabric was dipped into the scarlet dye, it would be changed in its identity from its original color to scarlet. The act of dipping it, resulting in changing its identity, was called *baptizō*. It is the Greek term from which we get our English word *baptism*.

Christ died for us on the cross. He was raised from the dead for us at the tomb. When we believed in the Savior's death and resurrection, we were "dipped" into the same scene. Our identity was changed. We didn't feel it, we didn't see it, we didn't hear it, but it occurred nevertheless. When we came to Christ, we were placed into Him as His death became ours, His victorious resurrection became ours, and His "awakening" to new life became our "awakening," His powerful walk became our powerful walk. Before we can experience the benefits of all that, we have to know it. The Christian life is not stumbling along, hoping to keep up with the Savior. He lives in me and I live in Him. And in this identification with Him, His power becomes mine. His very life becomes my life, guaranteeing that His victory over sin is mine to claim. I no longer need to live as a slave to sin.

Now if we have died with Christ, we believe that we shall also live with Him, knowing that Christ, having been raised from the dead, is never to die again; death no longer is master over Him. For the death that He died, He died to sin once for all; but the life that He lives, He lives to God. (vv. 8–10)

You will meet well-meaning Christians who teach about crucifying oneself. But I have good news for you: that has already been done. You are in Christ.

223

He was crucified once for all. He died for you so you never need to die again. Because we have our identification with Him, we have all the power needed to live the rest of our lives above the drag and dregs of slavery. Death to sin is an accomplished act, a finished fact. Theoretically, it has all been taken care of. A victorious walk begins with our knowing this fact. Christ's Emancipation Proclamation has put to death the whole idea of slavery to sin. Having died to sin's power, we are now free to serve our new Master:

And do not go on presenting the members of your body to sin as instruments of unrighteousness; but present yourselves to God as those alive from the dead, and your members as instruments of righteousness to God. For sin shall not be master over you, for you are not under law but under grace. (vv. 13–14)

Our bodies are not helpless victims of lustful urges and uncontrollable weaknesses. Those days ended when we became Christians. Remember, we've been emancipated! And since we have been emancipated, it is high time we start living like it. I remind you that our adversary doesn't want us to think like this. He would erase grace immediately if he could. But since he cannot, his strategy is to do everything in his power to deceive us into thinking like slaves. Why? Because when we start operating like free men and women, our old "master" can no longer control us.

A NECESSARY WARNING

I would love to tell you that change is easy, but I cannot. Old habits are terribly difficult to break. Thinking correctly takes courage. Furthermore, our adversary, Satan, won't back off easily. Neither will the legalists he uses. If you think the plantation slave owners following the Civil War were determined to keep their slaves, I'm here to tell you that today's grace killers are even more stubborn than they were. Count on it, the enemies of our souls despise this message of freedom. They hate grace, so be warned. In order for you to leave the security of slavery and ignorance and walk out into the new, risky fields of freedom and grace, you will need courage and inner resolve. My prayer is that God will give you an abundance of both. You're not alone in your quest for freedom. There are a lot of us taking this journey with you.

The sixteenth president made a comment shortly after the Emancipation Proclamation was passed by Congress early in 1863. Sounding more like Captain Ahab in Melville's novel *Moby Dick* than Abraham Lincoln delivering a speech, he warned:

> We are like whalers who have been on a long chase. We have at last got the harpoon into the monster, but we must now look how we steer, or with one flop of his tail he will send us all into eternity.[5]

The president proved himself a prophet with those words. His proclamation resulted in an escalation of the Civil War. He was absolutely correct. The declaration of freedom brought on even greater struggles and more bloodshed.

Such a warning is necessary. Who knows what battles you will encounter now that you have determined to live emancipated rather than enslaved. But the good news for many of you is this: at last we have gotten the harpoon into the monster. Now we must steer carefully and watch out for that wicked tail.

Appendix

HOW TO BEGIN A RELATIONSHIP WITH GOD

During His earthly ministry, Jesus was the perfect model of a person enjoying intimate fellowship with our heavenly Father and a close walk with Him. However, His example reveals how imperfect we are. Unlike Jesus, we are separated from God by sin, and we are powerless to restore this relationship on our own. We can never match the example of Jesus. However, we can enjoy intimate fellowship with God through His Son.

If you want to have a relationship with God, you need to understand four vital truths. Let's look at each marker in detail.

Our Spiritual Condition: Totally Depraved

The first truth is rather personal. One look in the mirror of Scripture, and our human condition becomes painfully clear:

> There is none righteous, not even one;
> There is none who understands,
> There is none who seeks for God;
> All have turned aside, together they have become useless;
> There is none who does good,
> There is not even one. (Romans 3:10–12)

We are all sinners through and through—totally depraved. Now, that doesn't mean we've committed every atrocity known to humankind. We're not as *bad* as we can be, just as *bad off* as we can be. Sin colors all our thoughts, motives, words, and actions.

You still don't believe it? Look around. Everything around us bears the smudge marks of our sinful nature. Despite our best effort to create a perfect world, crime statistics continue to soar, divorce rates keep climbing, and families keep crumbling.

Something has gone terribly wrong in our society and in ourselves, something deadly. Contrary to how the world would repackage it, "me-first" living doesn't equal rugged individuality and freedom; it equals death. As Paul said in his letter to the Romans, "The wages of sin is death" (6:23)—our spiritual and physical death that comes from God's righteous judgment of our sin, along with all the emotional and practical effects of the separation we experience on a daily basis.

God's Character: Infinitely Holy

How can God judge each of us for a sinful state we were born into? Our total depravity is only half the answer. The other half is God's infinite holiness.

The fact that we know things are not as they should be points us to a standard of goodness beyond ourselves. Our sense of injustice in life on this side of eternity implies a perfect standard of justice beyond our reality. That standard and source is God Himself. And God's standard of holiness contrasts starkly with our sinful condition.

Scripture says, "God is Light, and in Him there is no darkness at all" (1 John 1:5). He is absolutely holy—which creates a problem for us. If He's so pure, how can we who are so impure relate to Him?

Perhaps we could try to be better people, try to tilt the balance in favor of our good deeds, or seek out methods for self-improvement. Throughout history, people have attempted to live up to God's standard by keeping the Ten Commandments or living by their own code of ethics. Unfortunately, no one can come close to satisfying the demands of God's law. Romans 3:20 says, "For no one can ever be made right with God by doing what the law commands. The law simply shows us how sinful we are" (Romans 3:20 NLT).

Our Need: A Substitute

So here we are, sinners by nature and sinners by choice, trying to pull ourselves up by our own bootstraps to attain a relationship with our holy Creator. But every time we try, we fall flat on our faces. We can't live a good enough life to make up for our sin, because God's standard isn't "good enough"—it's perfection. And we can't make amends for the offense our sin has created without dying for it.

Who can get us out of this mess?

If someone could live perfectly, honoring God's law, and could bear sin's death penalty for us—in our place—then we would be saved from our predicament. But is there such a person? Thankfully, yes!

Meet your substitute—Jesus Christ. He is the One who suffered the punishment of death you deserve!

> [God] made Him who knew no sin to be sin on our behalf, so that we might become the righteousness of God in Him. (2 Corinthians 5:21)

God's Provision: A Savior

God rescued us by sending His Son, Jesus, to die for our sin on the cross (1 John 4:9–10). Jesus was fully human and fully God (John 1:1, 18), a truth that ensures His understanding of our weakness, His power to forgive, and His ability to bridge the gap between God and us (Romans 5:6–11). In short, we are "justified as a gift by His grace through the redemption which is in Christ Jesus" (Romans 3:24). Two words in this verse warrant further explanation: *justified* and *redemption*.

Justification is God's act of mercy in which He declares believing sinners righteous while they are still in their sinning state. Justification doesn't mean God *makes* us righteous so that we never sin again; rather, He *declares* us righteous—much like a judge pardons a guilty criminal. Because Jesus took our sin upon Himself and suffered our judgment on the cross, God forgives our debt and proclaims us pardoned.

Redemption is God's act of paying the ransom price to release us from our bondage of sin. Held hostage by Satan, we were shackled by the iron chains of sin and death. Like a loving parent whose child has been kidnapped, God willingly paid the ransom for you. And what a price He paid! He gave His only Son to bear our sins—past, present, and future. Jesus' death and resurrection broke our chains and set us free to become children of God (Romans 6:16–18, 22; Galatians 4:4–7).

PLACING YOUR FAITH IN CHRIST

These four truths describe how God has provided a way to Himself through His Son, Jesus Christ. Because the price has been paid in full by God, we must respond to His free gift of eternal life in total faith and confidence in Him to save us. We must step forward into the relationship with God that He has prepared for us—not by doing good works or being a good person, but by coming to Him just as we are and accepting His justification and redemption by faith.

> For by grace you have been saved through faith; and that not of yourselves,
> it is the gift of God; not as a result of works, so that no one may boast.
> (Ephesians 2:8–9)

We accept God's gift of salvation simply by placing our faith in Christ alone for the forgiveness of our sins.

Would you like to enter a relationship with your Creator by trusting Christ as your Savior? If so, here's a simple prayer you can use to express your faith:

Dear God,

I know my sin has put a barrier between You and me. Thank You for sending Your Son, Jesus, to pay the complete price for my sins as He died in my place. I trust in Jesus alone to forgive my sins, and I accept His gift of eternal life. I ask Jesus to be my personal Savior and the Lord of my life. I thank You for accepting me as I am and for Your commitment to make me the person I long to be.

In Jesus' name, amen.

No other decision you will ever make can compare with the one that puts you in a right relationship with God through His Son, Jesus Christ, who loved us and gave Himself for us!

Notes

Chapter 1 – Grace

1. Donald Grey Barnhouse, *Romans: Man's Ruin* (Grand Rapids: Eerdmans, 1952), 1: 72.
2. Sir Edward C. Burne-Jones, in *Let Me Illustrate,* Donald Grey Barnhouse (Westwood, N.J.: Revell, 1967), 145–46.
3. John Newton, "Amazing Grace" (1779).
4. Elisabeth Elliot, *The Liberty of Obedience* (Waco, TX: Word, 1968), 32.
5. Ibid., 33.
6. John Newton, "Amazing Grace" (1779).

Chapter 2 – Love

1. Gerhard Kittel and Gerhard Friedrich, eds., *Theological Dictionary of the New Testament,* ed. and trans. Geoffrey W. Bromiley (Grand Rapids: Eerdmans, 1973), 1: 37.
2. Earl D. Radmacher, Ronald Barclay Allen, and H. Wayne House, *The Nelson Study Bible: New King James Version,* (Nashville: Thomas Nelson, 1997), 1933.
3. Gerhard Kittel and Gerhard Friedrich, eds., *Theological Dictionary of the New Testament: Abridged in One Volume,* trans. Geoffrey W. Bromiley (Grand Rapids: Eerdmans, 1985), 1262.
4. Dallas Seminary Faculty, John F. Walvoord and Roy B. Zuck, eds., *The Bible Knowledge Commentary, New Testament Edition* (Wheaton: Victor, 1983), 535.
5. Kittel and Friedrich, *Theological Dictionary* 9: 483.
6. *Merriam-Webster's Collegiate Dictionary,* 10th ed., s.v. "charming."
7. Warren W. Wiersbe, *The Bible Exposition Commentary,* (Wheaton: Victor, 1989), 1: 611.
8. A. T. Robertson and Alfred Plummer, *A Critical and Exegetical Commentary on the First Epistle of St. Paul to the Corinthians,* International Critical Commentary, (Edinburgh, T. & T. Clark, 1914), 295.
9. C. S. Lewis, *The Four Loves* (New York: Harcourt, Brace & World, 1960), 169.
10. Anna Quindlen, *A Short Guide to a Happy Life* (New York: Random House, 2000), 4–7.

Chapter 3 – Joy

1. G. K. Chesterton, *Orthodoxy* (New York: Dodd, Mead and Co., 1954), 298.
2. Jane Canfield, in *Quote/Unquote*, comp. Lloyd Cory (Wheaton: Victor, 1977), 144.
3. Tim Hansel, *Holy Sweat* (Nashville: W Publishing Group, 1987), 58–59.

Chapter 4 – Fellowship and Friendship

1. Michael LeBoeuf, *How to Win Customers and Keep Them for Life* (New York: Berkley, 1987), 84–85.
2. Stuart Briscoe, *Bound for Joy: Philippians—Paul's Letter from Prison* (Glendale, CA: Regal, 1975), 92–93.
3. William Hendricksen, *New Testament Commentary* (Grand Rapids: Baker, 1962), 144–45.

Chapter 5 – God's Will

1. Garry Friesen with J. Robin Maxson, *Decision Making and the Will of God: A Biblical Alternative to the Traditional View* (Portland, OR: Multnomah Press, 1980), 244.

Chapter 6 – Intimacy

1. Eugene Peterson, *Run with the Horses* (Downers Grove, IL: InterVarsity, 1983), 16.
2. A. T. Robertson, *Word Pictures in the New Testament* (Grand Rapids: Baker, 1933), 299.
3. John R. W. Stott, *What Christ Thinks of the Church: Expository Addresses on the First Three Chapters of the Book of Revelation* (Colorado Springs: Shaw, 1990), 21.
4. Ibid., 22.
5. Ibid., 23.
6. Isaac Watts, "Am I a Soldier of the Cross?"
7. Henri J. M. Nouwen, *The Way of the Heart: Desert Spirituality and Contemporary Ministry* (New York: Seabury, 1981), 45–46.
8. Dallas Willard, *The Spirit of the Disciplines: Understanding How God Changes Lives* (San Francisco: Harper & Row, 1988), ix–xi. Reprinted by permission of HarperCollins Publishers, Inc.

Chapter 7 – Prayer

1. George A. Buttrick, quoted in *Devotional Classics: Selected Readings for Individuals and Groups*, ed. Richard J. Foster and James Bryan Smith (San Francisco: HarperSanFrancisco, 1993), 103.
2. E. M Bounds, *The Complete Works of E. M. Bounds on Prayer* (Grand Rapids: 1990), 93.
3. Douglas V. Steere, quoted in *Devotional Classics: Selected Readings for Individuals and Groups*, ed. Richard J. Foster and James Bryan Smith (San Francisco: HarperSanFrancisco, 1993), 89.

4. Ben Patterson, *Deepening Your Conversation with God* (Minneapolis: Bethany House, 1999), 22.

5. Dallas Willard, *The Spirit of the Disciplines: Understanding How God Changes Lives* (San Francisco: Harper & Row, 1988), 185–86. Reprinted by permission of HarperCollins Publishers, Inc.

6. R. Kent Hughes, *Disciplines of a Godly Man* (Wheaton: Crossway, 1991), 105. Used by permission. www.gnpcb.org.

7. Martin Luther, quoted in *Devotional Classics: Selected Readings for Individuals and Groups*, ed. Richard J. Foster and James Bryan Smith, (San Francisco: HarperSanFrancisco, 1993), 134.

8. Richard J. Foster, *Devotional Classics: Selected Readings for Individuals and Groups*, ed. Richard J. Foster and James Bryan Smith (San Francisco: HarperSanFrancisco, 1993), 137.

Chapter 8 – Humility

1. Philip Yancey and Paul Brand, *In the Likeness of God* (Grand Rapids, MI: Zondervan, 2004), 15.

2. J. Steven Wilkins, *Call of Duty: The Sterling Nobility of Robert E. Lee* (Nashville: Cumberland, 1997), 244.

3. William Barclay, *The Gospel of Mark* (Philadelphia: Westminster, 1956), 267.

4. Kenneth S. Davis, *Soldier of Democracy* (New York: Doubleday, 1945), 543.

Chapter 9 – Surrender

1. William Hendriksen, *Exposition of Philippians* (Grand Rapids: Baker, 1979), 100.

2. Arthur Bennett, ed., *The Valley of Vision: A Collection of Puritan Prayers and Devotions* (Carlisle, PA: Banner of Truth Trust, 1975), 91.

3. Peter Marshall, quoted in *The Best of Peter Marshall*, ed. Catherine Marshall (Grand Rapids: Baker, 1983), 141.

Chapter 10 – Self-Control

1. Sun Tzu, *The Art of War* (New York: Doubleday, 1988), 18.

2. Maxie Dunham, *The Communicator's Commentary* (Dallas: Word, 1981), 8:120.

Chapter 12 – Dealing with Failure, Suffering, Temptation, and Guilt

1. Kenneth S. Wuest, *In These Last Days*, vol. 4 in *Wuest's Word Studies from the Greek New Testament* (Grand Rapids: Eerdmans, 1966), 125–26.

2. Randy Alcorn, "Consequences of a Moral Tumble," *Leadership* 88, 46.

3. Stuart Briscoe, *Spiritual Stamina* (Portland, OR: Multnomah, 1988), 133.

4. Quoted in *More Children's Letters to God*, comp. Eric Marshall and Stuart Hample (New York: Simon and Schuster, 1967).

5. Quoted in William Barclay, *The Letters of James and Peter*, rev. ed., *The Daily Study Bible* Series (Philadelphia: Westminster, 1976), 203.

6. Warren W. Wiersbe, *Be Hopeful* (Wheaton: Victor, 1982), 57.

Chapter 13 – Overcoming Shame and Doubt

1. William Riley Wilson, *The Execution of Jesus: A Judicial, Literary and Historical Investigation* (New York: Simon & Schuster, 1970), 152.
2. Bernard of Clairvaux, "O Sacred Head, Now Wounded" (Nashville: Word Music/ Integrity Music, 1997), 316. Original source in public domain.
3. William Barclay, *The Gospel of John*, rev. ed. (Louisville: Westminster John Knox, 1975), 2:1–2. Used by permission.
4. Edward M. Plass, comp., *What Luther Says: An Anthology*, (St. Louis: Concordia, 1972), 426. Original source in public domain.
5. Alfred Tennyson, "In Memoriam," in *Baker's Pocket Treasury of Religious Verse*, Donald T. Kauffman, comp. (Grand Rapids: Baker, 1962), 174. Used by permission.
6. Daniel Taylor, *The Myth of Certainty* (Downers Grove, IL: InterVarsity, subsidiary rights owned by Daniel Taylor, 1986), 14–15. Used by permission.

Chapter 14 – Sacrifice: Personal and Financial

1. Dallas Willard, *The Spirit of the Disciplines: Understanding How God Changes Lives* (San Francisco: Harper & Row, 1988), 175. Reprinted by permission of HarperCollins Publishers Inc.
2. Reprinted from *The Pursuit of God* by A. W. Tozer, copyright © 1982, 1993 by Christian Publications, Inc. Used by permission of Christian Publications, Inc., 800.233.4443, www.christianpublications.com.
3. Elisabeth Elliot, *Through Gates of Splendor* (Carol Stream, IL: Tyndale, 1981), 259.

Closing: Living Free

1. Abraham Lincoln, in his second inaugural address, March 4, 1865, cited in Carl Sandburg, *Abraham Lincoln: The Prairie Years and the War Years* (New York: Harcourt, Brace & World, 1954), 664.
2. Ibid.
3. Shelby Foote, *The Civil War, A Narrative*, vol. 3 (New York: Vantage, 1986), 1045.
4. Gordon S. Seagrave, cited in *Quote Unquote.* comp. Lloyd Cory (Wheaton: Victor, 1977), 123. World rights reserved.
5. Abraham Lincoln in Washington, D.C., August 26, 1863, as cited in Henry Raymond, *The Life, Public Service and State Papers of Abraham Lincoln* (New York: Darby and Miller, 1865), 753.

Study Guide

Chapter 1—Grace

"If there is any singular truth that distinguishes Christianity from all other religions, all other systems of belief, it is *grace*."

1. Define *grace* in your own words.

2. "To show grace is to extend favor or kindness to one who doesn't deserve it and can never earn it." Why is it so difficult for us to accept something we do not deserve?

3. Which of the following "grace killers" affect your spiritual vitality?

   __ spoken words   __ written words   __ arrogance
   __ manipulation   __ intolerance   __ judgmental attitudes
   __ bullying   __ intimidation   __ narrow-mindedness

4. How does your experiencing these "grace killers" affect your freedom, spontaneity, and creativity?

5. There are four practical expectations you can anticipate as you get a firm grasp on grace. Describe how the realization of each of these expectations might affect your spiritual health.
   - You can expect to gain a greater appreciation for God's gifts to you and others.

- You can expect to spend less time and energy being critical of and concerned about others' choices.
- You can expect to become more tolerant and less judgmental.
- You can expect to take a giant step toward maturity.

6. Read 1 Corinthians 15:9–11 and then rewrite the passage from your own perspective.

7. After rewriting the passage, describe how your understanding of grace is changing.

8. Complete the following statements:
   - Because God does what He does by His grace, I will . . .
   - Because I am what I am by the grace of God, I will . . .
   - Because grace must be demonstrated in my attitudes and actions toward others, I will . . .

9. What is the difference between living by rules and living under grace?

10. Mark on the continuum below the degree to which you are experiencing God's grace today.

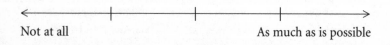

Not at all   As much as is possible

11. Take a few moments and reflect on what God has taught you through this lesson. List the three most important things you learned and how, when applied, they will affect your daily life.

Chapter 2—Love

"Love is a universal language. When expressed authentically, no words are necessary. Furthermore, love is no less essential to human life than air, food, or water."

1. One of the greatest descriptions of the priority of love is found in 1 Corinthians 13. Read verses 1–3 and describe how these verses compare to the priority you place on love.

2. *Agape* is the kind of love we experience with God. *The Nelson Study Bible* says, "True love puts up with people who would be easier to give up on." Describe a time when you have either given up on someone or been given up on by someone.

3. How would real *agape* love have changed the situation described above?

4. Read 1 Corinthians 13:4–7 and mark the characteristics of authentic love. Then, use the activity below to rate yourself in each characteristic.

	False									True
I am patient and kind.	1	2	3	4	5	6	7	8	9	10
I am not jealous.	1	2	3	4	5	6	7	8	9	10
I am not arrogant.	1	2	3	4	5	6	7	8	9	10
I am not prideful.	1	2	3	4	5	6	7	8	9	10
I am not rude.	1	2	3	4	5	6	7	8	9	10
I am not self-seeking.	1	2	3	4	5	6	7	8	9	10
I am not easily angered.	1	2	3	4	5	6	7	8	9	10
I don't keep records of wrongs.	1	2	3	4	5	6	7	8	9	10
I do not delight in evil.	1	2	3	4	5	6	7	8	9	10
I rejoice in truth.	1	2	3	4	5	6	7	8	9	10

Total the numbers you circled and write the total. The maximum score is 100. Based on an academic grading scale, how did you do on the "love test"?

5. Love isn't something we do; it's who we are as believers. When we have *agape* love, we will be more concerned with serving and helping than with inflating ourselves. This kind of love isn't arrogant. Think about your most recent expression of love. Was it more focused on what you received in return or on meeting the needs of someone else? Explain.

6. "*Agape* is the intersection of truth, salvation, and obedience to God." How does your love for other people affect their relationship with the Lord?

7. Have your words or actions toward another person ever interfered with his or her ability to see God for who He really is? If so, what would you do differently today?

8. Take a few moments and reflect on what God has taught you through this lesson. List the three most important things you learned and how, when applied, they will affect your daily life.

Chapter 3—Joy

"Visit most congregations today and search for signs of happiness and sounds of laughter and you often come away disappointed."

1. Which of the following statements is most often true of you?

___ My joy overwhelms my circumstances.
___ My circumstances overwhelm my joy.

2. What does your response say about the presence of God's joy in your life?

3. I would laugh more if only:

4. Read 2 Corinthians 11:23–28. Paul had more than enough reasons to give up and let his circumstances interrupt the work of God in and through his life. What kept Paul from giving up?

5. If you faced one or more of the circumstances Paul faced, would you be able to keep moving forward, or would you give up? Explain your response.

6. Paul was able to maintain his joy because he spent more time focused on God's strength than on his personal weakness. Because Paul was genuinely joyful, his joy was contagious. What attitude is most prevalent in your life?

7. What would happen if those around you "caught" your most prevalent attitude? Would their lives be made better or worse? Explain your response.

8. "Joyful people stay riveted to the present—the here and now, not the then and never." Are you more focused on what God is doing in your life or on things you did in the past?

9. How is your focus affecting the joy that should be flowing through your life and into the lives of others?

10. Read John 15:11. God's presence in our lives is accompanied by the joy that is part of His character. If your daily joy is a reflection of God's presence in your life, what would people who know you conclude about your relationship with God?

11. Take a few moments and reflect on what God has taught you through this lesson. List the three most important things you learned and how, when applied, they will affect your daily life.

Chapter 4—*Fellowship and Friendship*

"In spite of our high-tech world and efficient procedures, people remain the essential ingredient of life. When we forget that, a strange thing happens: we start treating people like inconveniences instead of assets."

1. Based on the quality of your relationships with other people, would you say that you view people as assets or inconveniences?

2. You probably are where you are today because of the influence of certain people. Take a moment to list some of those people and recount briefly how each influenced you.

3. Paul's life was made richer and more enjoyable through the presence of special friends—Luke, Timothy, Barnabas, Silas, Epaphroditus, and others. Each person was helpful to Paul, but the relationships were reciprocal—Paul made a difference in their lives too. In whose life are you making a difference? Describe the difference you are making.

4. Read Philippians 2:19–24. The relationship between Paul and Timothy was strong because of three foundational characteristics— they shared a similar vision, they had a mutual concern for others, and they had servant hearts. Consider your closest relationship and evaluate the strength of each characteristic.

	Weak								Strong	
We share a similar vision.	1	2	3	4	5	6	7	8	9	10
We are concerned about others.	1	2	3	4	5	6	7	8	9	10
We have servant hearts.	1	2	3	4	5	6	7	8	9	10

Add the numbers circled and write the total. Your score will range from a minimum of 3 to a maximum of 30. If you scored 0-10, your best relationship is weak. If you scored 11–20, your relationship is neutral. And 21-30 means your relationship is strong. Based on your

score, how can your relationship be strengthened in each of the three
characteristics?

5. In this chapter, we looked at three kinds of relationships that
deserve our attention. Consider the brief description of each and
identify a person in your life who fits the description. If you don't
have someone who fits, begin praying that God will make you
aware of the people He wants you to relate to.
   - Timothy is the person with whom we naturally connect. Who is
     your "Timothy"?
   - Epaphroditus is a person who comes to your rescue. Who is
     your "Epaphroditus"?
   - Jesus Christ is the One who offers salvation and can change
     your inner heart. Without Jesus, Timothy and Epaphroditus
     won't do you much good. Describe the quality of your
     relationship with Jesus.

6. Take a few moments and reflect on what God has taught you
through this lesson. List the three most important things you
learned and how, when applied, they will affect your daily life.

Chapter 5—God's Will

"But God offers a better way to live—one that requires faith as it lifts us above
the drag and grind of our immediate little world, opens new dimensions of
thought, and introduces a perspective without human limitations."

1. Read Isaiah 4:9, 12–13. Summarize those verses.

2. Since God is eternally consistent (2 Timothy 2:13), He cannot
contradict His own nature. Therefore, He can't cause us to sin, He
won't cause us to be dishonest, He wouldn't encourage us to
compromise our integrity to accomplish His plan, and so forth.
What is your strategy for knowing God's decreed will? Where do
you find it, and how much time do you spend studying it?

3. "No one is ultimately able to frustrate God's plan." What, then, are the consequences of a believer failing to do what God intended him or her to do?

4. Describe a time when you missed out on God's blessings because you failed to get involved in God's activity around you.

5. How did that experience make you feel? What was the effect of the experience on your relationship with God?

6. How would you describe God's permissive will?

7. Which of the following are optional for believers?

__ Sexual morality	__ Be joyful
__ Prayer	__ Submit to God's desires
__ Live according to God's ways	__ Love
__ Obey your parents	__ Marry a Christian
__ Work	__ Proclaim Christ
__ Worship	__ Give
__ Be grateful	__ Have no prejudice
__ Godly values	__ Meditate on Scripture
__ Support your family	__ Be holy

8. "The better you get to know the Word of God, the less confusing is the will of God." Based on your knowledge of the Word of God, how would you describe your knowledge of the will of God?

__ I know God's Word thoroughly and am living out God's will.
__ I need to spend more time in God's Word.
__ I am making up the rules as I go along. I do whatever I want and God understands.

9. Match the following prerequisites for doing the will of God with the correct scripture passage:

1. ___ You must be a Christian.
2. ___ You must be wise.
3. ___ You must want to do God's will.
4. ___ You must be willing to pray and wait.
5. ___ You must be willing to give up your creature comforts.
   a. John 7:17
   b. Acts 20:22–24
   c. Romans 8:14
   d. Matthew 7:7–8
   e. Ephesians 5:15–16

10. What makes risk so difficult for you?

11. Are you willing to make a major change in your life—assuming that it's the Lord's will?

12. Take a few moments and reflect on what God has taught you through this lesson. List the three most important things you learned and how, when applied, they will affect your daily life.

Chapter 6—Intimacy: Deepening Our Lives

"Your spiritual life may be in need of some major changes. A new perspective is essential in order to rekindle that first-love kind of relationship where God is real again, where you and He are on much closer speaking terms."

1. Read Revelation 2:2–5. If Jesus wrote a personal letter to you about your spiritual vitality, what would He say?

2. "God will never adjust His agenda to fit ours." Reflect on your daily life. In what ways do you sometimes choose your agenda over God's?

3. How do you define the word *discipline?* Paul told Timothy to discipline himself "for the purpose of godliness." When it comes to pursuing godliness, how would you characterize your pursuit?

___ I hope godliness is pursuing me.
___ I pursue godliness, but it's not the most important thing in my life.
___ Godliness is my most passionate pursuit.

4. When you face difficulties in life, do you first turn to your own knowledge or to God's wisdom? Explain your response.

5. "Discipline is training that corrects and perfects our mental faculties or molds our moral character." Consider each of the following activities and place a + by it if it contributes to the process described in the statement above or a – by it if it interferes with the process.

___ closest friendships	___ worship	___ small group
___ television	___ radio	___ music
___ Internet	___ hobbies	___ recreation
___ books	___ magazines	___ conversation
___ coworkers	___ neighbors	___ social activities

6. What are some immediate changes you should make so that you are pursuing a more intimate relationship with God?

7. Take a few moments and reflect on what God has taught you through this lesson. List the three most important things you learned and how, when applied, they will affect your daily life.

Chapter 7—Prayer: Calling Out

"A primary purpose of prayer is connecting with God in order to transfer His will into your life. It's collaborating with God to accomplish His goals."

1. Prayer must be God-centered, never self-centered. Think about your prayer life. What percentage of the time you spend in prayer focuses on you?

2. "God never hides His will. If we seek direction, He delights in providing it." About what are you praying right now?

3. What do you think is keeping you from hearing God's direction for your life?

4. Based on the way you pray, are you more focused on convincing God to do something you want or positioning yourself to do what God wants? Explain your response.

5. Read 1 Timothy 2:1–2. List some of the people for whom you should be praying.

6. Describe a time when God answered one of your prayers. How did you know God was responding?

7. Worry drains our energy and saps our spiritual vitality. Worry is a natural response to life's everyday concerns. Read Matthew 6:27. What was Jesus' advice regarding worry?

8. What happens to your prayer life when you are preoccupied with other concerns?

9. Use the words "nothing" and "everything" to complete the following statement: Worry about _____; pray about _____. Is this statement true or false in regard to the way you live?

10. Worry and prayer are opposite sides of the same coin. When you do one, you can't do the other. Our default response to life is worry. How can you replace worry with prayer?

11. The result of prayer is inexplicable peace. How would you describe your peacefulness right now?

    ___ I have no peace.

    ___ I am at peace when I'm asleep.

    ___ I experience more peace than anxiety.

    ___ I am experiencing God's peace to its fullest.

12. "Prayer is never a substitute for human responsibility." What are some things God might expect you to do in addition to praying for people and/or situations?

13. God promises He will hear us, He will be with us, and He will keep us at peace. Write a prayer expressing your gratitude for these three truths.

14. Take a few moments and reflect on what God has taught you through this lesson. List the three most important things you learned and how, when applied, they will affect your daily life.

Chapter 8—Humility: Bowing Low

"True humility comes from a place of strength and inner security. Humble people are fully aware of their gifts, their training, their experience, and all the attributes that make them successful at what they do. That security—that honest, healthy self-assessment—results in more than a humble constitution; it translates into actions that can be observed, actions that we will want to emulate."

1. What desires or aspirations compete with your desire for real humility?

2. True humility is the result of an intimate relationship with God. What does your humility say about the depth of your relationship with God? (See next page.)

__ I struggle with humility because my relationship with God isn't very strong.

__ Though I'm not there yet, I am growing in my relationship with God and in humility.

__ I believe real humility is unrealistic in today's world.

3. "We appreciate humility in others but rarely want it for ourselves." Is this true in your life? Explain your response.

4. What is the difference between humility and having low self-esteem? Which term best describes your attitude?

5. We discussed three biblical examples of humility. Which of these stories spoke most directly to you, and what did God say to you through it?

6. Because Mark 10 teaches that "we need to sit on promoting ourselves," I will . . .

7. Because Philippians 2 teaches that "we need to stand up for others," I will . . .

8. Because 1 Peter 5 teaches that "we need to bow low before our God," I will . . .

9. Take a few moments and reflect on what God has taught you through this lesson. List the three most important things you learned and how, when applied, they will affect your daily life.

Chapter 9—Surrender: Releasing Our Grip

"Paul tells us it is required of a steward that he be found *faithful*—not necessarily fruitful or full of charisma or excited or brimming with optimism, but faithful."

1. Read Hebrews 12:1. This verse calls attention to two things that interfere with a believer's spiritual vitality. What slows you down and keeps you from giving your best to those things that God says are important to Him?

2. What is your *signature sin*—the sin that seems to be more prevalent and easier to rationalize?

3. What is the connection between your signature sin and your pursuit of God's best?

4. Read Philippians 3:10 on page 118. Place an X on the line indicating where you are right now.

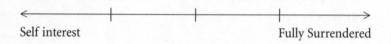

Self interest   Fully Surrendered

Now place an O on the line indicating where you want to be. What must you release to reach that goal?

5. Hebrews 12:2 says that believers must study Christ. Is your Bible study time more focused on information or transformation? Explain your response.

6. Hebrews 12:3 instructs us to compare ourselves to Christ. What will happen to your conversations, entertainment, social activities, schedule, worship, and so forth when you compare yourself to Christ?

7. Complete the following statements:
   - I agree that I must surrender my possessions, therefore I will:
   - I agree that I must surrender my position, therefore I will:
   - I agree that I must surrender my plans, therefore I will:
   - I agree that I must surrender my people, therefore I will:

8. Take a few moments and reflect on what God has taught you through this lesson. List the three most important things you learned and how, when applied, they will affect your daily life.

Chapter 10—*Self-Control: Holding Back*

"We have all exceeded the bounds of wisdom by failing to restrain ourselves. We all suffer from the same ailment: lack of self-control."

1. Read Romans 7:14-25. How does your life compare to the life Paul described?

2. Which fear most affects you—the fear of disappointing God or the fear of getting caught? Explain your response.

3. Read Galatians 5:17-21. "The flesh is a self-serving, nonbelieving, godless mind-set that lives by animal instinct. Its natural stance is facing away from God." This is your natural tendency. How do you protect yourself against yielding to this tendency?

   __ I don't; I just assume I'll be forgiven.
   __ I resist when I'm around others who expect me to resist.
   __ I know the avenues through which I am tempted and am eliminating the sources of temptation. As I grow in my relationship with God, I am sickened by the things that sicken Him.

4. Based on the way you have lived the past few days, which of the following is controlling your life? You can only choose one.

   __ the Holy Spirit
   __ my flesh and its desires

5. In Galatians 5:19-21, Paul identified the deeds of the flesh. Read the passage on page 133. List the attitudes or actions that are commonplace in your life.

6. Now read Galatians 5:22–23. Which list is more appealing to you—the deeds of the flesh or the fruit of the Spirit?

7. Based on your choice, what should be your attitude toward the Holy Spirit in your life?

___ I should want the Holy Spirit to control more of my life and me less of my life.
___ I should want the Holy Spirit to control less of my life and me more of my life.

8. God keeps you here for a purpose. What do you believe to be your purpose?

9. Is your daily life supporting or contradicting your purpose? Explain your response.

10. The first steps to living above the flesh are discussed. Work through the four steps and create some realistic action points that you will take to exercise better self-control.

11. Take a few moments and reflect on what God has taught you through this lesson. List the three most important things you learned and how, when applied, they will affect your daily life.

Chapter 11—Developing a Godly Moral Compass

"The Lord doesn't expect us to barter for His favor. His love isn't for sale."

1. The Bible is God's revelation of absolute truth containing God's directives and principles. What the Bible says is right is still right; what the Bible says is wrong, is still wrong. Defining right and wrong is God's prerogative and society has no say in the matter. Do you agree with that statement? Why or why not?

2. Read Micah 6:8. Rewrite that verse in your own words.

3. It is vital that God's people do what is right even when it isn't popular. Describe how you determine what is right.

4. As you seek to know God's will for your life, how do you expect Him to communicate to you?

5. How much time each day do you spend listening to God through reading His Word?

6. How had God transformed your personal convictions? What is the role of your personal convictions in following God's plan for your life?

7. How would you describe the spiritual character of your closest friends and advisors? Are those to whom you listen more or less tuned into the Holy Spirit than you?

8. Based on the spiritual health of those to whom you listen, how do you expect their advice to compare to God's real desires for you?

___ I expect their advice to point me toward God's desires.
___ I expect their advice to point me away from God's desires.

9. List the people you should be listening to and how you know they are tuned into God's Spirit.

10. Reflect on the last time you made a moral choice based on your understanding of God's definition of right and wrong. How did other people respond to your decision?

11. Rate the following priorities in the order in which you use them to make moral choices:

___ popularity   ___ personal desire   ___ obedience to God

12. Take a few moments and reflect on what God has taught you through this lesson. List the three most important things you learned and how, when applied, they will affect your daily life.

Chapter 12—Dealing with Failure, Suffering, Temptation, and Guilt

"God has given us a purpose for our existence, a reason to go on, even though that existence includes tough times. Living through suffering, we become sanctified—in other words, set apart for the glory of God. We gain perspective. We grow deeper. We grow up!"

1. We all agree life is tough. The apostle Peter's first letter offers us encouragement for facing the struggles that are part of our lives. Take a few moments to read 1 Peter. Describe a time when you have been mistreated because of your faith in God.

2. Why is it difficult for us to rejoice through our hard times?

3. Review the six reasons believers can rejoice through hard times. Which reason is most comforting to you, and why is that reason comforting?

4. When you face struggles, do you first respond with rejoicing or with resentment? Why?

5. Read John 17:14–15 and 1 John 2:15–17. What should be a believer's attitude toward the world?

6. Why is this attitude so hard to maintain?

7. What most often tempts you to embrace the world's ways?

8. How can you guard against the temptations that so easily distract you?

9. There are four techniques listed. Based on your most frequent temptations, what, specifically, should you do to implement each of the following techniques?
   - Pay close attention to what you look at.
   - Give greater thought to the consequences of sin than to its pleasures.
   - Begin each day by renewing your sense of reverence for God.
   - Periodically during each day focus fully on Christ.

10. Read 1 Peter 2:11–12. How should the fact that others are watching us affect our choices?

11. Because God is for me, I will:

12. Take a few moments and reflect on what God has taught you through this lesson. List the three most important things you learned and how, when applied, they will affect your daily life.

Chapter 13—Overcoming Shame and Doubt

"The sinless Son of God took all our sins on Himself when He died on the cross. It was there He endured the shame of the world. Every wicked deed done by humanity, He took on Himself when He suffered and died in our place."

1. Read John 8:1–11. What does this story teach about God's attitude toward us?

2. What does this story reveal about the attitudes of the religious people of that day?

3. When it comes to dealing with the sins of other people, do you most often exhibit the attitude of God or that of the religious leaders described in this story? Explain your response.

4. We all face condemnation, much of which is self-imposed. How does self-condemnation affect the vitality of your relationship with God?

5. There are two truths that will help you deal with your personal shame. Consider each statement and write a short prayer asking God to help you keep your focus on His love for you in light of these truths.
   - Those most unqualified to condemn you, will. Prayer:
   - The One most qualified to condemn you, won't. Prayer:

6. Read Matthew 11:28–30 and write what God says to you through these verses.

7. What do you believe is the relationship between faith and doubt?

8. What should be your response to your doubts about God?

9. "Times of doubting become schoolrooms of learning, those places where a new kind of faith is forged." What have you learned through your times of doubt?

10. Describe a time when you have risked and failed. What did you learn?

11. How does releasing things help you strengthen your faith?

12. Take a few moments and reflect on what God has taught you through this lesson. List the three most important things you learned and how, when applied, they will affect your daily life.

Chapter 14—*Sacrifice: Personal and Financial*

"I realized that life doesn't revolve around me—my comfort, my desires, my dreams, my plans. Clearly, it is all about Him."

1. Read Ephesians 5:1–2. How does this passage compare to the way you live your life?

2. We must apply the concept of sacrifice to three realms of life—personal, relational, and material. When you hear the word *sacrifice*, what thoughts first come to mind?

3. Read Matthew 6:19–33. What personal advice do you get from these verses? When it comes to meeting your needs, whom do you trust—yourself or God? Explain.

4. Read Genesis 22. What relationship principles do you see in this story?

5. "When one deals with personal and relational sacrifice, financial sacrifices naturally follow." In which area is it easier for you to make sacrifices? Why?

6. Why are people so defensive about sacrificing financially?

7. What does your attitude toward giving say about the depth of your relationship with God?

8. Take a few moments and reflect on what God has taught you through this lesson. List the three most important things you learned and how, when applied, they will affect your daily life.

Closing—*Living Free*

Write your personal commitment based on the study of this book and God's Word.

About the Author

Dr. Charles R. Swindoll is senior pastor of Stonebriar Community Church, chancellor of Dallas Theological Seminary, and the Bible teacher on the internationally syndicated radio program *Insight for Living*. He has written more than thirty best-selling books, such as *Strengthening Your Grip*, *Laugh Again*, *The Grace Awakening*, and the million-selling Great Lives from God's Word series. Chuck and his wife, Cynthia, live in Frisco, Texas.

CHARLES SWINDOLL'S MOST ENDURING,
WELL-KNOWN, AND PROFOUND WORK

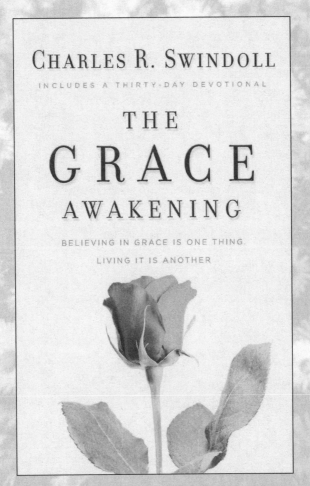

CHARLES R. SWINDOLL

INCLUDES A THIRTY-DAY DEVOTIONAL

THE

GRACE

AWAKENING

BELIEVING IN GRACE IS ONE THING.

LIVING IT IS ANOTHER

ISBN 978-1-4002-0293-5

20th Anniversary Edition Available Now

INCLUDES THE GRACE AWAKENING DEVOTIONAL